Treat It Gentle

Treat It Gentle

AN AUTOBIOGRAPHY
by Sidney Bechet

with a New Preface
by Rudi Blesh

Among those who
helped record and edit
the tapes on which this
book is based are Joan
Reid, Desmond Flower,
and John Ciardi.

A DA CAPO PAPERBACK

Library of Congress Cataloging in Publication Data

Béchet, Sidney.
  Treat it gentle.

  (A Da Capo paperback)
  Reprint of the 1st ed., 1960, published by Cassell,
London.
  "A catalogue of the recordings of Sidney Béchet,
compiled by David Mylne": p.
  1. Béchet, Sidney, 2. Jazz musicians—Correspondence.
I. Blesh, Rudi, 1899-   II. Title.
ML419.B23A3 1978   788'.66'0924 [B]   78-17561
ISBN 0-306-80086-1

ISBN: 0-306-80086-1

First Paperback Edition 1978

This Da Capo Press paperback edition of *Treat It Gentle* is an unabridged
republication, with the addition of a new preface by Rudi Blesh, of
the first edition published in New York in 1960. It is reprinted by
arrangement with Farrar, Straus & Giroux.

The drawing of Sidney Bechet on the title page is by
David Stone Martin and is reproduced by courtesy
of Folkways Records through Moses Asch.

Published by Da Capo Press, Inc.
A Subsidiary of Plenum Publishing Corporation
233 Spring Street, New York, N. Y. 10013

Preface

The autobiography of any great creative artist is a heritage of pure gold in the human cultural treasury. Such self-told stories are comparatively rare, however, among non-literary artists, and especially so in the case of musical creators.

In jazz the written autobiography is even rarer than in other musics. This has left, and is leaving, a sad lack in our archives of creativity. Granted that the story is in the music. Regrettably, where most of the music *was*, is now silence. Preserving that music was once impossible and later, though theoretically possible, was done infrequently. Even with artists as prodigally creative as Louis Armstrong and Sidney Bechet, far too little has been preserved through wax matrices and tape.

Any follower of live jazz knows how small a fraction of the musical story ever gets recorded: during many an evening in bistro or ginmill, or in private jam session, or even in moments during rehearsal, a memorable ballad or a night-shadowed blues sounds forth, then dies forever in silence. Moreover, the truly creative jazzman has never said his last musical word until he, too, is silenced by death.

Yet the written autobiography *can* supplement the music with facts and feelings and credos. Unfortunately, the important jazz autobiographies can be numbered on one's fingers. One thinks immediately of one of the most artistically and historically important—Jelly Roll Morton's long, rich Creole saga, captured in 1938 by Alan Lomax on 116 large longplay disks at the Library of Congress. One remembers, too, the stories of three white Chicagoans: Eddie Condon in *We Called It Music*, Milton Mezzrow in *Really the Blues*, and Benny Goodman in *The Kingdom of Swing* (as told to Irving Kolodin).

Precious parts of the story of Baby Dodds, the New Orleans drummer, were told to Larry Gara and are preserved in *Evergreen Review*. But for the rest of the long New Orleans story, from the 1890s to today, it is mainly autobiographical silence, with one notable—and fortunate—exception: that very paradigm of black New Orleans jazz, Louis Daniel Armstrong, the immortal Satchmo, left us not one, but two, books, *Swing That Music* (1936) and *Satchmo: My Life in New Orleans* (1954).

In 1960 the New Orleans autobiographical treasury was immeasurably enriched by the publication of the taped memoirs of one of the early Crescent City giants, soprano saxophone and clarinet master Sidney Bechet. This is the book we have here, *Treat It Gentle*, a volume whose modest size belies its bulk in history. Bechet, the handsome, mercurial Creole, relates a wealth of colorful and fascinating personal material and, in his story of jazz music from a creator's point of view, fleshes out the outlines of this American music.

Bechet goes far back beyond the specific origins of jazz into its shadowy beginnings during slavery, with engrossing and revelatory accounts of a slavetime black "musicianer," Omar, who happened to be Sidney's own grandfather. After reading these pages you will never forget him—the black serf who made his own drums in the ageless African mode and played on Sundays in New Orleans' legendary Congo Square (now known as Beauregard Square).

We are reminded of Alex Haley, as Sidney's memory takes us back to Omar, who heard in a dream his ancestral music in faraway Africa. "And when he awoke," says Bechet, "and remembered where he was—that chant, that memory, got mixed up in a kind of melody that had a crying inside itself." And, as Omar's grandson knew so well, it was a "voice from the other tribe calling, talking from somewhere else."

It was fortunate for us all when a history-minded jazz-lover, Miss Joan Reid, got to Sidney in his adopted France. She found him not only ready but eager to tell his story, and the story of his people and their music. He told her—and the world: "I want to tell you about this music before I go. A man don't have all the time in the world, and there's things he has to do before he can go happy."

Sidney Bechet, florid, handsome, and a jazz master, lived in his music—and outside of it—gustily, amorously, striding along his way. Like Albert Schweitzer, he placed supreme value on life itself; this he saw as a road with a bend, a road that one travels outward and then, in the fullness of one's years, back around again. It was music that carried Creole Sidney, the fiery and the wise, along that road, and it was music—something to trust and to "treat gentle"—that carried him back on the completing part of his journey.

These pages contain love and life and music, told as an autochthonous personal legend. Reading them makes me proud to have known Sidney Bechet as a friend. It will do no harm to repeat that we are all deeply indebted to Miss Joan Reid as well as to Mr. Desmond Flower and Mr. John Ciardi, who transcribed and arranged the taped material. Though rushed at the end by Bechet's approaching death, and then cut off short by that death, these words carry us close to the innermost spirit of jazz creation and to the consciousness of a great black artist.

Here, in his own words, is the "musicianer" who was the first to bring the New Orleans sound to Europe and who, as a twenty-two-year-old youth, was hailed by Ernest Ansermet in 1919 as a trail-blazing genius. The life of Sidney Bechet, so eloquently told in *Treat It Gentle*, was compounded of myth and poetry, with the full truth of each. In its own way, it comes out as music after all.

RUDI BLESH
New York City
April 1978

Foreword

by Desmond Flower

Sidney Bechet was first persuaded to tell his story some years ago by Miss Joan Reid, who succeeded in getting a very considerable amount of material on to tape. All who read this book must be grateful to her for her successful initiative in bringing Sidney to the recording machine, and for the amount of very hard work which she put in.

The task of putting Sidney's material into book form was later entrusted to me. I found the story to about 1936 complete; and that part of the book as it now appears, together with the final chapter, were passed by Sidney as being in the form in which he wished what he had to say to appear. Most of the story of the twenty years from 1936 also existed, but there were certain gaps. I therefore went to Paris, and Sidney recorded further material which enabled the remaining chapters to be completed. Sidney read and approved of these too, but said that there were some passages upon which he would like to enlarge, as he had more to say. He was not well, he said, but he would return to his tape-recorder as soon as his health permitted. Alas, that was not to be, for he was never again well enough to do what he intended.

The whole of this book as it now appears, was therefore complete and in Sidney's hands before his death. But there are a few parts of the later narrative which are little more than a recital of facts and dates. It is, of course, to these that he intended to return had he been given the strength to do so.

To have talked and worked with Sidney on this book was something for which I shall always be grateful. I first heard him play in 1931, but not until the preparation of this book did I have the pleasure of talking with him. He says of himself that he could sometimes be mean, and that he had his troubles, and his story does not belie this. But to meet him was an experience, for he was warm, wise, kind and gentle.

Contents

List of Illustrations

1. A Bend in the Road

You know there's people, they got the wrong idea of Jazz. They think it's all that red-light business. But that's not so. And the real story I've got to tell, it's right there. It's Jazz. *What* it is—how it come to be what it is.

People come up to me and they ask me, 'Are you going to play *Tin Roof Blues*?' They ask me, 'What's be-bop?' or what do I think of some record Louis Armstrong put out. But if I was to answer that, I'd have to go back a long way. That's why I have to tell a lot more than people would expect.

They come to tell me they like this record or that, and they ask me what I'm trying to do by my music. They ask me what's going to happen to Jazz? Where's it going? One night a man came to see me when I was playing in Paris; I'd known his son in New York. He came in with this party, and after the band had finished playing I got to talking with him. He started to tell me it meant a lot to him to hear me play; he'd had an experience he'd never had before. I told him I played like I always played. That's really all I can say.

But he was in a kind of feeling he wanted to talk. He was coming to me because there was something he wanted to know. So he told me he wanted to tell me a story, how he hadn't planned on coming to this place, this Vieux Colombier. He'd been off somewhere, very happy; his people, they had been enjoying themselves. And then someone suggested they come to hear me, that's what he said. And this man, he'd heard me, and I was still playing the old music, I was still playing New

Orleans. That's what he told me. 'This music is your music,' he said.

But, you know, no music is my music. It's everybody's who can feel it. You're here . . . well, if there's music, you feel it—then it's yours too. You got to be in the sun to feel the sun. It's that way with music too.

But what that man said started me thinking. I began to think there's a whole lot of people, all they've been hearing is how ragtime got started in New Orleans, and as far as they know it just stopped there. They get to think in a memory kind of way all about this Jazz; but these people don't seem to know it's more than a memory thing. They don't seem to know it's happening right there where they're listening to it, just as much as it ever did in memory.

This man that come to see me in the Vieux Colombier went on to tell me about the band, about the French kids. 'You gave them the spark,' he said. 'They didn't have it until you played.' And then he wanted to know what was going to happen to Jazz when people like me weren't around any more.

But you know, Jazz isn't just me. It isn't just any one person who plays it. There'll always be Jazz. It doesn't stop with me, it doesn't stop anywhere. You take a melody . . . people can feel a melody . . . as long as there's melody there's Jazz, there's rhythm. But this man didn't stop there; he went on to say it was me who made the music—me and the old bunch: Buddy Bolden, Kid Ory, La Rocca and all the others. That's where I tell him no. People's got an idea, I tell him, but it isn't like that; they think it started with one person—Bolden, Oliver, someone—but it wasn't like that.

I'm trying to explain it to this man, how it got started way back. I told him how my family beat time with their hands on drums . . . how that's Jazz too, how you can just beat on the table and it can be Jazz.

But what that man was saying . . . he was worried that if people like him don't hear about it, stumble on to it, just like he did that night when he was persuaded to come, it wasn't going to be around. 'Jazz comes out of an environment,' this man said. 'Something makes it. We don't have today what we should have to make it and keep it going. All we have to go on is a lot of legends. We'll remember river boats and never know how they were. We'll read about all those early days, and all we'll have is some bigger mystery except for maybe getting together with some friends from time to time and playing over all the records. We won't have anything of our own to add to it. The kids who take it up now, where are they going to go when they're looking for their background in Jazz? When they can't just walk down the street and hear it anywhere?'

'Maybe it stopped in New Orleans,' he said. 'Maybe there's no more of it except for a few of the old ones. Maybe its gone except for those who can remember it.'

Well, that's what this man had in his mind. But let me tell you one thing: Jazz, that's a name the white people have given to the music. What does Jazz mean to you when I come up behind you: 'Jazz,' I say, 'what does that do to you?' That doesn't explain the music.

There's two kinds of music. There's classic and there's ragtime. When I tell you ragtime, you can feel it, there's a spirit right in the word. It comes out of the Negro spirituals, out of Omar's way of singing, out of his rhythm. But Jazz— Jazz could mean any damn' thing: high times, screwing, ballroom. It used to be spelled *Jass*, which *was* screwing. But when you say ragtime, you're saying the music.

But here's what I really mean. All God's children got a crown. My race, their music . . . it's their way of giving you something, of showing you how to be happy. It's what they've got to make *them* happy. The spiritual, that's sad; but there's a way in it that's happy too. We can be told: 'Maybe you don't belong in Heaven, and you haven't got a place on this earth; you're not in our class, our race.' But somewhere, all God's children wear a crown, and someday we're going to wear ours too.

You know, the Negro doesn't want to cling to music. But he needs it; it means something; and *he* can mean something. He's always got to be honest, and people are always putting him to music. 'That's your place,' they say. How can you be honest to something when people are trying to make it unnatural for you?

But if you have a feeling for the music, you can understand him, and that's why he keeps it so important to himself. And he's always been trying. The black man, he's been learning his way from the beginning. A way of saying something from inside himself, as far back as time, as far back as Africa, in the jungle, and the way the drums talked across the jungle, the way they filled the whole air with a sound like the blood beating inside himself.

My story goes a long way back. It goes further back than I had anything to do with. My music is like that . . . I got it from something inherited, just like the stories my father gave down to me. And those stories are all I know about some of the things bringing me to where I am. And all my life I've been trying to explain about something, something I understand—the part of me that was there before I was. It was there waiting to be me. It was there waiting to be the music. It's that part I've been trying to explain to myself all my life.

I want to tell you about this music before I go. A man don't have all the time in the world, and there's things he has to do before he can go happy.

That's two very different things you know. Just going—that happens to everyone. But getting so you can go happy, getting so you can get done some of the things you meant to get done—that's something else.

It's like a man being born in a little place, just a bend in the road somewhere. After a while he begins to travel the road. He travels all the road there is and then he comes back. That man, he understands something when he gets back. He knows the road goes away and he knows the road comes back. He knows that road comes back just the same way it goes away.

But you take another man. He's been there in that bend in the road, and he never goes away. Time goes by and he's coming to the end of his days. He looks at that road and he doesn't really know what it is. He's missed it. That road, it got away from him. All he knows is how it starts off. He never gets to know where it goes and how it comes back, how it feels to

4

come back. He could be a good man, but there's something he hasn't been understanding. It's the road, or it's himself, or it's something else, but whatever it is, there's something he hasn't been trusting.

I can remember when I was young. I didn't have toys like others. I never had a toy to play with. I wouldn't have known what to do with a toy if you gave me one. I started once to write a song for a boy like that. The song, it was called *Sans Amis*. He had nothing to play with and no one to play with. But he had a song. He kept making that song over and over out of himself, changing it around, making it fit. That boy, he had this song about being lonely, and as soon as he had the song, he wasn't lonely any more. He was lucky. He was real well off; he had this thing he could trust, and so he could trust himself.

Oh, I can be mean—I know that. But not to the music. That's a thing you gotta trust. You gotta mean it, and you gotta treat it gentle. The music, it's that road. There's good things alongside it, and there's miseries. You stop by the way and you can't ever be sure what you're going to find waiting. But the music itself, the road itself—there's no stopping that. It goes on all the time. It's the thing that brings you to every-thing else. You have to trust that. There's no one ever came back who can't tell you that.

And when you get back, there's the river by the road. You're back where you started from and you're looking across the river, and you're getting yourself ready to go. I'm feeling I almost got myself happy enough inside now. I'm feeling I'm almost ready.

2. Omar

My grandfather—that's about the furthest I can remember back. My grandfather was a slave. But he was a man that could do anything. He could sing; he danced, he was a leader. It was natural to him; and everyone followed him.

Sundays when the slaves would meet—that was their free day—he beat out rhythms on drums at the Square—Congo Square they called it—and they'd all be gathered there around him. Everyone loved him. They waited for him to start things: dances, shouts, moods even. Anything he wanted to do, he'd lead them. He had a power. He was a strong man. His name was Omar.

Omar, he'd have these dreams about things. There was one time he had a dream about his right arm, about losing it at the elbow. After that, he'd only practice shooting with his left hand.

But maybe that don't belong here. What I'm saying is that he was a musician. No one had to explain notes or rhythm or feeling to him. It was all there inside him, something he was always sure of. All the things that was happening to him outside, they had to get there to be measured—there inside him where the music was.

He made his own drums out of skins of a pig or a horse hide. He knew horns. And when he wasn't working or hunting, he'd be trying them out. His master, he loved Omar. He thought so much of him that he kind of left him alone; and Omar did things his own way. He'd go hunting back in the bayous.

Bayou St. John or Bayou Pontchartrain. He'd go fishing back there. My grandfather, he was a free slave long before Emancipation. And he had his music and he could play it whenever he wanted.

Back in those days, it was like I said: Sundays was free for the slaves. They'd be sleeping and they'd never know the time, but there was a clock for them in the dawn when it would come, and the dawn it woke them natural like. All they felt, all that struggled to wake them up was knowing there was work all day until night. Sometimes, if they dreamed, things would come to them out of Africa, things they'd heard about or had seen. And in all that recollecting, somehow there wasn't any of it that didn't have part of a music-form in it. Maybe they'd hear someone from some tribe signalling to another, beating the drums for a feast maybe. They'd sleep, and it would come to them out of the bottom of that dream. They'd hear the drums of it, all sizes and all kinds of drums. They'd hear the chants and the dance calls. And always they'd hear that voice from the other tribe calling, talking across the air from somewhere else.

That was how the Negro communicated when he was back in Africa. He had no house, he had no telegram, no newspaper. But he had a drum, and he had a rhythm he could speak into the drum, and he could send it out through all the air to the rest of his people, and he could bring them to him. And when he got to the South, when he was a slave, just before he was waking, before the sun rode out in the sky, when there was just that morning silence over the fields with maybe a few birds in it—then, at that time, he was back there again, in Africa. Part of him was always there, standing still with his head turned to hear it, listening to someone from a distance, hearing something that was kind of a promise, even then. . . .

And when he awoke and remembered where he was—that chant, that memory, got mixed up in a kind of melody that had a crying inside itself. The part of him that was the tribe and the drums—that part moved on and became a spiritual. And the part of him that was where he was now, in the South, a slave—that part was the melody, the part of him that was different from his ancestors. That melody was what he had to live, every day, working, waiting for rest and joy, trying to understand that the distance he had to reach was not his own people, but white people. Day after day, like there was no end to it.

But Sunday mornings it was different. He'd wake up and start to be a slave and then maybe someone would tell him: 'Hell, no. Today's Sunday, man. It ain't Monday and it ain't Tuesday. Today's free day.' And then he'd hear drums from the square. First one drum, then another one answering it. Then a lot of drums. Then a voice, one voice. And then a refrain, a lot of voices joining and coming into each other. And all of it having to be heard. The music being born right inside itself, not knowing how it was getting to be music, one thing being responsible for another. Improvisation . . . that's what it was. It was primitive and it was crude, but down at the bottom of it—inside it, where it starts and gets into itself—down there it had the same thing there is at the bottom of ragtime. It was already born and making in the music they played at Congo Square.

And that square, in a way of speaking, it was my grandfather's square. He never had to hear it from a distance, because he was always ahead of the music there. It was there in his mind even before he got to the square and began performing it. It was *his* drum, *his* voice, *his* dancing. And people had to come, they couldn't move away from it. It was *all* the people, the masters too.

My grandfather was a young man then. He was young and he was strong and he hadn't any bowing to do to anybody. The only thing was, there was some who didn't want their slaves mixing with him, because he was so free and was treated so well by his master.

Another thing about this Congo Square—sometimes it was used for a selling-block. The masters would come there to buy and sell their slaves. My grandfather, though, never had anything like that. You know, someone was telling me once, from a book about Lincoln, something he said when he saw a mulatto girl being sold, how she was being treated, how she was all chained and pinched, and handled by the men what was thinking maybe of buying her. Lincoln, he was with two friends and he was watching, and he said, 'By God, boys, let's get away from this. If ever I get a chance to hit that thing, I'll hit it hard.'

Well, this one Sunday my father told me about, my grandfather was playing at this Congo Square. Everybody was mixing, just mixing as much as there could be. Some was dancing, if there was a feeling in them that way. Others, they were just hollering. But everybody, *everybody* was tapping their feet. Well, on this Sunday, in the midst of all this singing and dancing and drumming, my grandfather saw this girl.

She was standing sort of off by herself, just standing, and well . . . it come over him, it was one of those things. She was standing there, a little off by herself, and he just fell in love with her. Suddenly, everything he was doing, he was doing it for her. The girl, she must have been about thirteen or fourteen, all full of a kind of dream, like in the morning when no one's seen it. My grandfather came over to where she was and he danced and sang. Then he made her dance with him. The more there was of this dancing, the more happy he felt. What he was expressing—the language his feet and voice were making to tell her about himself—it was so rich inside him.

The girl was a slave, a maid for a young girl about her own age; they grew up together. But she didn't have any master like my grandfather had. Hers was mean to his people, watching them all the time. He wouldn't let them mix. It was like he had a fear of him; and mostly he watched this girl, noticing all what she did, all where she went; he wouldn't let anyone come around her.

That Sunday there—standing back some from the crowd, by the square, watching her dance—it came to him. He realized he wanted her for himself. Seeing her hesitate before dancing with my grandfather, that master, he wanted her. It seemed like everything she did sent itself inside him—her voice, soft, almost a hum, her arms, her body moving so strong in the rhythm. When the master saw my grandfather near to this girl, all with a power, dancing for her, and her responding, not being able to help herself, not wanting to . . . all at once the master, he got up to them and took her away.

My grandfather saw it all, saw what it was. He knew he wasn't supposed to talk to this girl or come to see her. And the girl was shy; she'd be frightened. He saw her being taken away. He'd seen her such a short time; it was such a short time he'd known all what he was singing and feeling and what it was leading up to in itself, inside him—to a kind of freedom, to a kind of time catching up to itself to where it was just itself and at peace. That feeling, it got too strong for him. He stopped the singing. He had to stop.

And people about him, they saw it. They'd seen what had happened. And so they started to moan, to let him know. They were moaning because something like that had happened to all of them.

There was an old woman come up to him then, some old hag. She was one of those witch women making brews. She made her living that way, by potions. She would sing into this potion, and bless it, and placate it, you know, and there would be a whole crowd around her when she did it back in the bayous, and they'd all be waiting to see what was going to happen to it; waiting to see if it was going to explode, waiting for it to show if things were going to work out, or if maybe there was an evil coming. The old woman came up to him and told him to come to her cabin the next day. She told it to him secret because it wasn't liked, that voodoo business. She said she was going to fix a potion for him, a love potion so that he could win this girl. She promised him to sing into it, and to praise over it, and to throw out the devils and bring down powers into it to work for him. And that way he would know, she said. If the powers said yes, then he would have the girl, and she would be his.

That old woman, came up to him and she danced around him a little, moving in different directions around him, but always coming back to him, making a chain around him, moaning some as she danced. She was all dried-up and skinny, but maybe she thought she'd be this girl if she made the potion right—she could have a part in all the loving. Some women are funny when they get old—they got to hear about everything, they got to know *all* what's going on; they can't bear to miss out on anything. That's how this old woman was about my grandfather. She touched him and she made him promise to come the next night, back there in the bayou where she made those brews. She danced around him and she was laughing and crying to herself. She was singing a love chant. Only it was more a wail. And then everybody in the square took to beating it out on drums, and she was wailing on, and they were all climbing up in the music like it was a tree and they wanting to shake it down and talk to the moon.

My grandfather left the square in the middle of all this. He went off alone, waiting for the next day. No one stopped him. There wasn't no one to bother him. The carts and flies and dogs, the slaves and the masters, they didn't need him.

All he thought about was this girl. He wanted to drop everything at her feet, like he had just come from somewhere far and was bringing it all to her, all that distance. He wanted to stop and listen, like there was a call from the bayous or the woods and he had heard it. She rode around with him all day like a wild bird on his shoulder.

The next day he was busy around the house and the fields, singing to himself—leaving to go watch the river and see how it had no need of the banks, how it carried itself along, not knowing how to do otherwise—moving because that was all it knew, like it was some tongue tasting off the earth and not wanting it.

And that evening he took off for this bayou where the old hag kept herself. There are lots of bayous in that country, and my grandfather knew them all. He knew them so well he could hide in them where no one could ever find him, all in that wild swamp like a jungle. If you've never been down in those bayous that's something to see. It's so even and calm there. There's big dark trees dripping in the water, funny lilies, things rotting, strange birds flying and swooping, bats, snakes—lots of snakes—and when the night come it's just like some burglar coming to steal what little light there is. There's such funny sounds, sounds like you never heard before. You're one place and you think you hear yourself away in another place. And that bayou—it's got to trust you and it's got to know you're trusting it, or it'll get you where you can't find yourself.

This night, when he went to get the potion, there wasn't much light. At that time of night a mist had got into the air. He went back into this one bayou, Bayou LeFourg, and the memory of this girl was following him. And when he got to this witch woman's place, there was a whole lot of slaves there, some free, some runaway—they was all chanting and moaning and beating on drums around this woman who had a big cast-iron pot she was boiling this potion in. They was all waiting to see what was going to happen, if this potion, it would give a sign—what all those roots and herbs and powders, they were going to do when the fire got them hot enough to throw out the devils.

Back there, outside her cabin with all the trees and no light and just the outline of that hut, this old woman started to sing. She bowed to the potion and started in waving her hands and moving her feet, and the rest of the people, soon they was waving and bowing too, cursing at the Evil, telling God where He could find them.

There was just the little light of the fire under the pot, burning just enough so you could see some of the legs moving and bowing and the hands reaching down, and the bottom of the witch woman's dress.

The whole thing there kept building and building up, and those people, they were telling themselves about things that were inside them. They were telling it out to the fire and the dark and the mist, and the only way they knew to tell it was by singing about a place where they all used to be happy once—how they used to stand listening in that place hearing sounds, like hooves when they ran over the ground, a sound of something running. They were trying to bring down some kind of witness to help them, and this love my grandfather felt for the girl started it all. Love was so important to these people, love was the only way to get close to someone. Sometimes it was the only way you could forget.

That's why there was this music in them; music was all they had to forget with. Or they could use it for a way of remembering that was as good as forgetting, a way that was another kind of forgetting. This music was their need, their want. But it had to have a pride too . . . they *needed* my grandfather to love this girl just like he needed her himself so they could bring themselves together and hope.

Then this potion exploded and it was a sign to them, and they set to clapping and shouting. Everyone came up to my grandfather and wanted to touch him to get a hold of some of the Power that was going to work for him. And then they started singing a praise.

The hag, she got some of this potion, put it in a little sack and tied it around his neck. He was to wear it there always for the potion to work. And my grandfather left there knowing that the girl was waiting for him, and that it was all going to be all right. He could hear what all the voices were doing behind him. Way off in the bayou he could still hear the voices where he left them, more quiet now, so deep—some real strain of love, some melody offering itself far back in the night.

The next few days there was to be a big ball for the white people at this girl's master's place. There was to be white musicians and lots of food and important people and everybody all dressed up. The girl was sent to town to get some things for it, but the master went along and the mistress too. The master, he wasn't letting her alone for a minute. But my grandfather followed him and he got a message to this girl that he would come around the evening of the ball. He knew she would be coming to town to buy goods for the ball and he had a friend who worked for his own master tell her. My grandfather, he was feeling the Love and the Power working in him and he was feeling strong. He had a confidence in him.

The day of the ball the whole place was busy, everybody fixing for the big doings, food being prepared, rooms being cleaned, furniture being arranged, the owners having their special clothes made ready. The girl was busy helping her mistress, ironing her things and helping her to pretty up, talking to her, listening to all the excitement and knowing that that evening my grandfather was coming to her. She was scared some, too. She could feel the master thinking about her, watching her. There wasn't none of that confidence in her, but there was an excitement. It was a song too, but it was a different song.

She was too inexperienced to know what my grandfather was out to do. But she had an instinct in her that had been born in her, it came as part of her heritage . . . there was so many girls before her, all having the same thing happening to them. She could sense it; she had an understanding for it. She'd never loved anyone or wanted to understand it for herself because she didn't want to be afraid. But this was all different inside her. It just seemed so much change was happening, but, you know, deep down inside herself, knowing my grandfather, she felt him like a safety inside herself, like he was a place you could rest in and be sure, like some of that confidence that was in him made a place for her too.

She had all this inside her but she kept it quiet—just went on doing her work like nothing was happening. The girl she worked for, her mistress, was so excited about the ball she didn't notice anything. But the master, his desire had kind of put him where he could feel her thoughts; he sensed something. I don't think that he had a hold of it, but there was some instinct in him too, and he was so jealous of my grandfather anyway that this girl was on his mind all the time. You understand, I think he enjoyed all this jealousy. He had a relish for it; he was a kind of sadist to himself, and this jealousy gave him a chance to work it out on other people.

The ball finally started. The musicianers were there playing their music, the kind of music that could fit indoors, the kind of music people would let inside their houses. It was quadrilles mostly and some reels, with maybe a tune like *Tiger Rag*, only different from what we know it today.

The guests started arriving. All the food and drinks was ready. There was the music inside and a whole lot of noise outside—the dogs barking, the carriages drawing up, a lot of voices talking and calling out. Bit by bit, things really got started. All the white people were inside dancing and talking, and all the slaves who had brought their people were outside talking to themselves and carrying on as much as they could, making jokes, gossiping.

And this girl, she slipped out of the house and went away back into the dark. She left the plantation hoping the lights from the big rooms wouldn't catch her when she passed them by, and she went running off into the woods at the edge of the bayous.

She was to meet him off there in the dark. They had made a meeting place near one of the bayous. And he wanted her. He was wanting her so bad, he hadn't waited where the meeting place was, but he had come most of the way she would have to come. He had been waiting on her all day and into the evening, walking around through the bayous in some kind of a spell. And the bayou seemed to know it. All the leaves were thick around one another, all the birds seemed to be going towards one another, and when the moon finally came out it wasn't full, but the light from it was inside him too. It was like that moon had too much light for itself to hold and had to get some of it inside him.

While he was waiting, he sang a little. It wasn't much of a song, not what we'd call a song. There wasn't much rhythm to it, but just pieces of melodies. It was moods he was making up out of himself. There wasn't anyone there to tell it to, but it was like he told it to her. He was finding the way of humming that feeling that the trees and the air were trying to give him, as if they wanted to be part of the power too. He was trying to say how he needed all this quiet of the bayou because so much of it was happening right inside himself. That's the way his song was; it was quiet and far off, but it was everywhere inside him.

So when it got near the time when the girl was to come, he couldn't stand it any longer. He got up and went to where she was coming. He went on almost clear to the house instead of waiting at the meeting place. And that's how he met her.

You know how to imagine the two of them seeing each

other, coming close. There's no describing it. It's just for two people. And right there where they were, right by the road she had come, they had each other. Right there where the night was to cool them and with all the trees dancing around them and over them like they was a tribe.

What they didn't know was that the master had followed her. He'd come after her, not so quick as she'd come because he didn't know the beginning of the bayou like she did, but guessing it, leading himself on by some craziness from want of her. And he came up on them where they was lying together. He swore at them and went to grab them, only he was so crazy he didn't know which one he wanted to grab, him or her. Her because she'd done murder inside him (all that kind of picture he had inside himself of the way she moved, all slow, all full, like some day in the middle of summer when it's got no hurry, of the way her eyes got when she was thinking of something, of her dancing there in Congo Square)—like I say he didn't know whether to grab her, or my grandfather (crazy mad at him because the girl had given herself). He stood there thinking all this at once until it exploded inside him, and then all at once he swung up with his gun and he made a grab at the girl, yanking her out of the way, and all in one motion he fired at my grandfather. And that ball, it hit in the arm my grandfather had had that dream about.

Maybe you won't believe it, but that's how it happened. My grandfather knew there was only one thing to do. He had to get away. He was trying to get the girl, get her so they could both run, but the master had a hold of her and he was trying to fix where my grandfather was so he could shoot at him again.

The girl was crying, wailing, telling my grandfather to go, moaning out, trying to free herself, scratching at the master, but just not being able to get free. My grandfather ran—ducking under the brush, holding his arm, and running off through the swamp with the master following. The girl ran too, not knowing where, wanting to go where my grandfather was going but not finding him in all that dark, feeling if she were to find the way the master would catch up with them both. She just ran around, hurt like some animal and wanting to hide. She could hear all the noise of the twigs and the branches, everything there had been between them breaking and crashing, becoming just a noise in the dark.

My grandfather kept on running. It was safe for him now; this bayou was so much a part of him. His arm was giving him trouble and it must have been all kinds of hell, pursued that way, not by something he could beat, but by that gun and by the colour of the hand that held it. He went running on like that, hating, worried over the girl, feeling guilty—all that love torn up just like that, hating all of a sudden even the bayou that was making it safe for him. But he kept on. I think it must be that he was proving out that thing, that survival of the fittest—not out of any book, but out of himself, out of a need he had of knowing he was able, knowing his way in the night. He was meaning to get away, to get strong and to come back. He was going to come back.

When he knew there was no finding him, he stopped and got his breath. He tied up his arm in some way and he took off for the hiding place of the runaway slaves, the ones who had been around when the witch woman was making her brew.

Oh, was he angry. He tore off that potion from himself and flung it into the water. He threw it off as far as he could with his left arm, but it didn't go far. It struck the water and something moved under the water . . . a 'gator disturbed by the splash and disturbing the water, and the ripples of it spread across the bayou moving like snakes in the moonlight and lay at his feet.

All that night he trekked through the bayou, feeling the night as if it was a breath that's wasted itself. At dawn he came upon these slaves that was hiding back there. He didn't explain nothing. Everybody back there, he had his own reason for being there, and every reason it explained every other somehow. There was no need of explanation. He just showed them his arm, and everyone understood everything he needed to.

They'd been hiding out in the bayou for all kinds of time, some of them just recent, but all of them meaning never to go back. They were going to stay there the rest of their lives. They had to stay back there anyhow, because about that time there were a lot of bandits, pirates who'd come in off the coast. The pirates were stealing and raiding off the towns and plantations, and these runaway slaves, they were taking the blame for it. There were posters up for them all around, offering rewards if someone were to catch any of them. Once in a while, these slaves would slip into town to some friend's house. But not often; mostly they stayed back in the bayou and made themselves hard to catch.

Well, my grandfather got to them. He knew most of them anyway. They fixed him up, but there wasn't much they could do for his arm: they had to cut it off later. It was just the way he had had the dream about it—you know, he had had the feeling right along, right from the time he had the dream. He lost his arm, but somehow he had been ready for it. He had a power in him, my grandfather, and he had a wish and a hate and it made him strong. He handled himself just as good not having that arm as when he did have it. There's some can be stopped by a scratch and there's some who just can't be stopped so long as they're living; and my grandfather, he wouldn't be stopped.

But I'm ahead of myself here. After this master had come upon my grandfather and this girl, and my grandfather had run off and the girl had run off too, stumbling around, cowering all crazy-like, he was trying to get another shot at my grandfather, and he was trying to find the girl. He was tumbling around too, not knowing what to do, and so he cried out.

That cry, it wasn't to say anything. The master knew my grandfather and the girl wouldn't answer. It was like another voice crying, like it was his own vexation crying out at the night. But there was people not too far off. They'd heard the shot and all the commotion, and they'd been coming out to see, and when the master cried out they heard him and they came up, breaking through the shrubs in all this dark. The three of them—my grandfather, the girl, her master—they hadn't been far back in the bayou, more or less just at the edge of it, and these people who'd heard the noise came trampling through and they found the master.

'What's happened?' they all wanted to know. 'Are you hurt?' 'What's going on?'

The master was mad, in a frenzy—my grandfather gone, the girl gone, everything he'd thought about himself happening between them happening right there and him coming on it, finished before he had a chance to do anything, and all that lust he'd had for the girl, someone else turning it all bitter—not the lust, but all that pleasure from thinking about it, all that pleasure he'd had warming inside himself all these weeks.

Maybe it's hard to blame him, even. People can't help feeling something when a pretty woman or someone passionate passes by right in front of them; maybe you try to tell yourself something different, but you know that's the truth. If you're a human person, it's just a natural thing to feel something that way.

Well, standing there that way with all those thoughts inside him, all mad, vain, and vexed and foolish, he cried out:

'Rape! One of my girls has been raped!'

Naturally no one would think he'd refer to a coloured girl as one of 'his' girls. They all thought right away he meant his *own* girl, his daughter. A white girl, she had been raped by a Negro—that's the way they got it. And right away it's the same old thing. Right away they are all out for a lynching. They set out after my grandfather right there. They was meaning to have their revenge.

It was too late then for the master to say anything. What he'd said satisfied him anyway. It was so that he was almost feeling good, and he got to believe it, and he followed after them, only he was trying to find this girl before they did so he could hide her.

All those trees there, they was standing like skeletons after the hide of the animal has disappeared. There was moonlight on their tops like blossoming, and there was the darkness under them, the light and the darkness somehow part of one thing that was darker than just plain dark, and all so still. And all that bayou—you could hear the white men's voices sounding from far off where they were chasing my grandfather, a noise way off disturbing the birds somewhere on the other side of the stillness.

Well, the master stumbled around, poking and feeling in the dark, and finally he came upon the girl. She hadn't gotten far. She was all cut up, her face bleeding, her hair all bunched up in some places and falling loose in others. She didn't know if she was some distance back in the bayou, or how far she was. She was dazed. She was just feeling lost. There was some evil happening, something bigger than she knew how to do with.

The man, her master, found her. He wasn't so sure if it was my grandfather or the girl. He swore and he yelled out: 'Stay where you are, nigger: I've got you!' And he pointed that gun, and the girl, paralysed like, just sitting there. Then all of a sudden she goes to move and the master saw it wasn't my grandfather. He came up to where she was crouching, sobbing to herself, and he hit her across the face to shock her, to quiet her so she wouldn't betray him and he took off his coat and wrapped her in it so her face wouldn't show.

Some of the men was still scattered around there poking about in the brush for my grandfather and they saw the master with the girl in his arms. He picked her up and he was carrying her like that in his arms, and when he crossed a patch of moonlight some of the men saw him and they came running up, wanting to help, all of them having this big excitement to put together, and all of them somehow feeling better about their excitement when they could talk about it, when they were together.

'Is she all right?' they said. 'We'll take her to a doctor.'

'We'll lynch that devil nigger as high as to . . .'

'We'll get him, don't you worry none.'

'We'll get the dogs after him.'

All that excitement, everyone talking, thinking if their own daughters were safe. But more than that, every man hearing a piece of his own excitement in what the other men were saying, feeling his excitement get bigger as he listened to it, every voice full of that excitement and a kind of righteousness;

and when you listen to voices like that, what they're saying, you can't tell the righteousness from the excitement: they're the same thing.

The master wrapped the coat around her closer so they wouldn't see. She wasn't one of those real dark girls anyway, and it was dark enough so the men couldn't tell. The master made out to pretend he was too ashamed for them to see, to help him bring her back. He acted it stubborn like, like it was the only right way. Wasn't it his own daughter?

The men got kind of humble and they let him go. They was trying to encourage him, trying to be all together in this thing. They wanted to understand this one thing about themselves, about having this thing, this excitement and righteousness, in common. Maybe then they each one of them would understand about his own self. They was going to see to it that my grandfather, his neck would be fixed good.

Well, the master carried this girl back through the swamps, stumbling over a piece of wood that had gone bad, almost tripping on a bush, not seeing his way too well. And walking along that way there was this feeling, this conviction growing inside him from the weight and the trouble and all the excitement behind him—he had this conviction he had been betrayed. He was feeling it was right and natural for the girl to be cut up and hit. She hadn't had any right going with my grandfather, a black man. That's how he thought of it: my grandfather was black. His lust had made him forget all about what colour *she* was. All he could remember was her eyes, all warm, all melody like when she was dancing—her hips, like sides to a moon, moving, swaying; her body, all about to topple over because of that love feeling she'd had when she was dancing. The master had that picture in his mind and he had that weight in his arms and they got to being the same thing inside him. He had the feeling that something that was his had been hurt and he'd had to go out and rescue it. It was right what he'd done.

He got back to his place, to the plantation, and all the lights and dancing and music, they were still carrying on. A couple of dogs set to barking, but he hushed them up. He cursed at all the voices and the laughter. Through the windows he could see his guests and he cursed them. They were going about flirting, amusing themselves, complimenting themselves on their importance and he could feel himself hating them. He was like some crazy man who was sick and had gotten away. He even rocked this girl in his arms, forgetting who she was, remembering only who he wanted her to be.

'We'll get him, honey,' he told her. 'We'll get even. Don't you worry; we'll strap him up good.'

He walked through the yard and into the kitchen. The slaves out in the yard fell away from him, not speaking, looking after him then looking at each other and shaking their heads. His face the way it was, the slaves didn't dare say anything. He took her into the kitchen and up the back stairs to a little room they kept for storing things—things they didn't use any more but weren't meaning to throw away.

He laid her down there and he wanted to forget about her now. Things, they became sharp to him now. He was beginning to have a danger for himself, what it was he had to do to put back this trouble he was feeling, all of it mixed up with the picture he had in him from the memory of what he had done— the bayou, her and my grandfather mating, the shot, the noise of brush being trampled, and all the people running. He didn't know what to do, what thing to go after first. He stood there thinking, trying to arrange everything in his mind.

It was quiet up there, he could hardly hear the music from downstairs. He looked at the dummies that his wife and his daughter used for modelling dresses. They were just standing there like something left over from a thing that was done. It was scaring him. Even the dummies were a reminding to him. There was always something left over. There was always something that could be put away only so far and no further. He would have to find his wife. He would have to send his wife to find her daughter and bring her upstairs, get her out of the way. He would have to talk to his wife.

When a man gets to feel a panic he acts in a quick way— things, they have to be cut away from him sharp, in a hurry, like he's got a knife. The master went down the stairs again fast. There was one of the slaves there cutting up fruit, not showing her face, only paring up a bowl full of fruit. He told the slave to hurry out and find his wife and tell her it was important, she had to come right back to the kitchen to talk to him.

The wife was worried; this didn't seem natural. She pardoned herself from her company, trying to be graceful in leaving so all in a hurry. She came back to the kitchen and her eyes were asking everything she didn't say. The master sent the slave outside and went over to the wife, up close. He's talking low and kind of fast.

'Where's Eveline?' he said.

'Why, she's inside,' the wife said. 'She's been dancing. She's been having a nice time. I believe she's . . .'

'Hush,' he said, 'that isn't it. Go get her. Bring her back here right away.'

The wife asked what had happened. She was wanting to know what it was, why he was sending for them both right then with all this ball on their hands and all these neighbours in the house. But the master, he was a man with his own made-up mind; he wasn't for no discussion of it just then.

'This isn't something you know about.' He said, 'Just do as I say.'

His wife, she had reason enough to know his ways. He was so often abrupt and she knew it only made it worse when she tried to bring her reason into it. She picked up her skirts, smoothing them a little, and she went. Everything had been going so nicely, all the furniture polished so well, the music kind of laughing and sighing so nice, the lights doing so well by her antiques, Eveline behaving so good—that part of things she knew about real well, the mistress things of making a house right. But this other, this was a thing she didn't understand. It was the thing in him she had never been able to understand, the thing she hadn't been brought up to understand.

When the three of them was back there in the kitchen, he ordered his wife to take Eveline to her room and keep her there, to lock her in. His wife wasn't liking the way this was turning out. He made it so easy for her to resent him, never making up to her for what her parents had done, giving her away to him, not having been fair, knowing she hadn't wanted to marry him. But there was nothing she could do. And she had a feeling things were going to be said that it was better Eveline didn't hear, things it wasn't right for her to hear. So she did like she was told. She took Eveline upstairs and put her to bed thinking her own thoughts, and when she came out of the room she turned the key in the lock and turned around and found her husband waiting for her in the hall.

He took her aside and he told her how it was. He told her that out there in the bayous, this girl, Eveline's maid, she had been raped. He'd come upon her and tried to save her, he said, but he'd been too late and the buck had gotten away. But he knew who it was and the whole countryside was out searching for him. He told her that the girl had been hurt, all cut up and crying and wounded and that in all that excitement when he'd tried to get this nigger after he'd shot at him, people had come running up and he'd cried out 'Rape!'

His wife interrupted him then, asking him how he was sure it was rape.

'The girl,' he said. He claimed the girl had told him that. And he told his wife not to interrupt any more, that the story wasn't finished.

So he went on. He told her how he cared for this girl, she was so close to Eveline, how he had always treated her like she was a daughter. And how it had shocked him when he found out what had been done to her, he was so mad with it, and how it was then he had cried out, not thinking, forgetting it was the girl who had been so close to the daughter and as if she had become the daughter for that instant. How it was then he had cried out: 'One of my girls has been raped!' and how people, they'd taken it for his daughter, for Eveline, and he had been so confused and mad still that he hadn't said anything, hadn't known what to say . . . .

And so that's how people were thinking it, he told her. That's why he had to talk to her. People, they were thinking now that Eveline, she had been raped.

And now all those people, he told her, they'd be coming around the house soon wanting to know was Eveline all right, or if there was any danger. And how could he tell them it was all a mistake? A man like him, he couldn't afford to lose face that way. He didn't dare tell them; it was frightening him. What if they refused to hunt for the black? It was important: he had to be caught. What if that nigger might want to avenge him . . . come back there and really try to get the daughter, or the wife, even try to shoot *him*. New Orleans and the country around it wouldn't be safe. And it wasn't much matter anyhow, one nigger more or less—wouldn't make much difference. You needed to put the terror in them once in a while, keep them where they knew they ought to be, else there might be ideas getting started in their heads—ideas you didn't want them to have.

Well, you know, he talked. He kept talking on and arguing with his wife. She got to pleading at times but he cut her off, getting sharper and sharper with her. And last of all he began threatening—wives, they had to help out their men, they had no place deciding things, thinking they knew better. 'You keep Eveline in there,' he told her. It was an order. There'd be so much confusion no one would know exactly when she had disappeared. 'I'll handle it all,' he told her, 'you just do as I say.'

So when the man who was acting as a kind of sheriff come up with some of the other men, the master was ready. There was some of the men who had been out by the bayou, and there was some others had come out from town with the sheriff, and there was some guests from the ball had heard something about it. They all come round, and the master met them and told them his daughter was upstairs and that a doctor was sent for. They could understand, he said, how no one was to see her. Her mother was with her, comforting her, trying to take away some of the shame. And he asked them please, not to say anything to the rest of the guests, the ones who hadn't heard anything already. They'd hear about it soon enough, he said. And he was so troubled . . . he felt he had to have a little time to collect himself. But right off he announced he was offering a reward for that nigger. Anyone who was to catch him or find out where he was keeping himself, he would get a nice piece.

The men left him then, and he went back to look for his wife. All this time the wife, she'd been thinking about all what was happening, trying to figure it out. She didn't trust his story. She felt there was too many places where it didn't hang together, all entire.

She got to wondering where the girl was, what he'd done with her, what it was the girl would have to say to her. But at the same time she wasn't trusting herself to decide anything. She wasn't daring to think, not even to herself, on any way of crossing her husband. Women in those days, they had no tradition that way. Maybe in other ways they got around it, but speaking up—that didn't happen. But this thing, it would be found out. She had that feeling for certain—that if the evil was big enough it couldn't stay hidden. She wasn't all that kind of an outside woman, but what she knew that.

So she went hunting through the rooms and hallways up there, wondering where he had put the girl. And he came up while she was searching. He found her there and demanded to know what she was doing, and the wife told him she was looking for the girl. Where had he put her? That girl, she might be hurt and need looking after.

The master was beginning to worry about the girl too. He wouldn't know what to do to fix her. So he brought the wife to the store-room and he unlocked the door and both of them stood there in the doorway, looking in out of the hallway light that picked its way from behind them among the clutter of things inside, falling between the dressmaker's dummies and some old furniture and not finding anything, seeming just to sink into that darkness, a frightening thing.

It scared them both when they found the girl there, she was lying so quiet and still, almost as if she wasn't breathing. It was hot in that room and it smelled like a piece of goods you pull out of a trunk that's been sealed a long time. They stood over the girl, looking at one another, and they could hear the slaves outside, out by the trees, singing to themselves, a soft singing, almost a hum. It was one of their spirituals: *Trouble time's come, pick up my burden, white man's riding out.*

The man picked up the girl and the woman led the way. They brought her to a small room they had, put her on the bed. The wife got some water and washed the girl's face and hands. She undressed her and put her to bed and sat by her. The man stood by the window, looking out, thinking.

It's the way of things sometimes. A man will go ten miles out of his way to spread harm to someone. He'll talk twelve hours and he won't spend one minute saying a good word. This master was like that. Here was this girl lying two steps away from him and downstairs there were all those people. He could tell the simple truth so easy like—how she wasn't sick from no rape, but she'd just been with a man she wanted. But the master knew he couldn't do that, and he knew he didn't want to. A man spends so much effort, so damn' much of his time doing all the *bad* he can, that when the times comes when there's some good he can do, he'd just as soon rope himself up to his own front door.

And when you start one of those lies, there's nothing you can do but go about getting it finished. It gets all out of your hands, and you're trying to catch at it every which way. But there's nothing you can do once it has got started. All the mending and repairing you do to it, trying to keep it where it started, trying to keep that one lie from becoming a thousand lies. But you can't do anything about it. You're just like a dog that's chasing rabbits when there's so many of them he doesn't know which one he's after.

So the master went downstairs. He went downstairs and he stopped the music and he called all his guests and said how sorry he was but something had come up in the family, an accident, it was terrible, his daughter had . . . a Negro had been there and done this thing . . . and they would excuse him, they would understand, but he needed the house quiet . . . there was this sorrow upon it . . . and how his wife was not feeling able . . . they would know how it was . . . .

The next day there were posters up all over town and around the plantations. There was a big reward offered and the posses were working out in all directions. You could hear the dogs working the bayou all day long trying to pick up a trail.

The slaves worked quiet, working hard, singing maybe, some plaint like *I'm worried*, waiting it out, wondering what really *had* happened, and not understanding. They all knew my grandfather and they couldn't understand. They all knew he had no business for a white girl. He just didn't have a need for a thing like that. It was a thing they couldn't understand except to fear it. There was a fear of it in the air.

You see, this master would realized that he *had* to say my grandfather raped his daughter or else no one would hunt after him. They all loved him too much. His own master would never allow it. But as it was, that master was in a spot: there was nothing he could do. The law was against him.

My grandfather's master tried to stop all that tracking down, the dogs and the posses. He knew my grandfather, knew he wouldn't do a thing like that. But all the people living there came up to him and showed him he had no right. The girl's master went over to the plantation and *he* told him he had no right; and so there was nothing my grandfather's master could do. My grandfather, he wasn't property any more; he couldn't be protected. It was all over, his being a free slave.

And the girl's master, it was just what he wanted. It was because of that he had to say it had been his daughter. Because there was still that hate in him. He had to see my grandfather brought down for what he had done, for what he had spoiled out of that dream the master had been storing up inside himself. He didn't care for the truth and he'd didn't care even for the girl any more. It was that thing he had felt die in himself out there in the bayou. He had felt it die out of him, like it was himself was being killed. And there was no resisting it any more. He had to have my grandfather; he had to see him dead if he was to ruin himself doing it.

And somehow the wife understood this. She stayed back at the plantation taking care of the girl, fixing things the best she could to make her comfortable. Sitting and waiting for the girl to come out of her shock. She never left the girl. She sat there through one night and into the day and feeling the next night settling in, waiting, letting the night say what it had to say when it hit all the buildings, the slaves in their cabins, and her even. Waiting and being half afraid what the girl would say when she got relaxed enough to talk.

She sat there thinking about her life, about the kind of child she had raised, about all the things she had done in the years that made up her life. And underneath all that she was feeling what kind of a man her husband was. Beginning to know for certain, and wishing life could give you a time to be young all over again so you could have it different.

And when the girl came to, when she stopped rambling inside herself from the shock and began to cry and to call my grandfather's name—not hateful like but in a kind of pain, crying his name like she was saying she had lost something, like everything had become unbearable . . . it was then the mistress knew she couldn't doubt any more. She sat in the night hearing the girl call my grandfather's name and she knew for certain. She heard it all in a kind of tenderness for the girl. This feeling she had, that they were losing something together, it filled her with a softness, a pity. That feeling, it's got no touch with how things are in the day. It was a night kind of knowing, like when you wake up in the dark and hear your own name, your own voice—and then when you get beyond that, when you get to calling a name that's not your own, but that's got even more of what's you in it, more of what's got your heart. . . .

'You love him?'

That was what the women asked. And the girl, she didn't answer outright. She cried. She clutched the covers and she cried as if the crying was far away inside her. And the woman left her then. She stopped watching out the nights with her.

All this time the search parties were fanning out through the bayous, dogs wailing and yelping, one calling to another. They'd find a part of his track and then it would lose itself in some swamp, and they'd find another and lose it again. Night and day, you could hear the pack calling from the bayous. And everyone living around there, they couldn't talk about nothing else, all of them waiting to hear what was happening, wondering if they'd found him yet, waiting to see how it would be.

The slaves felt a trouble on them. Nights, they was talking low to themselves, trying superstitions to keep away more evil, keeping under cover, trying to stay out of the white man's way. And days, they had their trouble on them. The overseers were being more cruel; the meals had less food to them; the work, they made it harder and there was more and more whip behind it. There was a whole lot more slaves getting beatings those days.

The only thing they had that couldn't be taken from them was their music. Their song, it was coming right up from the fields, settling itself in their feet and working right up, right up into their stomachs, their spirit, into their fear, into their longing. It was bewildered, this part in them. It was like it had no end, nowhere even to wait for an end, nowhere to hope for a change in things. But it had a beginning, and that much they understood . . . it was a feeling in them, a memory that came from a long way back. It was like they were trying to work the music back to its beginning and then start it over again, start it over and build it to a place where it could stop somehow, to a place where the music could put an end to itself and become another music, a new beginning that could begin *them* over again. There were chants and drums and voices—you could hear all that in it—and there was love and work and worry and waiting; there was being tired, and the sun, and the overseers following behind them so they didn't dare stop and look back. It was all in the music.

And back in the bayou where my grandfather was with the runaway slaves, there was music back there too. Those runaway slaves sensed the bayou warning them . . . *trouble, trouble* . . . the moon and the shadows and that heavy air, it was telling them an evil. And little by little they began to sing it.

Some of them had been at the square when my grandfather had sung for his girl. They'd seen him dance. They remembered that, and they took the melody and the music he'd had then; they took it and they sang it for him, beating out the time on their drums. It was just like they were in Africa again, like they was calling to one another, to another tribe, like they was trying to be with their people who was back there in the cabins, waiting all night to another dawn, working all day to another sunrest, working and waiting. Back there in the bayou, those runaway slaves took that glad song my grandfather had made and they sent it away into the night, sending it back to my grandfather, trying to give him the gladness and the power of it again.

My grandfather couldn't sing, though. They tried to bring him to where that place inside him had been, to the things a man promises himself, to the things that maybe happen just once. But all this worry he had, all this torment over the girl—there was all that in him blocking him from the place he meant to get to once. There was this terrible change in him; and the song just couldn't reach him.

Pretty soon word got around to them about the posters, about the reward, about how he had raped a white girl and how the whole countryside was after him. My grandfather couldn't understand it. He hadn't raped no white girl . . . what was happening back there? The girl, *his* girl . . . she hadn't told them to say that.

His mind jumped over one thing to another that was haunting him all the time . . . that memory of her and him, the way they had been together there at the beginning of the bayou . . . that calm place in the night before the night blew open on them. He looked up from that memory and he saw the bayou around him there where he was . . . the birds still meeting and flying over to one another, mosquitoes making their sounds as they swam around in the air, leaves and vines not letting one another go.

He'd look up from that memory and see all this living around him, all busy with itself, and he'd feel a question in him big as the whole earth: what was a man, what was he here for anyway? He'd sit there hitting at a bug, breaking a branch, running the soil through his hand. Everyone, they'd be silent watching him, wondering at him, not trying to get to him any more. They could feel the trouble of it in the air like big black wings, like a buzzard circling and circling over all the air, and they were waiting there to see where it would settle.

My grandfather could feel how they were, how they were waiting, and after a while he couldn't stand it no more. He'd get up and disappear off into the bayou where no one could see him. And it was like going into himself, walking through himself, waiting to see where it would all lead.

One day he was walking around that way, feeling all this misery tightening inside him. It was like a rusty wheel when it gets so tight it can't turn no more. He was feeling it lock inside him and he couldn't get it moving. He was wanting to see the girl, yearning for her, not living except for that. There was that part of him that was still free from all the torment, all the fear . . . it made that longing in him. And all at once it swelled up in him: he was walking around by himself and all at once he stopped where he was and he felt it change. It was like he'd gotten that wheel loose and turning at last. It was almost like he was free . . . and he knew he had a thing to do. He had to see her and talk to her. He had to take his chance and he had to hear her telling him she didn't have any part in all this, that nothing had changed inside her. He had to find her and take her away, or if she was safer where she was he had to let her be, but he had to talk to her, he had to feel her holding him.

He came back to the camp where those runaway slaves were, and he told them how it was . . . there was no helping it, he couldn't choose. One or two of them tried to keep him from going, but it didn't take no effect. They seemed to know it couldn't take no effect even as they was trying to stop him. So they watched him go and they sat there singing, knowing he'd be hearing them a long way gone. It was like they were following him, sending the song along with him to be a strength to him the way he had to go.

My grandfather could hear the song behind him, and it was like he could hear the silence ahead of him. He kept going through the bayou and bit by bit he felt the song fading out of the air and the silence taking it. He got to the place where he had to stop and strain to hear it . . . where he wasn't quite sure he *was* hearing it, but somehow still feeling the rhythm of it on the air. He felt it fade away and he felt the silence coming, and all at once he was strong again.

He went on fast as he could then, moving ahead, dodging the places where there might be some kind of a trail, breaking his way into swamps so he wouldn't leave much trace. It was dark in there. He'd look at things and it seemed like everything was inside some tunnel, a dark the trees made. The going wasn't very good in the dark and with all that tangled footing. And his arm was giving him trouble. But somehow he trusted that too—it was kind of like a sign—a place where all the trouble could catch itself and stop. So long as he could feel the hurt of it he had a thing to hold on to, a way of knowing what was real. Sometimes he thought he could hear things— the sound of a dog, a voice shouting. Maybe a bird would wake up and fly funny; he'd have the feeling when he was running about that something was pacing him. He'd watched rabbits when he had hunted for them, how they flattened back their ears and made their whole bodies slick-like, making less of themselves by tightening up so that nothing could get at them, not stone or bullet. My grandfather had that feeling on him, a thing hunting him.

Bit by bit, then, he was nearing the outskirts of the bayou. After that there'd be empty land, land that's got nothing mated to it, just dry-seeming grass; and behind that there'd be the plantations. New Orleans was off to the right. He knew that if he hit all that dry land there wouldn't be many trees for cover. He guessed they'd probably have that watched. It would be hell getting over all those fences. Even at night there'd be enough moon to make him seen. And day or night, there'd be dogs about.

Finally he hit out towards New Orleans, figuring on going to a plantation that was pretty close to town, to a cabin of a friend of his. If he was to mix with a lot of slaves it would give things a better chance to work for him. For a minute he was almost forgetting about that arm, how being a one-armed man would make him seen no matter how many he mingled with. For that minute, planning ahead, all eager, the fact slipped him. Then, just standing there, he felt it come back. He knew all over again who he was, what a dark there was for him. But he had to go on. There was no stopping there now.

He made it to his friend's place and woke him up. The fellow couldn't believe it. Surprise, it takes away liking a thing or disliking it; this fellow, he was supposed to feel good seeing my grandfather again. But even after the first shock, it was easier just to keep acting that surprise.

My grandfather woke him up and they just sat there, talking low. That fellow was talking up all about how worried he'd been—talking up to let my grandfather know what a friend he was, wanting my grandfather to share some of the bed. But all the while he was figuring something—a thing moving, taking shape in his mind, bending like all those black branches do when a rain is hitting the trees. That reward, that chance maybe a slave would have to get himself a little more freedom, if he was to bring in my grandfather. But this fellow didn't know how to go about it.

That fellow knew my grandfather. It wouldn't be easy. My grandfather wasn't too awful tired out, and even with just one arm, he was strong. And that fellow wasn't sure yet. It hadn't really come to him inside what he was out to do. He went on talking low, hearing the slaves in the other cabins just recent turned to sleep, seeing the lines of cabins like chicken coops outside his window, listening to my grandfather's voice in the dark.

My grandfather noticed how his friend was funny-acting, but he guessed it was because he was scared. He didn't worry about it any; there were too many questions he had to ask. Those questions didn't leave much room for other things. *Were they watching her plantation? People around, what were they thinking? How come this story about raping a white girl, how did it get started?* He sat there in the dark asking his friend and feeling the scaredness in the friend and breathing in the thick dark air. That air, it was like something pasted up and closed, thick and heavy; it was like it had been in a shoe a long time, there was something spoiled in it.

After a while there's no more to ask, and not much answer given. This friend made like he was turning in to sleep and he offered to share the bed, but my grandfather thanked him and sat up. Suddenly he was feeling like an old man who's lived too long and is scared awake by the noise of a clock falling. He felt a fear working into him from the night, a dark thing.

But he was a man and there was his woman out there and he didn't have time to worry out about what's wrong with the rest of everything. There was just that one thing that had to be done. He sat there in that dark, knowing that was the only thing. Then suddenly, there was no more thing to it: he got up from there and he took off, leaving his friend asleep. He skirted around the cabins and the fields, keeping clear of the big house, staying back in the shadows. There was a comfort to being on the move again; he could hear the night crooning to him like it was trying to rock him. Being out that way, finding his road in the dark, it was a comfort to him after that waiting. And when he reached that place where it was just grassland there between the bayous and the plantation, when he got there and was able to feel the wet of the grass touching him, feeling himself mighty now that he was on his way—when he got there he wanted to press that whole black night down on the ground like it was a towel. He felt a strength in him, a kind of knowing where he was going and how he was to get there. He got near to her plantation and stopped, wondering how he was to signal her, how he was to make himself known.

And while my grandfather was waiting, his friend was up there. He hadn't been sleeping at all and he'd known for sure where my grandfather was going; he'd gotten out of bed and raced ahead by the road and he was up there pounding at the big door at the front of the house where the girl was, banging on the knocker, trying to bring the master to open it, pounding away all in a fear, his hand beating against the door until suddenly without his ever knowing it, the door's not there and his hand is beating on nothing and he's pushing against a servant what had opened the door, the servant holding him back, amazed to see him there, telling him he must be crazy thinking to come to the front door that way. 'You crazy, man? Git around to the back door. You crazy?'

But he told the servant he had a right, there was something he had to tell the master, and he was sure going to stand right where he was when he told it.

But the master wasn't at home. His wife, the lady of the house, heard the noise and she came, moving slow through the hall, dressed all in some kind of dark lace, making her own shadows with her candle as she came. She asked him what it was he wanted: the master wasn't in, he was out in a searching party: she couldn't tell him more. She didn't say out in words what she felt seeing a Negro at her front door; she guessed it was all part of this thing. So many changes were happening. She felt tired. Everything she touched or saw seemed tired. She felt like she'd been breathing tired air—the way it was when she did things, climbed stairs or arranged for dinner or just went off to sit, wondering what her thoughts were working up to.

This slave went mad like, all crazy with eagerness and fearing it would go wrong. He had to hurry, he had to find out where the master was, he had to push down everything and take what was his to take—because if you don't take something when it's given to you, it comes back mean at you. You have to act quick, especially when there's a fear behind it, especially when you know a man might be learning what you're fixing to do to him.

That fellow ran off to try a whole lot of places where he might find the master. And this woman, the master's wife, went back into the library they had off their main room and played a piece on a piano they had, some ballad she'd learned when she was a girl. She touched the piano and she was thinking how pleasant the room wanted to be, how it wanted to put back all that dark that gathered to it. She sat there touching the piano with her fingers and let the piece play itself out, but in her mind she was thinking about the girl. Marie, her daughter's maid.

She sat there playing to herself, playing back the dark, and almost as if she was talking to the music she was whispering: *Those are Marie's thoughts. Every day, it's like this. Every day we know.* Where will it stop? she asked herself. Where can it stop? The hunting parties, the posters, the trouble building wider and wider; back there in the storeroom with her husband, with the girl lying there, she might have done something, it might have been different. But he had just told her to be quiet, commanded her, talked of marrying Eveline into a family down Florida way. It was to be done as he said, and he wasn't aiming to stop anything.

And now it had widened and it was beyond them. She sat touching the piano in that big room, and felt it about her: that girl's eyes, Marie, looking at her; Negroes pounding the front door almost before morning; the men gone on searching parties behind their dogs, tired and mad and hating. And a lie inside it all, waiting to break, insisting on being made known. She let her hand fall away from the piano and listened to the strings dying out of the air in that big room.

All this time my grandfather was waiting back there wondering how he was to do, trying to make out if there was any stirring, thinking how to reach the girl; he had come so far; there was that sickness of love tied to him like a ring when it won't come off because your finger's grown too tight. He didn't know how to do, but he couldn't wait any longer, he had to take his chance.

He ran then and crept up to the back of the house. There was no one about. Everything was like it was drowned in quiet. He crept up to the kitchen window and he looked in. He saw a servant come into the kitchen and he rapped on the window, gentle and fast. It frightened that servant plenty, his appearing that way, being who he was with half the country out hunting him. The servant began to moan a little prayer; she was scared this was a bad omen, that things was going to be worse still. But my grandfather spoke to her; he told her to go find the girl, Marie, he had to see her and he didn't have much time. The servant stopped her moaning some, but it was like she was afraid to move and my grandfather had to tell her all over again. He was beginning to get desperate now; he didn't know whether that servant woman was going off to betray him or if she was going off to call Marie, but she left him at last and he stood there waiting. It was like he was drowning. He couldn't tell what was coming to him out of the air, whether it would be Marie coming to answer that feeling in him or men suddenly jumping out of the night.

And then he heard a step inside the house and he saw the kitchen door turning, and it was over. It was Marie, her eyes as big as the night looking at him, her hands trembling when she touched him. For a minute then he took her to him, held her against him, feeling her arms go around him, feeling their bodies meet and soften and the bad feeling wearing itself out of them. There wasn't anything said, there wasn't anything to say.

After a while he led her away, back from the house and the side porch, back to a kind of spot that was dug up a bit from dogs scratching to make a hole. They lay there together in the dark, pressed into the ground, and at last they could talk out what they had to say. The girl told him all what the master had done, how it had happened, how there was a guard around the house; he'd been lucky, they'd gone off for a rest. They lay there talking the need out of themselves. He told Marie about the runaway slaves back there, how it had been with him. It hadn't made itself all clear to him yet, what she had told. It wasn't until he had been talking to her a while that he began to know it, feel it inside himself, all what the master had done to them, all the evil piling up from that one thing. He began to curse it. It came up like a thing from far off inside him, small at first, small and bitter, but building inside him, swelling and coming, making a feeling that when all that bitterness burst it would sour the world; thinking one lifetime, it wasn't enough to get rid of this story, to make it right.

The girl tried to soothe him. She told him about the mistress, how she'd been kind, how she knew what had really happened, knew they hadn't done nothing wrong; she'd help them. She touched his arm and she wanted to weep. But she was learning. She had no strength of her own, but somehow she had a strength to give. Almost it was a way of making things right, a hope. And he could feel it now, too. An answer, a part of an answer: or else it was a real answer, if only it could be made long enough. They were touching now, reaching. They had to have each other. And for that time, it *was* an answer. They had that to give, they were free inside themselves.

All this while the friend was out, going everywhere to find the master, asking everyone he saw where it would be best to look for him. Someone finally told him he'd gone to New Orleans and the fellow took off running as though to split, running till his breath got to be just one big pump inside him, pumping a need he had, that big feeling that he was changing himself, feeling he was becoming one of the master's kind. Soon now he could forget all about the fields, that sun that leaves a man with a tongue growing clear up from his stomach, the weed-chopping that takes a man's arms clear off his body, the cotton-picking that makes your fingers want to break. The reward, all that money, it would be coming to him.

He found the master, told him my grandfather was back there at the house, with the girl; it would be easy getting him —he could be surrounded like nothing. The reward, it would be his. . . .

The master didn't even talk to him, just looked at him like he wasn't there. He left him just standing there. He walked past him like he didn't exist.

This fellow's master, he was there too. He passed the fellow. 'You, git home,' he said. 'Git!' And he left him standing there like the other master had done. Not even looking at him.

They didn't waste any time. They had the whole country around there strung around like a rope. Where the bayous began, they got men to lay in cover. The whole land there, lying empty, like a freight yard without any trains. The quiet, it was almost shrill like, everyone so tense. Some people took to indoors; others got together, talking, laying bets, remembering stories they'd heard growing up or maybe that had happened a year ago, about a man being hunted, maybe escaping, maybe getting caught. Everyone had his own theory about what makes a Negro like that, making sure of their reasons for keeping him where he was. 'They haven't got enough with their own people,' they was saying. 'They want to come over to ours too.' And that something, it was something alien; they had no way of understanding; they didn't want to understand, anyway. It was a kind of assuring—assuring themselves *against* the black man, assuring for himself, or maybe *in*suring for himself.

That sort of conflict—you know, when you're not secure—like as a white man he'd feel inside himself, kept him from the Negro's music too. He didn't want it unless he could do it, too, do it better. But I don't want to get away from my story. There's so much books and speeches made about it, there's not much use talking about it all. I just play my music.

My grandfather, he was leaving the girl, holding her, telling her to wait out; God wouldn't just let them drop, as if they gave too much pain. 'You're mine,' he told her, 'and that makes it mine too, what I say. I can do anything I want in all the world when you're with me. And I'll get out of this. We'll have our time. . . .'

He left then, hunching himself over, running over the grounds. But the farther he got away from the plantation and got to where it started to be a little wilder, the more he felt like the weeds and grass somehow were trying to make a grab at him. And then he heard a shot, and he guessed what it was, there was an ambush for him, and he ran another way. He kept running and running and running: everyone after him, every way he went to go, getting cut off. He just had no way of getting safe, back into the bayous. Well, he kept on till he got to a clearing, right before the plantation of his friend. It was late and he was getting tired. Just an hour or two, some little rest he wanted, it was all—so he could figure something out. He crept up to his friend's cabin, went to him, shook him a little. And his friend there, he sprang up like, all quick; he hadn't been sleeping, but his eyes were closed; he was wondering what next move he was to take, lying there thinking, feeling positive about that reward, hearing the shot and thinking it was beginning then, they were after him, the reward would be coming.

'Who's that?' he said. My grandfather, he told him it was him—could he rest there a bit? . . . not much, just a little rest. The fellow, would he watch out for him? The whole country was after him; just give him an hour. . . .

So my grandfather, he couldn't help it, he started to sleep —not heavy like, but his eyes were closed, and he was forgetting some. And his friend there, lying on the cot, couldn't find anything to say to my grandfather, he was so shocked, having him appear like that. So he tried to lie quiet and let my grandfather sleep, remembering the master not saying anything to him when he'd told them where my grandfather was. It made him nervous, like he wasn't to be noticed; it kind of put him in a frenzy, how they weren't saying anything to him, like the only thing for him to do was get my grandfather himself—then they'd have to give him the reward.

My grandfather looked a hell of a lot different to his friend, lying there. There wasn't much to fear in him asleep, a one-armed man, wore out. He didn't have much to rejoice about now; he hadn't no right going with a girl that hadn't no approval, singing songs about it, getting everybody stirred up, everyone having to take a lot of misery just because of him and this girl.

And hearing that shot before, knowing it was shooting for my grandfather, it didn't make him so much alive somehow. As if that bullet was his death, and it had already been let loose, a thing that was already in the air. Somehow, even without hitting him, that shot had made a dead man of him. This friend sat there in the dark thinking, *He's dead . . . as good as dead . . . that shot already killed him.* Suddenly he heard himself saying it out loud and it frightened him. The whole night was frightening him.

41

He killed my grandfather. He killed him and he stood over him, looking at him. It hadn't even made a sound. He was still warm, even. There's not much to a man, the fellow thought; when he's through, there's not much to him.

He wiped up the blood and dragged and carried my grandfather out over the fields, sweat coming off him, to the master's house. He could hear lots of noise now. People were still out, hiding, waiting to catch my grandfather. Someone stopped him, and this friend told him he had my grandfather, they could all come in, he'd killed him. So the men that was around there, that one place, not too many, they started to follow; they couldn't believe it. They all come up to the master's place and this fellow took my grandfather off his shoulders and threw him on the ground. 'There he is. I got him. Where's the master? There's a reward to me who's got Omar.'

Well, the master came up. He'd left New Orleans by that time and the people he was talking to, trying to get everything together so my grandfather couldn't get away; and then when he came, having him dead right there that way, he didn't know what to do next . . . it was all so quick. A reward for a man, you know, at the time you set it up, it's all kind of far away. The reward and the man . . . then the man when he's dumped dead at your feet, nothing left to him, it's two different things.

His wife came up to him, angry; after what had happened, she wasn't able to stay outside of it any more. She wanted to know if he was going to tell them.

'Tell them,' she said, 'or I'll tell them myself.'

There had been too much night-waiting inside her. Marriage, duty—they'd gotten smaller inside the things she'd had to think about. She'd lived beyond herself and found a power inside herself; it had changed her.

'You tell them,' she said, 'now.'

And the master sensed it. He knew he couldn't command now. Somehow, even, he was wanting to say it himself, as if he had always meant to, as if saying it was part of what he'd been planning all along.

He stood there looking out at all those people, some with

their guns still: a whole lot of faces circled around the dead man, and the girl lying by him calling to him. And back of them the slaves . . . that damn' singing . . . *how* they was singing . . . something he could never set foot on. The whole place around was so busy—all that shouting, all the lights on in the house, the yard so crowded. All these things were giving him a pressure.

So he explained how, when it had all happened, he'd called out, 'one of my girls'—this coloured girl, she had been like a daughter. He hadn't meant his own daughter, Eveline. Later, when all the confusion came, he'd been too scared and confused, it had all gotten so he didn't know what to do; and he'd been so angry that Marie the coloured girl might have been hurt, he'd thought she *had* been raped. He hadn't known his wife had taken care of her . . . please try to understand him. It had been so dark in the bayou. He couldn't have seen who it was, just someone who needed some help. He'd left the girl as soon as he'd brought her to the house. He hadn't known.

He told it all, humbled himself as much as he could, said it all out of himself. And all the time he talked his eyes were on the girl, never looking up, staring hard at her as if every word he said was making her disappear, changing her into a mist and blowing her away. As if he were having done with her.

The people felt sick. They wanted to do something, but there was nothing they could. They just stood there—some arguing, some calling all kinds of things to the master, but by law, they couldn't get at him. Some didn't think it was too important, not enough to get people to taking sides, causing a lot of bad blood. So they cleared away finally. The man who was some kind of sheriff came back then; he asked questions, moved around a lot and kept people talking. But what was there to say?

And this fellow who'd killed my grandfather, he didn't get the reward. He was left there. They couldn't get him to leave, and finally they had to threaten him to make him clear out.

Some people who had got a love for Omar, they stayed wanting to fix up a funeral for him. They wanted to help out, a lot of them sorry, even before they knew that the girl hadn't been raped by Omar. But the master there told them no, he had to do it; he wanted to; it was the only way he had for making up for it some. It was a tragedy, he said; he wished it had never come around to him, no part of it. And so after a while there was only his wife and this girl. Everyone had left, and you could hear the mourning all the slaves were singing, trying to tell my grandfather to prepare a place for them, trying to give him some of their religion in case he'd got a need for it. They were singing, chanting again, beating themselves with their hands, beating on the ground, finding a way to let my grandfather go.

You know, things like that, they stay with you, more than if things happened natural like. In a way, it's what comes when people, they're living outside of themselves; maybe, living too much of everything at the same time, finding all kinds of laws instead of just the one there is.

My grandfather, he never tried to plan anything. Anything he did or tried happened because he couldn't help it, like he was trying to find things the same outside, as they were inside himself. And it wasn't weak things that happened. He just had a way of being happy or sad. He was like a piece of rhythm. Thinking about it, you see all kinds of things, ways to look at a life. Maybe in him things just hurried up to happen. Things what's dragged out a long time in most people, happened to him all in a little time.

And you know, he was a leader, he led the music. But still, as an idea, the way he played his horns, the way he beat on his drums, he was still a background music. It was still a music that hadn't broken loose, it hadn't stopped being scared. It was irresponsible in a way to all its worries.

It was an awful early beginning.

3. My Father

One night I was in Paris—I was playing at the Vieux Colombier—and I got to thinking that story inside me, about my grandfather Omar, and I got to talking it like almost I was playing the music, going back into it as it came. I got to talking it and looking at the room that way it was, all piled up for the night, the floor all swept, and only one light burning, and a sign over the piano saying:

THE PIANIST ACCEPTS CIGARETTES

I got to talking and there was some friends there. I was just talking like I was inside the music, just letting it come of itself, and remembering like that, all about my grandfather . . . you know, it's almost like I'm him.

And at the same time I was asking myself: 'Why am I here?' Well, just as soon as I asked the question I knew why. France, it's closer to Africa. I've wanted to be as close to it as I could. It's a mood, you'd call it, an atmosphere I wanted to put myself into. My grandfather, he was Africa. It was like getting back, and I wanted to get back as far as I could.

It's all true, all that I said about my grandfather. And it's all so mixed up with the music. In Paris it's like I can hear all what was happening to it when my grandfather was making it, back in those days when it had just been brought over from Africa and was still finding itself in the South. Those pieces of melody, that music my grandfather had for himself, the things the music was saying—it was all for something dear to you, something you just couldn't make unhappy. It was a thing to wear away your insides. Music like when one foot keeps coming up and going down on the ground when there's something stirring to make it move that way ... when all the leaves maybe are lying low and the wind is coming through them sombre like.

You take when a high note comes through—lifting and going and then stopping because there's no place else for it to go. That's stepping music—it's got to rush itself right off your voice or your horn because it's so excited. You can feel it. People, they go looking for music, you know, needing it. And the music—it's any damn' thing; it's whatever it is you need. Like when you're sad sometimes, you want to remember something, maybe something you was happy about once, and you find an old hat that your aunt once wore and left in a closet—it's just been left there, and she's dead. She was a beautiful woman and she used to wear this hat. She had it for glad times and she had it for bad times; it went a lot of places with her, and she left it behind. All the music I play is from what was finding itself in my grandfather's time. It was like water moving around a stone, all silent, waiting for the stone to wear away. Because all the strains that went to make up the spirituals, they were still unformed, still waiting for the heart of ragtime to grab them up, mix in with them, bring them out of where only a few people could feel the music and need it, bring it out to where it could say what it had to say.

It's like the Mississippi. It's got its own story. There's something it wants to tell. It's all those things and more, you could say, and some I don't know how to say. It's a way of living, a blood thing inside you.

That girl, Marie, she had a child. And my grandfather being dead, she had no name for it, nothing to christen it by. She was still staying there at that house when it came, and the master and his wife told her to take their name, Bechet, so the baby, it would have a name. And after that they let her alone, they let her do as she liked. She could stay there, bring up her child, have things like she wanted; everything would be taken care of, they told her.

She became free, almost the same as my grandfather. Only my grandfather, his freedom was different; it was the way he had to express it. He was free his own way, to look for his life, waiting for it. But she was only free back into herself, almost as if she had lived out her whole life and now she was free to remember it. She had this child, and it was Omar, too. She had a name from each side of her memory to give this child. Omar Bechet, he was my father.

Time went on. All the working, all the living, all the confusion . . . there was a hell of a lot of fuss and confusion about the time my father was growing up. It was right around Emancipation time. All the papers were taking sides, running cartoons of apes and things, screaming blood and gunpowder. A lot of people didn't want to lose the Negroes. The Negro, he was three billion dollars worth of property, and here was a law coming that was to take it all away. Who was to do the work then?

Well, they had the war, and it made a bitterness. A lot of people, they never could climb so high again after the war and they had a whole lot to say about that. It was a crime; it was all political; it was the end of America. What would anyone want with a lot of black people being free, people who couldn't even spell their names or read a book? And everything changed upside down . . . the soldiers being brought in to guard, sort of keep order, and making more bitterness just by being there.

But the Negroes, it had made them free. They wouldn't be bought and sold now, not ever again. If they could find a piece of land somewheres it would be theirs, they could work it for themselves—the ones anyway who had heard that slavery was against the law. A lot of Negroes, especially in back places, never did hear about it. But mostly there was this big change: a different feeling had got started.

> Go down Moses,
> Way down in Egypt land;
> Tell old Pharaoh,
> Let my people go. . . .

It was years they'd been singing that. And suddenly there was a different way of singing it. You could feel a new way of happiness in the lines. All that waiting, all that time when that song was far-off music, waiting music, suffering music; and all at once it was there, it had arrived. It was joy music now. It was Free Day . . . Emancipation.

And New Orleans just bust wide open. A real time was had. They heard the music, and the music told them about it. They heard that music from bands marching up and down the streets and they knew what music it was. It was laughing out loud up and down all the streets, laughing like two people just finding out about each other . . . like something that had found a short-cut after travelling through all the distance there was. That music, it wasn't spirituals or blues or ragtime, but everything all at once, each one putting something over on the other. That one day the music had progressed all the way up to the point where it is today, all the way up from what it had been in the beginning to the place where it could be itself.

Maybe that's not easy to understand. White people, they don't have the memory that needs to understand it. But that's what the music is . . . a lost thing finding itself. It's like a man with no place of his own. He wanders the world and he's a stranger wherever he is; he's a stranger right in the place where he was born. But then something happens to him and he finds a place, *his* place. He stands in front of it and he crosses the door, going inside. That's where the music was that day—it was taking him through the door; he was coming home.

Marie, she was there with the boy, both of them all excited. She was wanting to cry with all that dancing and shouting, the drinking, everybody running in and out, passing every which ways right in front of her. Some of those people didn't even know what Emancipation was; they just knew there was a hell of a parade going on, a whole lot of laughing and singing, a whole lot of music being happier than the music had ever been before.

When my father told me about it, years after, I always

48

thought I wanted to write a song about it. I got the music for that song, but I haven't got all the words. I got just a few:

> Today, today, is Emancipation Day.
> Our thanks, our thanks, O Lord, to thee—
> O Lord, O Lord, how happy we will be,
> A Free Day, a Free Day that's happened to me—

That's all I got. But you got to imagine you was hearing that day to understand the music. That's what it is: it's that day's music the way my father could tell about it, the way he could make me hear it.

That was 1863, and my father was about eight at the time. He was old enough to remember. There was all that excitement, and then the settling down. Even with Emancipation people had their living to get done. A lot of the Negroes were taking off, moving around, trying to find a new way. Others just stayed where they were, doing what they were used to doing, not knowing any other thing to do. A lot of people found Emancipation day hadn't made much change.

My father had been growing up as good as free. His mother had been left some money and she was fixed nice. Those people, the master and his wife, had taken care of her. They had let her do just what she wanted, and when they died they'd seen to it that she wouldn't have a whole lot of worry how to take care of herself and the boy. She'd stayed on with them after the trouble with my grandfather. There just wasn't much else she could choose; there was nowhere to go. And those people there, the man and his wife, they were trying to make it up to her. It was almost like they were trying to tell her without putting it into words that they wanted her to come over to them and do their forgetting. Time changes a man, and that master he acted a very different way after all that trouble. It was like some part of the evil had been washed away out of him by all that had happened; and the evil had left a kind of sorrow in its place, a gentler thing.

Even after Emancipation, my grandmother stayed on there, bringing up the boy, doing little things around the house. She was really free then, but it didn't seem to change nothing; she still didn't have anything to go away to, and she was sort of used to it there. In a way, even, she was content; not struggling against anybody or anything, just staying on around the house and fields and that edge of bayou. She wasn't forgetting my grandfather and she wasn't trying to think about him conscious like; she just found a part of him in all that land around, feeling something like maybe the trees do standing around a field, mourning some and wondering what's become of the ones that were there before the field was made.

My grandmother had this money she'd been given, and so after the people died and the boy, Omar, he was growing up, she finally did move away, and she got a place of her own. The boy used to play in the woods and by the river there, making little boats and things, wandering about, racing off to hear the music whenever it was being played or sung. Seems like there was always music around New Orleans in those days. All those people who had been slaves, they needed the music more than ever now; it was like they were trying to find out in this music what they were supposed to do with this freedom: playing the music and listening to it—waiting for it to express what they needed to learn, once they had learned it wasn't just white people the music had to reach to, nor even to their own people, but straight out to life and to what a man does with his life when it finally *is* his.

My father fooled around with horns and the instruments they had, and he sang along with them—the spirituals and all the shouts—and he danced, too; he had a feeling for it. Around that time he was going to a pay school, a private school for both white and black. His mother paid for it from some of the money her master had left her. He was learning there, speaking and writing fluent, both English and French, having a very good education. When he finished this school, he had to decide to take up a trade, some work that would make his living. Well, he had tried to play cornet; he'd fooled around with it, but he never became much good at it. He just couldn't *play* music. He had a real understanding of it, a real

50

feeling, but he couldn't play it. Music was his pleasure, but it wasn't something for a living; so he took up being a shoe-maker—not repairing them, but making them, designing them, all kinds. All his life he stayed close to the music. And all the time he wasn't around where the music was, he was there at his shop making those fine shoes like he knew how. That shop was over on Esplanade Avenue there in New Orleans. Oh, he made a many a fine shoe in that shop, but where he really lived, where he really learned who he was inside himself—that was always where the music was being played. That was his real life. He understood it so well—he could sing or whistle, he could hum out what he'd only heard once; he could remember it and put it all together. He knew what was good music and what was bad, what was real and what was faking itself. Sometimes he got impatient with the music. He'd always had his way, and he was just naturally strong in himself—he wasn't a man for holding back, and when he sensed the music holding back it made an itch in him. It was like he had a feeling of knowing where the music wanted to go, where it should go; he had more feeling that way than many of the musicianers, and it troubled him when it held back, when it didn't reach out for what was happening to it. It had so many new things to say—all what was going on around the Mississippi, the time what was coming: he knew the music had to reach out to say those things.

People think you got to play music to understand it. That isn't right; all you've got to have is a love for it. That understanding my father had for it—more understanding than many a musicianer who was playing it—and that made it just as important to him as if he *was* playing it.

But dancing—that was another thing. That was something he did himself; he could dance awful well, just dance himself on out. People got a pleasure out of watching him. There was one time—I remember this so plain—I was awful young and I asked my mother (she was so light you almost couldn't see she was coloured, Octoroon they call it), I up and asked her: 'Why did you marry that black man?' My mother, she was an awful understanding woman. She could have answered all kinds of things from that one thing I asked her. She could have had me growing up full of a lot of confused ideas without ever understanding something awful important in life. But she had a better way. She just looked at me and said, 'Well, your father, when I saw him, he was wearing such pretty shoes. I just saw those shoes, and he was dancing so well. All I could see was the shoes and how he was dancing, and I fell in love with him.'

When my father was a young man, the bands they were having in those days was mostly music that wanted to talk to you and me, but it still didn't know how. But it's just like if I've lived all my life in one place, I've never taken a trip. Then if I go somewhere, I know there's other places than where I am; but before I take this trip, I don't know nothing else. Well, back in those days, the musicianers were playing all among themselves, meeting mostly at one house, playing all night . . . but mostly, even though they knew different times were coming, knew there'd been a change, they were mostly staying together.

You know, there was one house where they all met, where my father got them all together. It was in the section called 'back o' town'. We just called it 'back o' town'.

'Where're you goin'?'

'Oh, nowhere, just back o' town.'

Well, right across from this house was a police station. You could hear the music, there, coming across the street, but mostly there was no complaints. Once in a while one of those old hens who don't like themselves would put in a complaint to the police, but nothing was ever done about it. The police working there never bothered; they'd come on out in the street most of the time to listen to it, and they joked with the musicianers, taking life real easy.

Sometimes in this house, they'd have contests like, they'd put a jug of wine in the centre of the floor and cut figures around it. 'Cutting figures', that's what it was called. They'd dance around this jug of wine, a whole lot of kind of steps, dance as close to it as they could and still not touch it or knock it over. The man who touched it, he'd have to go out

52

and buy another gallon, buy more wine for everybody, the musicianers too—and then there'd be some more dancing. My father used to win a lot of prizes there. It wasn't no woman party. It wasn't nothing like that. There wouldn't *be* any women where these men got together. It was music and this cutting figures. Maybe somebody's wife would show up, but it wasn't any sporting place like Lulu White's. Those sporting places, it was mostly pianos you heard there, but these musicianers meeting at this house back o' town, they just brought their friends, just to relax. Those bands, those days, there wasn't any piano to them: it was guitar, bass, violin, drum, trombone, cornet—that was the original orchestra.

People have got an idea that the music started in whore-houses. Well, there was a district there, you know, and the houses in it, they'd all have someone playing a guitar or a mandolin, or a piano . . . someone singing maybe; but they didn't have orchestras, and the musicianers never played regular there. There was Tom Anderson; he had one of those cabaret-like places—saloons. He had practically everything there, card-rooms, bar, a hop-room—and he had music. Sometimes you'd hear accordion, guitar, mandolin, sometimes bass, maybe a violin; other times you'd hear someone singing there. It wasn't a whorehouse but you'd hear *whorehouse* music there. Lulu White, she wanted orchestras; sometimes she'd hire one, but it still wasn't a steady thing. The musicianers would go to those houses just whenever they didn't have a regular engagement or some gig they was playing, when there was no party or picnic or ball to play at. But in those days there was always some party going, some fish fry, and there was always some picnic around the lakes—Milneburg or Spanish Fort Lake.

All that what's been written about you got to play your instrument in a whorehouse, it's all wrong. Just going there for work sometimes, or to one of those cabarets over by Franklin Street when there was nothing else doing, that was all there was. I could pass one of those houses and hear a band and the next night I could pass by again and I wouldn't hear that same band, it wouldn't be there. So how can you say Jazz started in whorehouses when the musicianers didn't have no real need for them? It's just like a man, you know: he doesn't go to a whorehouse unless there's just nothing else for him. He's just letting something bad out, some feeling he isn't wanted somewhere. This Jazz was just like a man. No, it wasn't red-light districts were making ragtime. Musicianers weren't *going* there to make it. The only thing that was holding them back from playing it for everyone was the same thing that was always holding it back. A lot of those houses, sure, they wanted to hear it, they wanted the musicianers.

But Jazz didn't come from a peephole in one of them. You know, you take a woman. Say she's got a light dress on; maybe it's summer—if you look through her dress and see she's a woman, it's not her fault; it's not her fault you're looking to see how she is. And if she moves, and you watch her, all the time thinking about having her, that isn't her fault either. That's your mind putting something else on something very natural; that's a fact and shouldn't be made out of shape. And that's Jazz too. If people want to take a melody and think what it's saying is trash, that ain't the fault of the melody. Sure, there's pieces like *Easy Rider* or *Jockey Blues* that have got lyrics you'd call 'dirty'. Lots of them, they're exhibition-like, they're for show—a novelty to attract attention. But it's not those lyrics or those blues that really enter into your heart. The ones that really do that, they're about sad things—about loving someone and it turns out bad, or wanting and not knowing what you're wanting. Something sincere, like loving a woman, there's nothing dirty in that.

One night—my father happened not to be there that night—they had a new policeman on the beat; I guess he wanted to show he was new and he didn't like coloured people anyway. Well, this man who had music all the time was sitting on the stoop that evening, just sitting there. The musicianers, they hadn't come there yet that night.

And this policeman walked up to the man. 'Go on inside,' he told him.

The man, he was sitting there; it was his own stoop, and he didn't pay any attention.

'You be inside by the time I get back or there'll be trouble.' And the policeman went off, walking slow, on his beat. And when he came back the man was still sitting there. The policeman told him again, 'Go inside,' and he took out his club and hit him, and the man jumped up and grabbed the club away from him and started hitting the policeman back with it. And people started running up. It's something you can't hardly help thinking, when you see a black man and a white man fighting. If you see two men who are white, at first you wait; you don't know which one is right. But on a street like that, a black man—he's hitting the other, it's hard to think what started it, how it happened or *who's* right. The decision is easily made that the black man is wrong. That was one of those things of that time.

Well, soon there was a riot. The police from across the street started running over; other people came, and a lot of people were killed. But the man got into his house, and he boarded it up, and he got his gun and fired from his windows; his mother there, she reloaded his gun for him, and this thing kept up for hours and days. Man, that was something, I'm telling you! There was a whole square of houses, all connected, and around all this square there wasn't a space but four or five inches apart that didn't have a bullet hole. It looked like some corners I've seen in Paris after World War II after they got finished defending it there.

Well, they put out an alarm for him, the whole city knew about it. Policemen came from all over. There was a whole mob of them around, ambushing the house. This was going on and the man wouldn't come out; he just wouldn't come out and he wouldn't give himself up. A priest came and pleaded with him, saying to stop all the shooting because so many people were getting hurt and getting killed from all the fuss. But he *still* wouldn't come out. And finally his house was set on fire, and they all thought he was dead. But you know, they never did get him. To this day, they don't know what happened to him. No one's ever seen him, they've never found him, no part of him. He got away . . . maybe through some house there that connected with his.

That day my father was at work at his shoe place. Everyone knew about the riot, all the trouble there was. And the people he was working for had so much feeling for him, they called a friend of theirs—he ran a funeral place—and they called a hearse for him so he wouldn't get killed, or the police wouldn't put him in jail—the streets weren't safe that night—and that's how he came home.

Well very often, you know, the musicianers had opportunities to play engagements all over New Orleans. There was one place they went a lot, they used to call it *Irish Channel*. Well, they'd be passing through the section, and one of the Irishmen, he'd see a musicianer coming by and he'd stop him. 'Hey, Nigger, where you going? What you got there with you —that your bass?' Anything they figured was yours—music, singing, dance—they'd make you do that: you do that at the point of a revolver. If they felt you were happy doing it, they really felt you were *their* Nigger: You was in their house and they was making you play—that's the funny thing, you know: making you stop it, and begin it, making you stop in the middle and do it all over again.

But that night my father came home in the hearse—I can remember awful good that expression on my mother's face! But then something was always happening around. There's another time even—this one time, I remember, it was my uncle; he's dead now. But he used to sing awful good; he had a nice voice. One time he was going home and he passed in front of the opera house. They was having an opera, and he stood out in front of it, in the street, and all of a sudden, wanting to like that, something he couldn't help himself, he started to sing along one part, one of the main parts. He was singing pretty loud and a lot of people heard him. You could hear him all inside the opera house, too. A couple of people, they came out to see what was going on. And then a couple of policemen came along, and they arrested him: he wasn't supposed to be doing that, disturbing things. They brought him to a police station, and he was going to have to pay a fine, maybe stay overnight. But you know, it was funny, the police captain liked music very much—he knew a lot about opera, and when they told him my uncle had been singing like that, in front of the opera house, as a joke, at first, he asked my uncle to sing, and he liked my uncle's voice so much, he let him go. My uncle didn't have to pay that fine. He just walked out of the station. Oh, yes, there was always something; New Orleans, there was always something happening.

That's the kind of man he was, my father, back in his young-man days. And about then he took to spending a lot of time along the river. That was the time these river boats was steaming up and down the river, making a real big splash when they came in to a landing. It was a gay time, the kind of time my father just naturally loved.

These boats, used to have contests, for music. One boat would line up alongside another and they'd play at each other, not too serious . . . sort of to amuse the people who was paying to ride on the boats. White musicianers they were at that time. There wasn't anything but white musicianers on the boats then, but they'd go along the Mississippi, and they'd hear the singing of the Negroes by the river, and some of it reached them. They'd be the songs of the Negroes working, or maybe just going about their business, maybe just resting . . . there'd be all that kind of music like it was some part of the Mississippi itself, something the river wanted to say. And it had an effect, you know; it just naturally had to have an effect on whoever heard it.

There's been so much that's been written and sung about the Mississippi, all romantic and wonderful somehow. But there's a lot of misery there too, a lot of the bad times and the hurt that's been living there beside the river. And the Negroes by the river, working, singing around, they had to have something to wash away their troubles: they'd let the Mississippi carry some of it for them.

That music was so strong, there was such a want for it that there was no moving away from it. The people on the boats couldn't help listening. Some of them, maybe, they were

not showing their liking, not all of them. There were some
even who didn't want to hear it at all. But it was one of those
things that kind of comes in and robs you; it takes something
in you without your even knowing it. And that's the way it
was. Pretty soon the people wanted to hear more of it; they
wanted to know more about it.

My father, when he wasn't working at his trade or down at
the steamboat landing, spent all his time among the Negro
musicianers. By that time he'd gotten himself so well known
and so liked down at the steamboat landing that the manager
of one of those boats had come to depend on him. My father
took care of all kinds of arrangements for him. But all the time
he could, he was off listening to what the musicianers were
doing to those old traditional songs, how they were making a
new spirit from them. My father often found jobs for some of
those musicianers. Many a time he'd start things going, getting
up a dance or a contest. And because he worked down on the
river too, and the manager was so fond of him, he got up an
idea to put coloured musicianers on this one boat . . . put them
on and really let them stir things up, let the music show a lot
of things what had been happening to it since Emancipation,
bring some of the good times to move along the river with the
boats.

That's how he got up a band one day, and that was the
first coloured band that had been put on a boat. That boat,
it got started on its excursion and all the people were waiting
to have their big time and expecting to hear the old band, when
all of a sudden they heard this new music. They'd never
heard anything like it . . . at first they didn't know what to
make of it. It was something they'd heard about all right, and
it was supposed to be bad. *Jass*, that wasn't a pretty word.
There was lots of other names for it too, and at first some of
those people got mad and demanded their money back—
they hadn't paid to come and hear that; it was bad enough
when they'd had to listen to some of it, something like it,
coming in from across the river. But after a while, you know,
everyone, they couldn't help themselves—they were liking it
and they were feeling good. The music was coming out to

meet them and it got a welcome. Pretty soon they were having a time there. The tunes they were playing . . . *Salty Dog*, that would be one . . . just playing on out, coaxing and bragging some, but all natural too, all so warm.

Then another boat came alongside this one. It had heard all the goings on. That other boat, it had white musicianers and the people on her were leaning over trying to hear the new music, and the musicianers were mad. A whole lot of people were feeling mad about it . . . a lot of business was going to be taken away. Negroes, playing on a boat, it wasn't right; mixing that way, it could lead to a lot of trouble. And those people who had been enjoying the music, letting themselves feel friendly to it, all of a sudden they felt they ought to get ashamed. It was just like when you were a kid and you'd been out all day—maybe you were supposed to have been at school, and you came in and your mother was there wanting to know where you'd been. Well, you'd been fishing and you hadn't ought to have been. You just can't come right out and say what you've been doing, so you pull out a string of fish and *then* you say 'I've been fishing'. Well, those people, they couldn't even feel they could bring out a string of fish. They just felt guilty and they didn't want to hear any more. What was happening was making them feel kind of ashamed, so all they could do was get mad.

But those coloured musicianers kept on playing, and pretty soon the people on the boat, even the white musicianers themselves, began to go with the music. They couldn't stay mad. The music, *it* wasn't mad, it hadn't got any threat to it; there was just simple things in it, a lot of moods, a lot of feelings people had inside themselves. And so the white band, it played too, and the people, they gave in and pretty soon there was all kinds of dancing and hell raising, everybody having a whole lot of fun, answering to all that rhythm there, feeling all that melody carry them along.

That's how my father wanted it. He just filled his house with music, and when it wasn't being played at home he'd be off somewhere else where it was being played. Like I said, he wasn't a musicianer, but he really had a feeling for it. He lived right on, too, and died in 1923. I was just hitting New York, coming back from Europe, when it happened. There I was then, a musicianer travelling all over. And there he was dead and I was taking the train back to New Orleans. A long way. A long way home. But that was what he wanted for me, what he'd always wanted for me.

4. The Second Line

Everyone in our house liked music. When they heard it played right, they answered to it from way down inside themselves. If my brothers weren't around the house playing, they was out playing somewhere else. My father, my mother, and me too—we was all the same about music. Even when I was just a little kid I was always running out to where the music was going on, chasing after the parades. Sometimes I'd get into the second line of the parade and just go along.

The second line of the parade, that was a thing you don't see any more. There used to be big parades all over New Orleans—a band playing, people dancing and strutting and shouting, waving their hands, kids following along waving flags. One of those parades would start down the street, and all kinds of people when they saw it pass would forget all about what they was doing and just take off after it, just joining in the fun. You know how it is—a parade, it just makes you stop anything you're doing; you stop working, eating, any damn' thing, and you run on out, and if you can't get in it you just get as close as you can.

In those days people just made up parades for the pleasure. They'd all get together and everyone would put some money into it, maybe a dollar, and they'd make plans for stopping off at one place for one thing, and at some other place for something else—drinks or cake or some food. They'd have maybe six places they was scheduled to go to.

And those that didn't have money, they couldn't get in the

parade. But they enjoyed it just as much as those that were doing it—more, some of them. And those people, they were called 'second liners'. They had to make their own parade with broomsticks, kerchiefs, tin pans, any old damn' thing. And they'd take off shouting, singing, following along the sidewalk, going off on side streets when they was told they had no business being on the sidewalks or along the kerbs like that, or maybe when the police would try to break them up. Then they'd go off one way and join the parade away up and start all over again. They'd be having their own damn' parade, taking what was going on in the street and doing something different with it, tearing it up kind of, having their fun. They'd be the second line of the parade.

When I was just a kid I used to get in on a lot of those second lines, singing, dancing, hollering—oh, it just couldn't be stopped! But sometimes you had to watch out: the police, sometimes they did nothing but smile, other times they just weren't taking anything for pleasure.

The police would come by sometimes and, like I say, some of them didn't do nothing to stop what was going on, but others used to beat up the people and break them up and get them moving away from there. You'd just never knew which it would be with those police. But somehow they never did touch the musicianers; I never did see that happen.

Once, I remember, Buddy Bolden was out there singing and playing. He was singing a song of his that got to be real famous, *I Thought I Heard Buddy Bolden Say*. The words to that, they wasn't considered too nice. A lot of mothers would hear their kids singing when they came home:

> I thought I heard Buddy Bolden say,
> 'Funky Butt, Funky Butt, take it away. . . .'

And if the kids were scratched up at all or hurt some, the mothers they'd know right away where their kids had been, because as often as not someone did get scratched up when they hung around listening to these contests or to the advertising the bands did for some dance hall or something. This time I remember, I was down there around Canal Street somewheres—I was awful little then—and a policeman come along and he looked at my head and he looked at my ass, and he smacked me good with that stick he was carrying. I ran home then and I was really hurting some, I couldn't even sit down for dinner that night; and my mother, she took one look at me and she knew right away where I'd been.

Then there were the funerals. There used to be a lot of clubs in New Orleans, social clubs. They used to meet regular. They had nights for ladies; they played cards, they had concerts—a piano player or two or three musicians; it all depended what night in the week it was. Sometimes they used to have very serious meetings, and talk about how to do something good for members and the club and different things. When a member died, naturally all the members would meet at the club. They would have a brass band, the Onward Brass Band or Allen's Brass Band, and they would go from the club to the house of the member which was dead, and would play not dance music but mortuary music until they got to be about a block from the residence of the dead person. Then the big drum would just give tempo as they approached. The members would all go in to see the corpse, and then they would take him out to the cemetery with funeral marches. And they'd bury him, and as soon as he was buried they would leave the cemetery with that piece *Didn't He Ramble*. That was a lovely piece and it's really the story about a bull. This bull, all through his life he rambled and rambled until the butcher cut him down. Well, that really meant that this member he rambled till the Lord cut him down; and that was the end of that.

Sometimes we'd have what they called in those days 'bucking contests'; that was long before they talked about 'cutting contests'. One band, it would come right up in front of the other and play at it, and the first band it would play right back, until finally one band just had to give in. And the one that didn't give in, all the people, they'd rush up to it and give it drinks and food and holler for more, wanting more, not having enough. There just couldn't be enough for those people back there. And that band was best that played the best *together*. No matter what kind of music it was, if the band could keep it together, that made it the best. That band, it would know its numbers and know its foundation and it would know *itself*.

And those bands, they could play anything that was wanted—waltzes, shorties, marches, *any*thing. Lots of times it was the Creole musicianers. They'd be the ones, their band, who'd win. And like I say, they had to be ready for anything. You take a band like Manuel Perez's; they'd have engagements at dance halls, theatres, for churches even. And they'd have to play tunes that could fit in, tunes like maybe *Have You Seen My Lovin' Henry?*, *Fiddle Up on Your Violin*, or *I'm Gonna See My Sweetie Tonight*. Tunes like that you could one-step to. You had to have a reserve of knowing how to play anything with a lot of feeling and understanding. And one thing—that one thing you just can't describe—the feeling there was to a good band that made it able to do anything better than the next band, knowing how to do something without being told.

Some bands, they played compositions, some of Scott Joplin's numbers what had been arranged already. Or they played stand-bys like *Maple Leaf* or *High Society*, pieces they had memorized, they had them put down in a fixed way.

But if a band could play numbers that weren't arranged, or even numbers that were, but do them in their own way, free and sure, with a kind of inspired improvising—that was the band that would naturally win in the bucking contests.

In Perez's band they used to play all kinds of numbers. Numbers like *Black Smoke, Pineapple Rag, Canadian Capers*. Those were shorties really. In a way of speaking they were more of a challenge. Or not a challenge exactly, but they made what they were doing fuller just because they *could* play them too when other bands they didn't know how. Those were numbers for people to dance to. Their mood, it was different, the kind of feeling they demanded. Perez, he had a band could do anything. There was one number, it was English. It's one everybody knows. *Lightning Bug* it's called. Perez, he'd three-time that until it was really beautiful to hear.

Well, the people listening to them, they'd follow wherever they marched along playing, and finally they'd just win out. It was always the public who decided. You was always being judged. It would make you tremble when one of those bands, it came into sight. Say you was somebody standing there, a spectator—you'd be hearing two bands maybe advertising for different theatres or a dance or just being out there. One of them it would come up in front of the other and face it, and you'd hear both of them. There'd be the two. And then you'd start noticing onliest the one. Somehow you'd just hear it better. Maybe it was clearer, maybe it was just giving you a lot more feeling. That band, it would be so gay and fine—the men in it, there was nothing they was depending on but themselves. They didn't have to play after some arrangement. Almost it was like they was playing ahead of themselves. And so they'd have more confidence and there would be a richness to what they were doing. And so you'd want to hear it closer and you'd get up nearer. And then, it seemed it was *all* you was hearing. It was the only one that came through. And the other band, it would get away farther and farther until finally you just didn't hear it at all.

There was another kind of bucking contest too. There'd be those parades of different clubs and often times it would happen that two or three clubs, they would be parading the same day and they'd have engaged these different brass bands. Allen's Brass Band, it was one that was very well known. The Onward, that used to be another. The Excelsior, that was one. And those bands, the men in them, waiting for that parade to start, they'd all have that excited feeling, knowing they could play good, that they was going to please the people who would be about there that day. They had no fears. But the musicianers from other bands, bands that had just been gotten up for that day—they were just a bunch of men who was going to play, and that was a difference; they wouldn't have that sure feeling inside. Bands like the ones I named, they were organized and they had the preference at these club parades.

And those clubs, maybe the Lions Club or the Odd Fellows

or the Swells or the Magnolias, the men who were their
members, they'd all have their full dress suits on with sashes
that would go down to their knees, and they'd have this
Grand Marshal who was the leader of the club. He'd have the
longest sash. He'd have a sash that would go right down to his
shoe tops and it would have gold bangles on it. And on his
shoulder, he'd have an emblem, maybe a gold lion. That was
his badge. But most of all, the way you could tell the Marshal,
it was from how he walked. The Marshal, he'd be a man that
really could strut.

It was really a question of that: the best strutter in the
club, he'd be the Grand Marshal. He'd be a man who could
prance when he walked, a man that could really fool and
surprise you. He'd keep time to the music, but all along he'd
keep a strutting and moving so you'd never know what he was
going to be doing next. Naturally, the music, it m..kes you
strut, but it's *him* too, the way he's strutting, it gets you.
It's what you want from a parade: you want to *see* it as well
as hear it. And all those fancy steps he'd have—oh, that was
really something!—ways he'd have of turning around himself.
People, they got a whole lot of pleasure out of just watching
him, hearing the music and seeing him strut and other members
of the club coming behind him, strutting and marching, some
riding on horses but getting down to march a while, galli-
vanting there in real style. It would have your eyes just the
same as your ears for waiting.

And people everywhere, they'd be coming from every
direction. They'd just appear. It was like Congo Square again,
only modern, different. The times, they had changed. But the
happiness, the excitement—that was the same thing all the
time.

And so these parades march along. You'd be in the band for
this one club say, you'd be stationed to be somewhere at a
certain time, and another band it would be stationed at some
other place, maybe somewhere almost on the other side of
town. And the time would come you'd have fixed to start
both, and you'd move off and start by going to some member
of the club's house, stopping off there for a drink or a talk or

to eat and have a little fun, and then go on again. The other band, it would be doing the same. Both of you would be moving to the meeting place. And the people, they'd be up by Claiborne Avenue and St. Philip. They know you'd be coming there. You *had* to pass some time. It was a parade and you'd be going to where the people were because naturally if you have a parade you were going out to be seen. And you timed it to reach there the same time as another band. And that's where the hell starts, because if two bands meet, there's got to be this bucking contest.

The way it was fixed, one of the bands, it would stop, face around, and then go up close to the other, go right through it, one band going uptown and the other downtown.

The Grand Marshal, he'd be leading the club and when he got to some corner or some turn, he'd have a way of tricking his knee, of turning all around, prancing—he'd fool you. You wouldn't be knowing if he was going left or right. Oftentimes, the second lines running along after the parade, they'd go complete right after he'd turned left. And that was a big part of it—him stepping and twisting and having you guessing all along. The way he could move, that was doing something for you. He led it.

And people they'd be singing along, dancing, drinking, toasting. That Marshal, he'd lead his club's band up to the other one, and the leader, he'd go through with him. Manuel Perez, for example, he had his Onward Band—other bands, they'd tremble to face him. A brass band, it was twenty pieces, you know. And the leader, he'd take his band right in amongst the other, and he'd stop. You'd be standing there on Claiborne Avenue and the bands, they'd come closer to each other, keep coming closer, and you'd be hearing the two of them, first one in a way, then the next. And then they'd get closer and you couldn't make them out any more. And then they'd be right in together, one line between another, and then it was just noise, just everything all at once. They'd be forty instruments all bucking at one another. And then you'd have to catch your breath: they'd be separating themselves.

Then came the beauty of it. That was the part that really

took something right out of you. You'd hear mostly one band, so clear, so good, making you happier, sadder, whatever way it wanted you to feel. It would come out of the bucking and it would still be playing all together. None of the musicianers would be confused, none of them would have mixed up the music, they would all be in time.

And that other band, getting scared, knowing it couldn't go on further, it was finished. It couldn't be trying any harder, it was there still doing its best, but hearing the other band, say some good band like the Onward—it had thrown them off. It wasn't a band any more. It was just some excited musicianers. It would have three or six different tempos going. The men, they didn't know their music and they didn't know their feeling and they couldn't hear the next man. Every man, he'd be thrown back on his own trying to find whatever number it was they had started out to play. But that number, it wasn't there any more. There was nothing to be recognized.

And the people, they just let that band be. They didn't care to hear it. They'd all be gone after the other band, crowding around it, cheering the musicianers, waiting to give them drinks and food. All of them feeling good about the music, how that band it kept the music together.

And being able to play in that kind of band, it was more than a learning kind of thing. You know, when you learn something, you can go just as far. When you've finished that, there's not much else you can do unless you know how to get hold of something inside you that isn't learned. It has to be there inside you without any need of learning. The band that played what it knew, it didn't have enough. In the end it would get confused; it was finished. And the people, they could tell.

But how it was they could tell—that was the music too. It was what they had of the music inside themselves. There wasn't any personality attraction thing to it. The music, it was the onliest thing that counted. The music, it was having a time for itself. It was moving. It was being free and natural.

That's how I was growing up. I used to go down by the

river, too, and catch fish, cat fish. And then there was those
swamps I used to go into after black fish. We called them Shoe
Picks. We used to believe if you caught them and kept them in
moss, put moss all over them, they'd turn into snakes . . . all
those crazy things a kid takes into his head. But all that was
nothing but the kind of fooling around a kid will do, the kind
of thing a kid has to do. It's a kind of memory-making thing
every kid has in his own way and puts away inside him, and
years later it calls a man far back into himself, every man his
own way. It's nothing important in itself, but it's there and it
makes itself important . . . it's the first things you found out
about and somehow those things, they stay on at the bottom
of everything else.

My brothers played in the Silver Bells Band: that was my
brother Leonard's band. He had my brother Joe on guitar,
Sidney Desvigne cornet and Adolf de Massilliere on drums.
Leonard, he played trombone in his band, but he'd also bought
a clarinet one time and he was sort of learning to play it. He
used to keep it locked up when he was away, but I wasn't
ready to be kept out of anything—I was about six at the time
—I found the key to the dresser he had the clarinet locked
up in, and I'd take it out of the drawer and go practice with
it around the back of the house. There was a place under
the porch where I could get myself out of the way, and
I'd sit there teaching myself about the clarinet, all how it
worked.

One day I was under there and my mother came around
back to where I was playing and she found me out. 'What are
you doing with your brother's clarinet!' she said. It really
frightened her seeing me with it because she knew I wasn't
supposed to have it and she was just sure it would be broken
and she could already hear what my brother would be saying
when he came home. She just didn't like the idea of touching
something that wasn't yours. But she'd already heard me
playing a little when she came around the house, and instead
of making me put the clarinet back right away, she made me
play some more for her. It was afternoon and there was no
one around. She stayed out there with me and listened a good

while, and she saw I could handle it. I played a tune called *I Don't Know Where I'm Going But I'm On My Way*.

So she got to talking to me, how she wanted my brother to hear me that night, how she was going to arrange something so we'd all play together and I could keep the clarinet. She sat there with me in the afternoon and talked about a lot of things and there was a something in her voice, a kind of happiness at finding I could handle it. I couldn't ever forget that time, the way she was, the feeling I had that the two of us, we were suddenly finding such a lot of one another.

That night my brothers were playing at home. Leonard, my brother, was always going from the trombone to the clarinet when he was with us, sort of feeling it out. Well, I asked to play his clarinet and my mother said, 'Oh, let him play it,' and I played and he heard me and all at once he stopped playing himself and looked at me; he was really surprised.

There was another time I remember. It was my brother's birthday and there was to be a big party, all a surprise—he wasn't told anything about it. My aunts and my mother and her friends had cakes special made for it, special shell fish, a whole lot of food prepared. Everybody in the neighbourhood had been invited and they were all going to spring in on our lawn to surprise my brother. And the best of all—there was to be a band. It was Freddie Keppard's Band had been hired for it.

All that day I was racing around among the women watching all this preparing for the party, being real excited about all the going on, the way a kid will be when something's to happen. And then the people began to arrive—it was a real big party. And finally the band came in. They set themselves inside the house and waited, and when my brother came home they let go all at once and the people came jumping out shouting *Surprise!* Well, it really did surprise him—all that going on, people running around, the music. And after all that had gotten under way, the party sort of settled down to the music.

There was dancing, people getting together, things being

real lively. The people, they were all over the house and the lawn. And the band was playing back in the kitchen.

As it happened, it had been understood that the clarinettist —that was George Baquet, he was a fine musicianer— wouldn't show up till later; he had another engagement on a parade. So the band went along playing without him for a time, but it got going real good. The music just took off and went ahead, being real happy about itself.

I stood around there hearing them play. I was standing back by myself in the entry to the kitchen, and I couldn't help myself. This was a band that was answering all its own questions. The way they played, it got me terrible strong. It was something I couldn't change and something I just couldn't do anything about. I knew I was too young for *them*, but I sure wanted to play along with them all the same. So I sneaked away. If I can't play with them, I told myself, I'll just play along with their music. I sneaked off and got the clarinet and went into the front room where nobody was at. It was a sort of dentist's office—my brother was studying to be a dentist too. I went in there and I sat down in the dentist's chair—it was dark in there—and I began to follow right along with the band with that clarinet of my brother's what he had given me.

At first no one heard me; but then, the way I was told it, people began to take notice. They hear the clarinet, but they knew George Baquet hadn't shown up yet. Well, they figured maybe he *had* shown up, or maybe some other musicianer was taking George Baquet's place. And then the men in Keppard's band, *they* noticed it and began to look at each other. Who the hell was playing? Maybe they thought it was a joke of Baquet's, maybe he was back somewheres else in the house where the party was going on. The musicianers, they were having their own damn' party in the kitchen. There were people there too, but mostly the crowd was out front.

All this time I didn't know anything about what all was happening; they told me about that later. I was just having myself a hell of a good time, improvising, following along, not thinking a worry. It was just entire natural to me just a whole lot of happiness to be playing in their orchestra—

they didn't even have to know it; just me, I wanted to know it.

But they prowled all around and at last they found me. They opened the door and they couldn't believe their eyes. At first they couldn't see anything—the dentist chair was so big and the room so dark. But I was still playing along like there was still music going on, only I was playing real soft-like. They stood there looking at me as if they couldn't believe it yet, and finally one of them laughed and said: 'Well, you're awful little, but we heard you, and you were sure playing like hell.'

So they brought me back there, back into the kitchen with them and they put me in a chair by the window, and they gave me a drink. And then it was almost the same, almost the same thing only now it was the big thing—it was real: I was back there with them, I was playing in their orchestra; they were all still so surprised they didn't know what to make of it. Me, I was just happy—I was really there, I was playing along with *them*.

I'll never forget that feeling I had back there in the kitchen with those men, playing along. Those men, they were masters. Ragtime didn't have to look for a home when they were playing it. They really gave me the feeling of being discontented until I'd be able to work regular with them. Oh, it was grand!

And then after a while Baquet showed up. There was an alley right in back of the house and the kitchen it opened on to it, and being summer the window was open. Baquet came along this alley and *he* heard the clarinet and he wondered who was playing it, who the hell was taking his place. He stuck his head in the window and he looked around. He *heard* it, but he couldn't *see* it. He kept looking from side to side, but there was just no clarinet where he could see it. But then he looked down: he saw me there in the chair—he just saw my head. He saw me and he couldn't believe his eyes; about all he could see was the clarinet.

Well, I guess that was a surprise for him too, but he came on in, and he took out his clarinet and he ran his hand over my head and he just laughed. And he kept me there all evening, playing right along beside of him. That night, I guess I was the richest kid in New Orleans. You couldn't have bought me for a sky full of new moons, and I was six years old. At the end Baquet asked my mother if he could give me some lessons; and my mother said, 'That's real kind of you, Monsieur Baquet, but I don't know how we'd pay you.' And Baquet said, 'You just let Sidney come to me, and he and I will fix that up.' And in the end that's what we did.

Well, there I was a musicianer; and before long I was going around seeing all the men, sometimes we'd go into the men's room and I'd see how they had themselves all wrapped up. Some of them had their privates bandaged and there'd be sort of a strong odour-like, something like that iodoform. I'd see that but I didn't say anything mostly. I'd ask maybe one of them some time, 'What's that!' and he'd give me some answer. I never did know exactly, but I guessed that's what being a man was and I got to thinking. I wanted to be a man so bad: I had to have some disease! I did find out that much. I was all hot to have me a disease!

One time I went home and I looked in the cabinet in the bathroom, thinking about that. I didn't know for sure how to get me a disease, but I wanted anyhow to put something on myself and wrap myself up and then have them see me. I was going to show them I was something too.

I looked around in the cabinet and I didn't find anything at first, nothing in particular, but I figured anything would do, so I finally got something down from the shelf—it was musterol. I looked at it; it smelled pretty much like the iodoform stuff my brother used to give in his dentist office, so I put it on.

My God, that did it! I was fixed good! How that stuff did burn! I got it off just as soon as I could stop dancing from the pain, but was I sore. My mother heard me, and she came racing in. I just couldn't tell her what it was for, I had no way of telling her. I don't know what it was I said to her, but I never did tell anyone right up to now. That was my secret. But she did find out I had put it on and she made off like she thought I was going crazy. 'What did you do that for?'

she kept asking me in French. 'Are you crazy?' She just couldn't understand.

But after a while it stopped burning and I saw I was going to be all right; I began to feel different then. When I got around with the men, they couldn't help seeing me all bandaged up. They'd look at one another and they'd look at me. 'What happened to you?' they'd say. 'What all you gone and picked up?'

And me, I just act like it wasn't nothing. 'Oh,' I'd say, 'I went with some gal.' I was really feeling big those times.

But I still didn't know really. So much of how things were I didn't understand at all. I'd hear the men . . . they was always talking about their women, and I'd see how they all had such pretty women, how some of them, they was married and all. I wanted to have a girl of my own. I wanted awful bad to be like the men. So one time when I was about fourteen—it was long after that time with the musterol—I saw a chance to get myself a girl. That was really something, the way I did. One of those real kid-crazy things.

There was this girl I had seen around. She was pregnant. The fellow she'd been going with had just gone off and left her. I got to thinking about that, how it was really something for her, being left like that; so I figured *I'd* marry her. I figured I'd go tell her father I was the one who had done it. I'd make a confession, I figured, and that would fix it for sure. I wanted so bad to have a wife.

So one evening I went over to the house where she was living and I asked to talk to her father. He come out then and we sat talking for a while and I told him finally I was the father of the child. This was to be a man-to-man talk, I made him understand, and I was setting to do the right thing. I wanted to marry her, I said, and we'd have a real wedding.

He didn't answer. He didn't say anything at all about what he was thinking. He sat there quiet-like for a while and then he told me to wait some. He left me there and he went off and bought a gallon of wine, and he came back and said, 'Here, let's drink some of this.' Then he took a drink and I took a drink and we sat up that way most of the night, sitting there on the porch passing the wine back and forth and talking around, all about everything, just talking. I'd never been used to so much wine and it sort of got my tongue loose. I told him all how sorry I was this thing had happened; but it would be all right, I told him; I was aiming to do the only decent thing. I told him all how it was with me getting along in the world. 'I'm sure I can support a wife,' I told him, man-to-man. 'I'm working pretty regular,' I said. 'I earn seventy-five cents, a dollar a night in the district.' I made him understand how it was, how I was a *district man.* That's really something, I made him see. That was supposed to convince him I was really a man so's he'd be all the more willing to let me marry this girl.

Meanwhile we kept passing the wine-gallon back and forth and I talked and talked, and I finally just talked myself to sleep right there on the porch.

That man, he let me go on, and when I was sound asleep he picked me right up in his arms and carried me home. I wasn't living at home then, but being how I was drunk by this time, that's where he took me. My mother told me about it later. He took me home and he put me to bed and he explained to her all about what I'd wanted to see him about.

'You tell him not to do anything like that again,' he told her. 'He's a nice boy, but he's sure desperate! You got to have a talk with him. You got to tell him to be careful about going around doing a thing like that. Someday he's liable to get himself a real trouble. It just happen,' he said, 'I know the boy who's harmed my daughter. It wasn't your boy at all.' And then he left.

I had a hell of a time the next morning explaining to my mother why I'd wanted to marry this girl. I was kind of embarrassed anyway. I tried to explain to her that *everyone*, they're married, and I wanted to be married too. And here was this girl needing a man, I told her—well, why couldn't I be the father without making it? I couldn't see that made any difference. That just didn't enter into it. What was I to know about all that? I just wanted to be like everyone else that had himself a wife.

My mother, she said about everything she *could* say. She was real understanding about how it all was. She explained that ain't the way at all, how you got to court a girl; you got to meet her first, be with her a time, and how marriage follows after that.

'Why'd you want to marry a girl you don't know anything about?' she said. And she went on to explain all sorts of things, trying to make me understand.

But, you know, mostly I think about that man, how he acted about everything. Most fathers would have had the shotgun out for the first male that came along ringing the bell. But that man, he acted so wonderful understanding about everything . . . he just let me talk and talk, let me go on about anything I wanted to say, anything I needed to say. All those things I'd be thinking about—he didn't care what it was; he just let me talk it out. I've thought about him many a time; we became real good friends later. There was a kind of understanding about him.

But I didn't have to do those crazy things to be a Jazz musicianer. I did them because I was a kid and I wanted to be a man, that's all. I wanted to be like everyone else. Nowadays young musicianers think they've just naturally got to act crazy if you want to play. They've got reefers and they've got gin and they've got women and they've got all that crazy jive-talk, all that stuff about 'gate' and 'tea' and being real 'cool'. Five hours of conversation, one minute of playing— that's what it amounts to.

But if you really mean to play your instrument, this jive business has got nothing to do with it. If you really mean to play, you've got to do some remembering. There's no one that can't remember something crazy he's done sometime. But remembering it, that's one thing—you can put that in the music. Being crazy, that's something else. That don't make any music at all.

5. Growing Up

For a while my brother kept me with him playing in his band. I was too small to go wandering around some of the places we had to play late at night, but my brother, he'd bring me to where we had the engagements and he'd bring me back home again. It was my first steady playing with a band and that's something what's important to a kid—the first thing—but it wasn't long before I could see there was other bands who were doing more to advance ragtime, playing it with a better feeling. I'd listen and I'd get the feeling terrible strong that I wanted to play how they were playing. I wanted to play in those bands and my brother he insisted I had to play in his band. It made me many a problem in those days.

About that time, too, I played a lot with Buddy Petit. He played cornet. He was quite a character, and we became great friends. His father, Joe Petit, was a fine musicianer too; he played valve trombone, which was used quite a bit around those times, but you don't see it much nowadays. Joe Petit was a very popular guy; I guess he founded just about every good band there was in those days—the Eagle, the Imperial, the Superior and the Olympia among them—and after the band was formed and everything was straightened out, he would just pull out and go on to something else.

Well, his son Buddy Petit was a very, very good trumpet player; even Louis used to take off his hat to him. We used to get together and just play along, learning how to put ourselves together, finding so many things in the music, so many

ways of coming to the music. After a while the two of us
organized the Young Olympia Band, unbeknownst to my
brother. We were all young kids, and we had a lot of success.
We were seven pieces, the old original Olympia: John Marrero
guitar, a violin, Simon Marrero on bass, Arnold de Pas on
drums, Ernest Kelly, trombone, and Buddy and myself. We
played all kinds of engagements, balls, banquets, and even
parades—though these we didn't do with the small bands, we
got together a brass band. I'd always catch hell from my
brother when he'd find I was playing in them. Many a time
he'd come to catch me at it and drag me off. Often, you
know, both those bands would have engagements to play the
same nights in different places. Naturally, I was supposed
to be playing with my brother, but he'd come along and
find me playing with the Young Olympia. He wasn't pleased
none at all by that. Oh, he had a great deal to say when that
happened.

There was so much trouble after that on account of my
wanting to play with the Young Olympia, wanting to go on
my own. I didn't care to have trouble with my brother, but it
was like I just couldn't help myself. There was so much more
of what I was looking for in other bands, so much more of
what I was needing. Some of it, maybe it was just plain
biggity. When you're growing up that happens . . . you keep
looking for bigger ways, grander ways to free yourself. You're
just busting to get off on your own. But there was more than
that too. When you come up against something you *know*
you can grow inside of for a real long while . . . something like
a really fine orchestra that makes you really happy . . . that's
more than just being biggity . . . that's like waiting for your
life, almost as if you know where it is and you have to go to it.
And then, when someone tries to hold you back, then you
get impatient, you get that feeling terrible strong that whoever it is, he mustn't be let to hold you back. But you don't
know how to say that is the way it really is. And that's when
the biggity comes out . . . you say all kinds of crazy things,
words you'd rather hadn't been said . . . but it's not really
biggity. It's just that you're confused. And you can't stop.

That's what you know before everything else . . . you can't let yourself be stopped, not by anyone.

Well, all those things put together . . . I wasn't more than nine, ten, eleven, something like that. . . . I was already beginning to want to live away from home so I wouldn't be having that trouble . . . so my feelings, they could lead me straight. Well, that was all too early yet . . . it wasn't time. All the same I was beginning to look around, wondering to see how it could be managed.

Meantime I used to go over regular to George Baquet's. He didn't live too far from me. I'd go over two, three times a week to have him give me a lesson. I used to bring him that Bull Durham tobacco. He had a real fondness for that. He wouldn't take any money so I'd bring two or three packs every time I went for a lesson and he was always glad to have it.

I did that for a while, but the way it turned out, it seemed he just couldn't learn me nothing. You've got to understand what I mean about that. Baquet was a hell of a fine music-ianer; he played awful fine. But he wasn't exactly a real ragtime player. What he played, it wasn't really Jazz . . . he stuck real close to the line in a way. He played things more classic-like, straight out how it was written. And he played it very serious. He was much more that way than Big Eye Louis. When Baquet played it, there wasn't none of those growls and buzzes which is a part of ragtime music, which is a way the musicianer has of replacing different feelings he finds inside the music and inside himself . . . all those inter-preting moans and groans and happy sounds. There wasn't none of that in the way he played. I don't know if it was that Baquet *couldn't* do it, all I know is he *didn't* do it. After a time I didn't go there any more.

There was Big Eye Louis Nelson then. I took some lessons from him, but that wasn't for long either.

And Lorenzo Tio, he gave me lessons. I hung around his house a lot. We used to talk a lot together, and we'd play to all hours. Lorenzo Tio, he was real good to me. Once I remem-ber I went in for one of these 'Amateur Talent' contests at the theatre. I went on and did a song and a dance act, but I can't have done it very well because the master of ceremonies, he asked me if there was anything else I could do. Well, I said yes, I could play the clarinet, but I hadn't brought mine with me. Lorenzo Tio, he was playing in the pit orchestra, so I walked over and asked him if I could borrow his. So he said yes, and I won the contest and the first prize of $25.00. Man, that seemed a lot of money to me then when I was all that young!

But you know, it's a funny thing about teaching, about all those lessons. They didn't really do for me. They weren't doing what had to be done. I guess you come right down to it, a musicianer just has to learn for himself, just by playing and listening.

Being a teacher, that's an awful hard thing to learn. There's so many kinds of teachers, many of them saying the opposite from one another. A good teacher has got to be able to know what a person *can* be taught. Everyone has his own way of learning, but a teacher is most interested in teaching the normal way, the way the average person learns. And there's some people, they're lacking in knowing how to do things the average way. It don't make no sense to them. Or else other times, a teacher only knows how *he's* learned something . . . maybe how he's *supposed* to have learned it. That kind of teacher comes along and says: 'Here now; you hold your instrument *this* way. That's the way to play that thing.' Well, you don't know how to play it that way. You know how to play it your own way, and he wants you to play it his way. Well, you take it . . . you hold it his way . . . you try to play it that way, but you can't. Nothing comes out. There's no music. That way he's wanting you to hold it just don't fit. So you turn it around . . . you pick it up and hold it like *you* want. Right there it's all changed. Right away you know what to do with it . . . you really got something now. You're playing maybe what he wants, or how he wants to hear you, only you're doing it your own way. And that's what counts . . . having a way that *is* your own . . . all the way to you from inside your own self.

Take a piano player: tell him, 'No, keep your hands flat.

Play like this. Whoever heard of doing it that way?' You tell him that and you whack him on the fingers so he'll keep it flat down like he's supposed to. You do him that way and the first thing you know he can't play at all.

But you take the same man, give him a chance to do it his own way, leave him be . . . if there's anything inside him, that man, he'll go to town, he'll *make* something.

The way I see it, whatever way you do something best, that's the way to do it. There isn't but just that one way. Teachers, they mostly forget that. Some of those teachers I had, they was real musicianers, but they all of them tried to make me do their way.

And there's another thing . . . a part of the same thing really. When I was getting all those lessons and things, some person—a teacher—he would tell me: 'Look at the music.' He'd want me to read one note, and I'd see the whole page. Hell, I ain't never learned to read one note after the other. 'Look at A,' they'd say, and I'd see the whole thing. The notes, they were nothing: I'd seen them already. I'd take a look at the page and from there on I'd be on my own just playing and improvising.

And that's the way it has to be. There ain't no one can write down for you what you need to know to make the music over again. There ain't no one can write down the feeling you have to have. That's from inside yourself, and you can't play note by note like something written down. The music has to let you be . . . you've got to stay free inside it.

It wasn't long after that, when I was about twelve, that I was going out playing with different bands. If I had any distance to go where we was playing at, one of my brothers would take me over and come get me to take me back. There was some tough sections those days.

One of those times I was playing with John Robichaux's Orchestra. We were at a place called St. Catherine's Hall then, and to get to it I had to go through part of the red-light section, the part of it along by Rampart Street and Claiborne Avenue, all in between those two streets and Canal and

Franklin. There wasn't any real danger of getting into trouble there, but my mother didn't want me going through there alone; I was too young, she said. So she and my brother and my next older brother, Omar—he was Omar too—they would take turns walking me to this place where I was to play at St. Catherine's Hall.

I didn't know what all those women were doing hanging around the doorways in front of those houses. I'd go through and see them all there, standing around the way they do, waiting. They was all wearing those real short skirts and I saw them about, and it's the first time I recall any wondering about women like that. I was going through there and I looked at all those women and I asked my mother, 'What are all those little girls doing standing like that?' I was just wondering about those skirts. They didn't *look* like little girls really, but I hadn't ever seen no women wearing clothes like that so I just up and asked my mother. I forget what she answered. All I remember is that we finally got to St. Catherine's, but I was beginning to wonder what it was all about.

And a little after that I'd be staying away from home sometimes, playing engagements away. My mother made an arrangement for me to stay with my aunt, so later when I'd leave my aunt's place and go away on my own, it wasn't so hard for her. She'd got used to it by then. But when I was staying with my aunt, having more freedom like, I'd go off places and I'd hear things, and I'd wonder some. There wasn't anything like that at my aunt's house—nothing being said that I needed to wonder anything about, but just being off and hearing people, growing up kind of; I'd hear things and not know how it was, but I was wondering.

Then a while later, I was maybe fourteen then, I was playing at Billy Phillips' 101 Ranch over on Franklin Street. George Baquet was there, along with Freddie Keppard. They was there together up to the time Freddie left New Orleans and went North. Joe Oliver was around too. He was playing in the Magnolia Orchestra right opposite from Billy Phillips' 101. After Freddie left New Orleans I played with Joe in the Olympia Orchestra at Pete Lala's over on Iberville Street.

Pete's brother, Johnny Lala had a place too; his was the Twenty-Five Club.

Those days, too, we played at a lot of halls . . . places like Perseverance Hall, Downtown Economy Hall, New Hall, Oddfellows Hall. I got to hear a little about all sorts of things here and there, but it was all confused; I really didn't know nothing at all, what it was about.

Around 1908 I started playing with Bunk Johnson in the Eagle Orchestra. That used to be Buddy Bolden's band, and Buddy made such an impression around there that people never did stop thinking of it as his band, even long after he got taken. But under Bunk Johnson the band was the Eagle Orchestra. They played real fine too. They were great musicianers.

That Buddy Bolden—everyone in New Orleans knew about him. He was a real walk-around man. He could play, that was true; but, well, he was more a showman: he was a hell of a good showman. You take someone, if he's thumping and stamping on the stand with his foot and making faces and doing something with his hand, waving and what not—you look at him, you notice him more, it's more than hearing his music. You take another man: he may be playing as good— he can be playing better—but you hear the other one more because you're so busy watching him. Buddy, he was a hell of a good showman. If he forgot something, he'd make something else. It didn't matter to him whether it was especially fitting or not what he made up, he'd just go ahead and do it, and he'd make you forget all about whatever it was *he* had forgotten. But there was others that played much better. Maybe they didn't have so much name, so much flash about them, but they played a lot deeper into the music.

Manuel Perez was one. He played much better cornet than Buddy. Perez, he was a musicianer; he was *sincere*. He stuck to his instrument. You hear a record, you know—you don't see all that stamping and face-making; you just hear the music. And that's the same of today; you take someone that's grinning and stomping and moving around the stand where the *music* should be going—for the moment you're lost from the music, you're so busy watching him fool around. But you get his same record and try to listen to the music then, and there's no music there. But Manuel Perez, there wasn't none of that in him. He was really sincere. He really played his cornet.

Buddy, you know, before he died he was in an insane asylum. Buddy used to drink awful heavy, and it got him in the end. He lived it fast, Buddy did. And that's another reason why he was so popular, why you hear his name so much: it was the way he lived his life. The things he'd do, they got him a lot of attention. You was always hearing, for example, how he had three or four women living with him in the same house. He'd walk down the street and one woman, she'd have his trumpet, and another, she'd carry his watch, and another, she'd have his handkerchief, and maybe there'd be another one who wouldn't have nothing to carry, but she'd be there all the same hoping to carry something home. That's the kind of man he was. He could drink, and he had stories he knew— he was a real storyteller—and he just couldn't go anywhere without making a big splash, and he didn't give a damn about anything. And he could play too. He took ragtime up some; but he couldn't follow through on it, he wasn't able. There was a lot of reasons for that, mostly personal I guess, but when it came right down to the music he just wasn't able.

There was others after him, they played real cornet. There was Perez . . . he didn't need to do things showman-like; he didn't even try. And after Buddy died Freddie Keppard was King. Freddie kind of took Buddy's way some; he played practically the same way as Buddy, but he played, he *really* played. And then there was Joe Oliver. And then after him Louis came along.

There's still that question today, that Buddy Bolden question, all about what's showmanship and what's music. What I say is, you've got to be the music first. Play your instrument and after that go ahead and perform all you please, if you call it performing, or showmanship, or whatever you want to call it. Personality—hell, you've got personalities everywhere. If you can blow a note and perform at the same time—if you can do that, you're entitled to all the personality they'll give you; but it's got to be the instrument that comes first.

It's like I'm driving a car and I'm so busy waving my hand to you and thinking about my nice car and all how good and classy I look in it, before you know it I've backed myself right into a haberdashery and all I got for myself is some trouble. That's how it is with this showmanship business. But a man, if he's an artist, he don't worry about that. I don't care what kind of an artist he is—if he really means it, the thing what he's looking for in the art form has to come first. He has to be sincere about that.

Manuel Perez, he was an artist. It takes a lot out of a man to be an artist. Maybe Buddy Bolden was an artist and maybe he wasn't, but it took too much out of him—that and the drinking; in the end he had to be put in the insane asylum.

And there was so many that went that way. But Manuel Perez, the way he ended was a terrible thing. If you could have seen it, it would have broken your heart. Manuel had been such a handsome man. You'd see his face and there'd be nothing in it you would want to see missing in a man's face. And the way he walked—so fine, so proud. He never done any drinking either, or coming up behind women. You never heard anything about his private life except that he was married. There was none of this parading of himself, the way Buddy Bolden used to advertise himself. But out there, when they had some parade, you'd see how Manuel really was . . . you'd see him and you'd know that was a *man* you was seeing. It was something to remember.

And about the time Manuel was around, there'd been a fellow called Fanon who used to hang around the band. He'd never been a musicianer, he was idiot-like, but he knew pretty well what he wanted; he knew he wanted to listen to the music. You could do anything to him; you could tease him, make him do all sorts of things. And he was goosey; if you just pointed your fingers at him goose pimples would jump out on him and run wild. He was pitiful to see. And Manuel, that man who walked so proud, he had a stroke and *he* turned out that way. He was just like this Fanon in the end.

I was down in New Orleans and I saw Manuel before he died. I saw him and I couldn't bear to see him; it was something awful. He just began to slobber at the mouth when you spoke to him. He wasn't an old man either . . . fifty-nine, 'long about there. His wife was taking care of him, and it made you want to cry the way she spoke to him, the way she had to speak to him. She was keeping him with her, refusing to lock him up; but he'd had it all . . . he'd had everything but the crazyhouse, everything but that. All that was left of him was that slobber and this jabber he got to talking with no sense in it. And when he looked at you there wasn't anything in his eyes . . . it was like they were missing from his face, and his face, it had just come apart.

And after a while you get to thinking, there were so many of them went like that. You get to asking: Why is it that it could happen? Why was it that it did happen? What was it took hold of a musicianer that way, took a real man and just emptied him out of himself leaving a thing you wouldn't want to look at? People ask me if it's something in the music. How do you answer that? Sometimes I lay at night thinking about it, thinking someday I'll get the right answer. It's so funny, you know . . . you're hearing all so much about it all the time, so many mysterious things, until you get so you stop asking the one question that could find out. Sometimes it's the same way finding some clue as it is going through some old drawer looking for something. You get to looking and you get so busy coming across old letters and mementoes and pictures that you forget for a while what it was you were after.

But that question, it's what has to be answered: why so many of these men who were really great and who really played—when they went, they just went crazy. So many of them. There was Benny Raphael, Scott Joplin, Armand J. Piron; and there was that Fanon . . . he wasn't a musicianer, but he loved it so awful much.

The way it happens, it's a hard thing to get at. But you know, when a man's been giving his whole life to something he loves, his whole heart and soul, putting aside all the troubles that come to him, putting aside everything but the music—

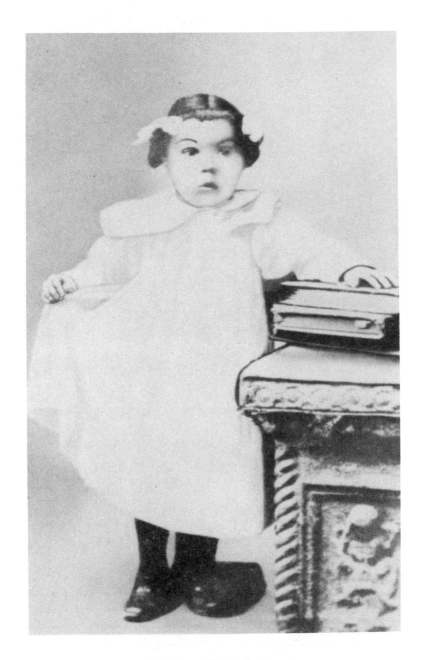

Sidney Bechet, 1900

Benny Peyton's band in London, 1919. Sidney Bechet is on the extreme right; Benny Peyton is to his immediate left

The *Ballets Nègres*, Paris, 1925. Sidney Bechet is second from the right

Sidney Bechet, 1926

just doing that one thing so he can be giving some happiness, so he can be *making* some happiness—when he does that all his life, and then something comes along to stop him: that's when it hits. It's something like a poverty, only it's a poverty *inside* himself; there's nothing he's got any more; there's nothing and there's no one, and he's forgotten.

It's a thing that won't be given an easy answer, but whatever the answer is, whatever it is tears a man to pieces—that thing is inside the man himself. Maybe the music makes it worse and maybe not; it depends who the man is. There's that sadness, that lost place in the music, and there's many a musicianer who can't think about anything else. But there's a way of laughing in it too. That laughing don't hide the lost place, it don't put it out of sight, it don't even try . . . it goes along with that lost place. Maybe it's where the lost place wants to be. The kind of laughing a man has to find inside himself. That's in the music too, and there was a many a fine musicianer who knew how to laugh with it.

Alphonse Picou, he was one. He was a real musicianer. He was the first to take the piccolo part of *High Society*—the brass band arrangement—and play it on a clarinet. That was to become the standard clarinet part of *High Society*. That's the way it has been played ever since.

Alphonse was much the same age as Manuel and started playing at the same time; but, there, he's just the way he's always been. He's a man; what it seems like, he can't do nothing but have a time for himself. Life, that's just his pleasure. I guess he owns about half of New Orleans now, dyes his hair every six months, walks around just enjoying himself. He's been married two or three times by now, and he's the kind of man who can still want to be married again. I guess when he's a hundred and ten, he'll still be strutting and showing among the ladies. He just always was that way and there he is. He never was anything like Manuel. Alphonse was just cutting up, carrying on, drinking, everything there was. He was a smiling man . . . there was just no trouble big enough for him to take notice of it for long.

And like I say, he was a musicianer, a real musicianer. And

that's how come I ask myself, why one man goes one way and another man goes so different. How come if it's like some people say, if it's the music that's supposed to do those bad things to a man? There ain't nothing bad in the music, nothing a man has to be punished for.

Well, back in those days, except for Buddy Bolden's band there wasn't much of this Teddy So-and-so's Hotshots, or Hill's such-and-such; instead they'd have some name like Imperial Orchestra, or the Peerless, or the Magnolia, or the Superior, or the Olympia. Every band was trying to find some name that was one higher than the next one. And all the musicianers they'd wear these hats with an emblem on them and the name of the band all blazed out, except it was always called an Orchestra, and they'd have that abbreviated to *Orch. Imperial Orch* it would say on the hats, and there'd be some emblem to go with the name.

Naturally the Eagle Orch had an eagle for its emblem—that was to represent America —and when I showed up to play my first time they told me to go get myself a uniform cap with the emblem. I didn't need to be told twice. I was real proud of myself: there I was, working in the Eagle Orch. I was on my way to have an emblem made up, and I went to this old lady in the neighbourhood who used to do some sewing and she said sure, she could make it up, She had it done real soon, too, and I looked at it and I tried it on and I took it off to look at it again. I just couldn't get done admiring it. It was a beautiful thing!

Finally I put it on and went marching out of there down to where the band was playing. I was feeling eight feet tall. Walking along that way I had a feeling everybody on the street was doing nothing else but look at me; and me, I was really there to be looked at. By the time I got to where the band was I was going like a troop of cavalry. I marched in there and I sat down to play with the men and I was going along real fine when suddenly I found that everybody was looking at me. They took one look at my hat and suddenly they just couldn't see anything else: everybody was having a time with me.

'Lookit that!' they said.

'Man, oh man, we got us a real live rooster.'

'Tell this boy to get an eagle on his hat, and what's he come back with but a chicken?'

Well, I hadn't noticed before. I hadn't exactly remembered what an eagle looked like. It *had* been an eagle when I first looked at it, but I looked at theirs and I looked at mine, and I saw it *was* a chicken; it was awful like a chicken.

I hadn't thought about it, but all at once I realized what a poor impression I'd done my first thing with the band, and I decided I was really going to show them. The next day I set out to get myself a real eagle: I'd get myself about the *eaglest* eagle I could find. So I went off to where they had the army barracks and those stores for the army, and I bought myself one of those officer hats. *There* was an eagle for them, and I marched up and down letting people have a look at it. It not only had an eagle, it had the stars and stripes below it too; it was the prettiest thing I ever did see.

I went back to where the band was then, and I was really set to show them; but as soon as I walked in they just burst out laughing. I thought they just never would get done with all that teasing and razzing. They even made up a song for me:

> Told that boy to come down here with an eagle—
> he comes back with a damn' chicken!
> That isn't enough for him—
> he comes back with the *whole* regiment!
> That damn' Creole—
> he comes in with the *whole* United States Army!

Oh, they didn't forget that for months. The next day after that I went out to a man who made hats and uniforms regular for the bands. I finally got myself straightened out there, but the boys in the band hadn't any mind to forget about it. Every once in a while they'd just start up all over to have themselves a time about it—

'Where's that chicken?' somebody would say.

'That ain't no chicken, man—that's the whole United States Army!'

Oh, they had a time with me. But they was real musicianers. I sure was proud to be playing with them.

I was about seventeen when I first started playing with the Eagle Orchestra. I was living at home, and Bunk Johnson came and promised my mother he would watch out for me: he'd come by for me when we was to play and he'd take me back. Then, a little later, I stopped living at home and stayed at different places around town, playing with the Eagle Orchestra when they had a place to play at, and playing with other bands when we didn't have an engagement. I was really learning a whole lot . . . there was so many a fine musicianer around New Orleans then, so much a man could learn from. But I was getting restless.

I'd been hearing so much about up North, about this place and that place. I was having an itch to go. I stayed on there a while, playing along with many great musicianers, growing into the music, thinking I'd be going off one of those days, but wanting to take the most I could with me. There was so much to play, so much to listen to.

There was Bunk Johnson I spoke about already. He was a great blues player. He drank awful heavy, but he always took good care of me. Bunk was the quietest man, even with all his drinking. He'd been around New Orleans some time, but nobody ever did know where he'd come from. A lot of musicianers when they were down in New Orleans, you never could tell where they came from. All you'd know was how they'd be living somewheres uptown or back o' town, or near such and such a street. I never did know about Bunk; but when he was playing the blues, that was something I did know. That was some place I'd been to myself.

There was lots of musicianers like that, men I knew and played with and listened to without ever knowing where they were from. Kid Ory was one. I was staying up in the Garden District about the time I used to see a lot of him: that was uptown, over by Carlson Street. I had this girl I was staying with then, and many a time I'd run into Kid Ory on the street and right off he'd start talking Creole. I never knew where he learned that. 'Where'd you learn that?' I'd say. He'd just laugh. 'Man,' he'd say, 'I am Creole. Don't you know a Creole when you see him?'

That went on for years. He was always joking me about it, and I was always wondering where he'd learned to talk like that. It wasn't till years later I found out he really was Creole. I don't know why that surprised me. I'd just always thought it was his joke with me, that he'd picked up that talk from somewhere, from some woman he'd been with maybe.

The Creoles made many a fine musicianer. There was Manuel Perez, Lorenzo Tio, Alphonse Picou, René Batiste (he was manager of the Imperial Orchestra), Benny Raphael, Vic Gaspard, his brother Oke—oh, many a one. They were damn' fine . . . they were some of the best for ragtime. Somehow ragtime had a way of being easy for the Creoles; but when it came to the blues you couldn't beat Bunk or the Eagle Orchestra. I listened to all of them and I played with most of them. I was learning so much those days. There were the Carey brothers, Jack and Mutt, they had a band I played with sometimes up around Carlson Street. They had drums, clarinet, trumpet, and guitar—Tommy Benton, he played the guitar. Other times I went with Joe Oliver and we played at Pete Lala's Theatre, that was a picture vaudeville theatre.

It was Bunk Johnson who was the first to make me acquainted with Louis Armstrong. Bunk told me about this quartet Louis was singing in. 'Sidney,' he said, 'I want you to go hear a little quartet, how they sing and harmonize.' He knew I was crazy about singing harmony. He'd take me out to those circuses whenever they came into town and they had any singing in them, and he'd take me to vaudeville and all. Whenever there was some quartet or opera, or some harmony, or some big band somewhere, we'd always go.

Louis was living over on Perdido Street and then, like I said, he was singing in this quartet. They were real good . . . they had a way. There was a fellow singing there, Little Mack was his name, he was the lead; he became a hell of a good drummer later. And Louis, he sang tenor then.

I went many a time to hear this quartet sing and I got to like Louis a whole lot, he was damn' nice. I was a little older than him. At that time he sort of looked up to me, me playing in bands and being with the big men.

One time, a little after I started going to hear this quartet, I ran into Louis on the street and I asked him home for dinner. I wanted him and the quartet to come around so my family could hear them sing.

Well, Louis, he sort of hemmed around, and said he couldn't make it. I could see there was something troubling him and finally he let it out. 'Look, Sidney,' he says, 'I don't have any shoes . . . these I got, they won't get me there.' Well I said that was easy fixed and gave him fifty cents to get his shoes repaired, and he went off promising me he would come.

Well, I don't know what it was, but he never showed up. We lived way across on the other side of town and that was a hell of a distance to walk. And it's that way you see . . . it's a little thing, and there's big things around it, but it keeps coming back. You're playing some number and it starts going—sometimes it goes right back to the street and played about those shoes. When you're playing about it maybe you don't know it is about that. But then, later, you're thinking about it, and it comes to you. It's not a describing music, nothing like that. Maybe nobody else could ever tell it was about that. But thinking back, you know the music was how you felt about remembering that time on that street . . . remembering it from a way back.

A while later there was a drummer, a great big fellow who was a famous character called Black Benny; he didn't have a regular band of his own, but he used to play around with different outfits, and sometimes he played with us in Bunk's Band at Buddy Bartelot's place. And he said to me one day, 'You think you can play. But I know a little boy right around the corner from my place, he can play *High Society* better than you.' So I said, 'Well, I'd like to see that boy.' He said 'All right, come over with me.' And we went, and it was Louis. And I'll be doggone if he didn't play *High Society* on the cornet. I mean, you know, that it was originally a piccolo part but it was done, like I said, by Picou on clarinet. It was very hard for clarinet to do, and really unthinkable for cornet to do at those times. But Louis, he did it. So I was very pleased about it. I had a little job for an advertisement that I was doing twice a week for a picture theatre, the Ivory Theatre right by my house on Race Street. And the lady I was working for, she used to give me $2.00. So I hired Louis to come with me on this advertising, and, you know, it was wonderful. Anyway, I gave him 50 c., I gave the drummer, Little Mack, 50 c. and that meant I made a dollar; the leader always kept the double. That was the first time I ever heard Louis play the cornet. He played the cornet then, though he went to the trumpet later. We went out and bought some beer with the money and got those sandwiches, Poor Boys, they're called—a half a loaf of bread split open and stuffed with ham. We really had good times.

Of course, Louis was playing the cornet a bit before he went into that Jones school, but it was, you know, how kids play. The school helped, it really started him up; you know, it's like at home if you have an instrument around all the time— it helps a boy make up his mind what he will do if you give him an idea. They were well looked after in that school, and they even had their own outfit which used to go out and play.

Around about that time, too, Louis changed where he was living; he moved over by Franklin Street, across the street from the Parish Prison. At that time I saw a lot of Louis; I liked him fine. He was a good musicianer.

It wasn't long after that advertisement business at the Ivory Theatre that Louis began to hang about Bunk's band where we all were at Buddy Bartelot's. This would be around 1913. Louis used to try to play like Bunk a little, and Bunk would give him lessons too. He'd stay behind the piano mostly, keeping out of sight. He did that because people used to come visiting from all over—people from out of town, people from New Orleans too, all sorts of parties and things, some of them with police escorts—they'd come down to the club and if they came down and they saw him, just a little kid like that in short pants, there'd be trouble. Me, I was wearing long pants—that made me a man; but if the police saw kids in short pants, they chased them out!

I was still young, but I got around quite a lot then, making myself known, exchanging things with other musicianers. There was Johnny Dodds about that time, he was with Kid Ory when I was with the Eagle Orchestra. Johnny, he's said I influenced him, that he got a lot of inspiration from me. Well, I'm proud to be told that. There was Jimmy Noone there too, I influenced him—that's what people who have written books have said he told them. Larry Shields was another; he used to come to me for lessons. I won't be more modest than I am; I'm glad to be told I've given this influence. But I wasn't thinking much about that in those days. I was playing around, walking around, just sort of waiting. There was this feeling that I had, how I wanted to be starting out, but the chance never did quite come along then.

6. I'm On My Way

You know, there's this mood about the music, a kind of need to be moving. You just can't set it down and hold it. Those Dixieland musicianers, they tried to do that; they tried to write the music down and kind of freeze it. Even when they didn't arrange it to death, they didn't have any place to send it; that's why they lost it. You just can't keep the music unless you move with it.

There was a fellow like that when I was waiting around New Orleans. I'd been kind of giving lessons to Albert Nicholas—they wasn't lessons exactly either; it was just that Albert was younger than me, and afternoons we'd sit together on the back steps and we'd play along together and I'd kind of advise him. Well, Albert had this uncle who was called Wooden Joe and he was always trying to play the clarinet with us; he really wanted to damn' bad, but somehow it just wasn't the thing for him. After a while he gave it up. Later he became a real good trumpet player.

But what I had in mind about this Wooden Joe—he never could move with the music. All he ever knew was the type numbers of the time when he learned to play; he never could break with them. He was real good for that, and it was all right so long as it was that time, but after that, when things got different, when there was new things coming into the music—then it was just too bad; Wooden Joe just wasn't there. A man that plays like that, his music gets too complacent-like; the music, it's got this itch to be going in it—when it loses that, there's not much left. Those days I was getting that itch pretty strong. I really wanted to be moving. And finally I saw my chance, and I took it.

I Don't Know Where I'm Going, But I'm On My Way. That's the first piece I ever played when I picked up a clarinet, and that's the first piece I played when I first left New Orleans, and of all the places I could have imagined it was in a dime store. If I played that piece in one dime store I played it in a dozen.

It was Clarence Williams started all that playing I did in dime stores. Clarence had his own place on Rampart Street; I worked with him a while there, but it sure was a rough place. Anyway, he'd written some songs and he wanted to take them all over in a small show so people could hear them. He was all fired up about how popular his songs would be when people had got used to hearing them that way. He had it all worked out that after they'd come popular that way, he could make a regular travelling show to go all over. He had me convinced it *would* be a regular show. There was Louis Wade, who played piano, too —the both of us wanted to go North and we thought we *were* going North. We'd heard all about how the North was freer, and we were wanting to go real bad. But my God, where do we end up but in Texas. . . . Louis played piano, I played clarinet, and Clarence sang; we played dances, shows and one-night stands, and in dime stores all over Texas peddling these songs. For a while there it was, nothing but one dime store after another.

The way it was—day after day in all those dime stores— we began to get pretty tired of it. I was ready to move on and Louis, he was ready to move, so when the show made Galveston, we jumped it and joined some kind of carnival they had going through there, and we travelled with it to Plantersville, Texas. And that's where we got stuck: we woke up one morning and the carnival, it was gone. We had been staying with a lady that put some people up in her house, and when we went down to the carnival ground in the morning, it was just an empty field. I learned later there had been some sheriff who had come around and told them they had to clear out. And so there we were.

I didn't know what to do, and Louis didn't have any ideas; but it was early in the day and we stopped off at a store to buy some cigarettes so we could sit and think where we were going next. We walked into this store and we found we'd walked right into a kind of court they were holding there—they didn't have any place else in that town, so the magistrate or whoever it was brought his court into the store, and so we had to wait for the court to be over before we could buy the cigarettes. We walked into this store with the court going on, and right away we saw these two white men there that we knew. The night before that, there had been some kind of a party at this lady's home where we were staying and these two white men had been there. There was two girls that lived in the house regular, and these men had come to see the girls. Louis and me, we had been playing at the carnival, and we came back fast as we could because of the police not leaving us alone if we were out much after dark. We came along pretty fast that way and Louis sort of had his mind on one of those girls, talking about her. Then we came up to the house and we could see them through the window. They're all inside there, fooling around; and they're all of them eating those wild cherries, just the kind of cherries you get from a backyard or a field. But the way they're doing it, kind of making a play out of eating them, holding them up by the stem for one another, to me it's like they were courting. Louis didn't like it any, but there's nothing he can do. We just stood there for a while watching them through the window—those two men and the two girls sitting there with just one big light on in the kitchen behind them, eating cherries that way and fooling around. After a while we went to bed, and Louis talked some about white men coming and their way of visiting and then after a while he fell asleep.

The next morning we walked into this store and there they all were again, the four of them. One of those girls had a husband and when he'd found out about that visiting the white men had done, he'd hit her or something. Whatever it was, there'd been some trouble and this court was meeting to decide it.

We stood there listening some, and Louis began to get disgusted. Seems like what it was—this white man, the one that had been with the girl, he was put out because of this trouble and he'd meant to fix the husband. That wasn't what the girl wanted, but that's what the whole thing was coming down to. I didn't understand all of this, but Louis explained it to me and then I could understand it some. Louis was still thinking about this girl; there was a picture of her sort of hanging around in his mind and he could see this was nothing for him to be mixed up in.

'Sidney,' he said to me, 'I'm getting away from this town.'

I could see he was plenty upset about this business. It was like he was knowing he couldn't keep himself from getting mad and making trouble unless he got out of there.

'I have a little money saved in Beaumont,' he said. 'When I get there I'll send for you just as soon as I can.'

Then he turned away and just walked out of there, going fast and not looking back any.

So I was left there. I was feeling lost and I was feeling scared too. What was I to do now? Louis didn't give me any chance to go with him and I couldn't think of where to go by myself. It was all so sudden. And while I was standing there this white man—this interfering man that was out to fix that girl's husband—called over to me.

'Hey, *you* there,' he says, 'what do you want?'

I couldn't tell what was going on and I couldn't think of anything to say. I was thinking I'd better get out too, but I had got to say something so I said, 'Who, me?' That's all I could think of . . . just that, and wanting to be out of there.

'Yes, you!' he said.

I opened my mouth trying to find what to say, but before I could get any kind of answer out he tossed some money on the floor.

'Go on down to the hardware store and tell the man I want fifty yards of well-rope,' he said.

I picked the money out of the sawdust and I did like I was told. I was afraid he was going to make trouble for me. He'd got that look. I got on down to the store and I lugged back all that rope . . . it was damn' heavy and it was a real hot day. All the way back I was worrying about what this man would think of next, if he was fixing to work up any meanness. But when I get back he took the rope and he let me go. He didn't say a word and I didn't wait around to hear if he should think of anything else. I got out of there fast, glad to have seen the last of him.

But the way it turned out, it wasn't the last of him. There was this boy in town that I'd made acquaintance with and I'd been to his house and brought my clarinet and I'd played. We'd had a good time that way, and when he heard how I was alone and out of money, he rounded up some people for a kind of dance, charging them money to get in, and I was to play for them. He had it all arranged, but I was a little concerned. I didn't want to do it. A thing like that, a dance, it would be ending late and we wasn't supposed to be out on the street after dark. It wasn't safe. This boy, he was urging me and I wanted to, but being a little scared at the same time, thinking about that interfering man and how near I'd been to trouble, maybe. But finally this boy promised he'd see to it I got home safe. He said he'd have somebody that was well known walk me home in case the police stopped me, and finally I agreed to play.

I thought it was to be a dance just for ourselves, for Negroes, but I got there and the first thing I saw was this interfering white man. He was there having himself a time, acting real friendly like. But a man like that, his name is trouble. Whatever bad thing comes upon you, that's his amusement. He won't stay with his own, and he won't let you be.

But I'd got my playing to do and after a while I stopped worrying about him. I played along and there was some real dancing going on . . . we were all having a good time. When it was all over, the boy gave me the money for playing because he knew I had got nothing, and then he told me he'd got it fixed; this white man was to walk me home. Right off I started to say I didn't like it, but before I could think what to say, this man came over to take me along. He was full up on whisky and was acting real friendly like, but I didn't dare say no to him, and so we went along together.

The route we'd got to go lay along the railroad tracks. The only way back. This man, he was kidding me about being scared. Well, we went along that way, and it was dark out there. It was so dark you could hardly see where to walk, and this man, either he'd got cat's eyes or he was too drunk to care, because he was dancing around telling me all kinds of crazy stories to scare me and having himself a real time. We got on a ways and we came to a place where there's rows and rows of those cross-stiles piled up by the tracks, just stacks of these cross-stiles. I was walking along and all at once these stacks sort of came at me out of the dark, just black and weird and sudden. Well, I was plenty scared and this man saw that. It's what he'd been wanting, and he set out to make it real good. He was walking along beside me and all at once he disappeared and then he jumped out at me from behind one of those stacks of stiles making what's supposed to be ghost noises. He was making like it's spirits hunting me. That's his joke.

But it wasn't being a joke to me. All that yelling and screaming he was doing in and out of those big black stacks . . . all the land around lying so still and empty with not a house anywhere, not another person near . . . nothing but that kind of stubble you find around railroads and a little of that glisten the tracks have at night—well it *did* scare me, it really did, and all at once when he jumped out on me that way I let go. I'd picked up a stick and I just lashed at him when he came jumping. I felt that stick hit and I knew I'd fixed him good. He made a grab at me and I swung that stick again, and then I didn't know what I was doing. I swung around some, but he wasn't there any more and I figured he'd dodged behind one of those stacks and I didn't know where he'd be coming from next if he was coming. I ran out of there fast. I wasn't worrying any more about where to put my feet; I ran off through the dark, and I kept running for a mile, maybe a mile and a half, until I had to catch my breath, until I'd got out of sight of all those piles of cross-stiles that looked like they were big evil things growing up out of the earth.

And there I was, just the way it always is with trouble. Somehow, there's just no need to go looking for trouble. The way it is, trouble comes looking for you. I hadn't wanted any dealing with that man.

First off I was wondering what to do next, and not knowing. I didn't know where to go and I didn't dare to be around there, come morning; I was *really* scared now. I wanted to catch some train and get to Galveston. One of my brothers, he was living there; he was married and all . . . been there some time. He had a job playing guitar in some place there. That's the only thing I could think of, but I didn't know anything about catching trains. I didn't even know which way the trains would be going to Galveston. I didn't know what to do.

But just then, as luck would have it, a freight came by where I was and it stopped for watering right there. I wasn't waiting to find out where it was going. All I wanted was to be out of there fast. I remembered hearing talk about how it was done, so I waited there till it was all set to go, and then just as it was starting to roll I swung on between two box-cars far back, and I just held on. I rode along that way for a while and then I looked up: it was the brakeman, he'd seen me. He didn't know whether I was young or old or strong or weak or white or black; all he knew was he didn't want me there, and he was leaning down from the top of the car swinging his club and trying to hit me off. I was holding on to this ladder that runs up the car and I was looking up, dodging that club, and was looking down seeing the cinders streak by under me. I just took a grip on the ladder and I wouldn't let him hit me off. I was just frozen there; there was the cinders under me and there was the club over me, and it was like I'd just closed my mind to all but just holding on. He could have killed me, but I'd have died holding on to that bar.

But something seemed to come over him; I was pretty small and maybe he saw I wasn't anyone who needed to be feared of. Or maybe he could tell from the way I was frozen there, that I wasn't any real hobo. He stopped swinging that club and he flashed some kind of lantern he had. I guess there

wasn't much more to be seen than the whites of my eyes—
they must have been covering my whole face about then. I
guess maybe he took me for even younger than I was. Anyhow, he came down then and he made me climb up the ladder
and go ahead over the tops of the cars. I was plenty scared,
but once he came down there I knew I had to do like he said.
So I went crawling along holding on to that raised walk they
got along the tops of those cars and he came walking along
behind me like I was his prisoner. The train was beginning
to sway some, and I was holding on to that walk hard, but he
was just coming on behind me like he was walking a beat and
thinking nothing of it. There was all that smoke laying back
over the train from the engine, and there was that swaying
and there was the brakeman behind me, coming on, fixing to
do whatever he meant to do. And all that day and all that
night, it seemed like it had been going on so long it couldn't
ever end.

But the way it turned out, he was being friendly. He moved
me back all the way to the caboose and when we got there he
took me inside. And there I was, with all my luck changed
again. One minute I was crawling along the top there in all
that smoke wondering if he was going to throw me off, and the
next I was sitting inside the caboose like I was a passenger.
And on top of everything else I found out that train there was
going straight to Galveston. That kind of changing around, the
way luck goes faster than you can figure it, it just won't be
understood. You start doing a thing and sometimes there's
nothing happens, and sometimes there's trouble busting
faster than you know it, and sometimes it's luck comes
busting. It's nothing you can figure. The onliest thing I've
ever been sure of how it was going is the music; that's something a man can make himself if he has the feeling.

Well, I was in this caboose and there were some other men
there talking about how they were going to turn me in to the
authorities when we got to the next place, but somehow I got
the feeling now it was just talk they're making. They said
they're going to fix me, but they didn't *sound* like it. Or maybe
that was just the way I was feeling. I'd been so scared that

last while there . . . all what had been happening . . . that I just didn't have any more scare in me. Coming into that caboose, it was like getting free chicken after all else what had been doing.

Then this brakeman saw my clarinet case sticking up out of my pants and he wanted to know what was inside it, and as soon as I told him he wanted to hear me play, and that did it— if I had any doubt before I knew it was gone when I saw him sitting there listening to the music. It was noisy in that caboose, but the clarinet had a tone that cut through those train sounds, and I could tell these men, they were enjoying the music real good.

And that's how it was at last. I sat there all relaxed, playing up a good time all the way into Galveston. Everything was changed. The brakeman even took me aside and told me how to do when we got to Galveston, how to go out of the yards there without running much chance of bumping into some railroad detective there what might be out looking for tramps. As luck would have it, I did bump right straight into one of them almost the minute I walked around the next train, and for a minute there I thought I was back in my troubles all over again. I explained how I'd been riding with this brake-man. I claimed he was a friend of my brother's and that he'd brought me along so I could play for him, and I showed the detective the clarinet, and after a while he sort of waved his hand and let me go.

Well, I hadn't been out of New Orleans very long—it wasn't two months since I started out with Clarence Williams—but that night when I walked out of the freight yard in Galveston and went to hunt up my brother, it felt like I'd been away from home just about forever. I was still nothing but a kid, and all this changing, all this trouble and luck and suddenness, it was confusing me. That wasn't the thing I'd been looking for. And still it was something for the music, something happening all the time to my people, a thing the music had to know for sure. There had to be a memory of it behind the music. Omar's trouble was big; and my trouble was little when you look way back on it, but right then it had been more trouble than I knew what to do with. In a way it taught me a whole lot about Omar's trouble in a way I couldn't have known about until I'd had some trouble of my own.

Still and all, I was young then; I wasn't for worrying long. Sometimes when I was playing the music I knew what it was that I was remembering. Other times, I was just being a kid, forgetting a thing almost before it was over. Somehow it seems like I always *understood* more when the music was playing and I was inside it, bringing it on out to itself.

But right then, walking around Galveston with all this changing behind me, it was almost like it never had happened. All I knew was I was hungry. So I got something to eat. And then I hunted up my brother and I started living with him.

We played some together, working here and there in different places, only I was supposed to be in early because I was still pretty young. My brother was real insistent about my coming home before it got late. All the same, I got to fooling around one night and the first thing I know I'd stayed out long after hours. I'd just been talking along with somebody here and somebody there, and when I thought to ask someone what the time was, he'd tell me it was after midnight, and then I didn't dare go home; so I'd go around from one place to another—bars, diners—putting it off, but knowing I got to think about doing it sooner or later. Then in one of these places I met up with this Mexican. He couldn't speak a word of English hardly and he was having a hell of a time making himself understood, but I liked talking to him. He'd got the kind of laugh about him you can't help wanting to see happen.

We talked along one way and another and I found out he had no place to stay and no money. Well, I couldn't take him home with me—my brother and my sister-in-law they'd really give it to me then. But I couldn't just leave him like that, so I explained to him the best I could, making all kinds of motions and sign language, that he was supposed to follow me and wait for me to see if the coast was clear. Maybe that way I could sort of sneak him in. He was pretty drunk. By this time we were both of us pretty drunk and not making too much sense, but after a while he got the idea and started in following me, like I'd said he was to do, and we started out.

My brother lived in a strange sort of place. Some of those streets in Galveston, they run by alphabet, and there was this M Street and on the corner there, there was this big house that some rich people lived in. It was really a beautiful house, mansion like. And running off right beside this house there was a little entrance. It was just a drive—if you didn't know it was there, you could miss it easy. And just off this entrance there was something like a street in there, M and a Half Street it was called. Where my brother was living, it was this M and a Half Street right there in back of the big house. The people that owned the big house owned these small houses there and they kept their help in them and they rented them out some too, to coloured people.

Well, I was just getting to the end of this M Street with this Mexican behind me. I needed to sneak in first and see if my sister-in-law was sleeping, or if they're watching out for me. I'd explained all this to the Mexican, but everytime I looked around he was coming on right behind me. Well, I was standing there waving my hands a whole lot, and two policemen right across the street came over.

'Where you think you're going?' they said.

So I told them.

'I live here,' I said, 'my brother, he lives here.'

They just laughed. They pointed to the big house and said 'In there, eh?'

I tried to explain, but they weren't listening. They just grabbed us right there and took us both off to the jail.

We hadn't more than got inside the door than they went to work on the Mexican. One of them punched him in the stomach and at the same time the other one hit him right back of the neck, and then they beat him and kicked him on the floor till he couldn't get up. His face, it was so full of blood you couldn't see what he looked like. One of these detectives what was doing the beating up had only got one hand. Later on I found out he'd had some trouble over in Mexican Town there in Galveston and gotten shot in the hand and had to have the hand cut off to the wrist, and ever since then, if he got hold of any Mexican, he took his revenge all over again.

At the time, though, I didn't know that. I was just standing there frozen up with fear thinking they'd be doing the same to me next, that it would be me lying on the floor with my face kicked in. But in the end they just locked me up without laying a hand to me. I guess maybe they thought I was too young. Or they'd had all the blood they wanted from the Mexican. Anyhow when they finished with him all they did was to ask me questions. The Mexican was still lying on the floor, and every once in a while one of the detectives gave him a kick to see if he'd come to again, and then turned to me with his questions. I tried to tell them about this M and a Half Street, and they just laughed and said there wasn't no such place. I'd sobered up for sure by then, worrying what they'd do next and I tried to explain, but they weren't listening to any explanations. I told them the Mexican wasn't responsible for anything, that I was just bringing him home with me, but all they did was to give him another kick where he was lying there and after a while they threw him into the bull-pen and they shoved me in after him and slammed the door. But they didn't hurt me none. They even let me keep my clarinet.

And it was while I was in jail there that I played the first blues I ever played with a lot of guys singing and no other instruments, just the singing. And, oh my God, what singing that was! It was my first experience that way, hearing someone right next to me start up singing . . . *Got a life full of so much punishment, Got me a feeling. Come down Jesus. Oh, why don't they put God on this earth where you can find Him easier.* Hearing someone else come in after a minute, just hearing his voice in the dark and knowing right away his life has a long way to go. Seeing someone hungry and beat-up, seeing his face all bloody and knowing he can't speak your language to tell you what it is, knowing that the only way he has to explain himself is being human, suffering and waiting. . . .

I'll never forget what those blues did to me. I can't remember every single line, but some I remember. And how it was, the thing it was saying inside itself—I remember that entire. This blues was different from anything I ever heard. Someone's woman left town, or someone's man, he'd gone around to another door . . . then there was something that took every thought I had out of my mind until it had me so close inside it I could *taste* how it felt . . . I was seeing the chains and that gallows, feeling the tears on my own face, rejoicing in the Angel the Lord sent down for that sinner. Oh my God, that was a blues. The way they sang it there, it was something you would send down to earth if it had been given to you to be God. What you'd send to your son in trouble if he was on earth and you was in Heaven.

This blues was all about a man that kept getting himself in different kinds of trouble. It started like this:

> Tied in a hundred feet of chain,
> Every link of the chain was initial to his name.
> Warden come early that morning for him to be hung
> On account of something he hadn't done.

There was about twenty verses to it. It went on to tell the whole story—how the warden brings him to the gallows and how the poor man he's praying to the sheriff, pleading, telling him he hasn't done the wrong. And the sheriff believes the man . . . that he's innocent. He tries to help him, but there's no proof. It was the same old, old thing. Finally, at the end of it, at the final closing of the verse it went:

> The man prays to the Lord to hear his cry
> And the Lord says, 'Go down Angel, that man's got
>   no right to die.'

Well, it would be easy for me to tell you some lyrics, make up other ones, just fill it in and fake it for you. But that won't do—that's not the way I'd want. You got to hear it for yourself, you got to *feel* that singing, and I got no way to make that possible for you in a book way. But what you've got to realize is this blues, it had a memory to it; it was like I was talking to one of these people come to hear us play.

I got to talking to him once and I told him about this blues, about the memory, and he said, 'Yes. It has a myth quality.' Well, that's just a name for it, but what it really was, it was that man. He was more than just a man. He was like every man that's been done a wrong. Inside him he'd got the memory of all the wrong that's been done to all my people. That's what the memory is . . . when I remember that man, I'm remembering myself, a feeling I've always had. When a blues is good, that kind of memory just grows up inside it. That's when you can't help yourself . . . you just can't ever forget it. There's nothing about that night I could ever forget.

The next morning I woke up and looked around this bull-pen. There was every kind of man in there for every kind of reason. Some of them, it pained me just to look at them. And that Mexican was stretched out there, terribly beat up, looking like something that wasn't really a man any more. Oh, it was a pitiful thing, and all I could do was stand there wishing for some way of helping him and knowing there was nothing that could be done.

Then after a while my brother came to get me out. Somebody had told him where I'd been the evening before and that I was in jail, so he came and explained about this M and a Half Street; they finally learned there was such a street, they believed it and they let me out then. But they kept the Mexican there. I couldn't ever learn what happened to him.

I'd had my brother's guitar that evening before. He'd had an appointment he had to get to and he'd left it with me to bring home and that's how I'd really met up with this Mexican. He could play the guitar; he'd been singing those Spanish songs, and all I'd wanted was to stand around listening to him. That's how we started going around from place to place, him singing those songs and playing the guitar. It was a lucky thing I'd left the guitar with the bar-tender in the last place we'd been. A guitar's a big thing, and I didn't want to be seen out at night lugging any big package. I was sober enough to think of that, and it was a good thing. If that Mexican had been carrying the guitar when he was picked up there's no saying what those detectives would have done to it, had they thought it was his. I get to thinking about that Mexican from time to time; I sure brought that boy bad luck, but he sure could play hell out of that guitar.

Anyway, my brother got me out of jail, and we went over to get his guitar, and on the way he explained to me all about how he had this job that would bring us both back to New Orleans. He'd had a letter and he was to go down and pick up with a band there, and he was wanting to take me along so we could play together. Well, I hadn't been out of New Orleans long but there never was anyone who could have been readier to go back. The way things go, I was to find myself itching to move along again after I'd been home a while, but at the time I got out of the jail I had no part of any itch left to me; I was awful ready to be back in New Orleans.

My brother on different occasions had been able to get familiar with hoboing and, from what I'd told him about how I came to Galveston, he was thinking *I* had experience at it too, so he told me he wanted to hobo it back. He didn't have enough money to get us both back to New Orleans as passengers, and he had to leave some money with his wife till he could send for her, so he was figuring to catch a freight and ride it free.

Well, I couldn't tell him I didn't really know the first thing about it, and I figured I'd just watch what he did and do the same thing—that ought to come out about right—so after we were all fixed to leave I went down to the freight yard with him and we waited around till he'd picked out the right freight, and just as it started to move we ran for it. My brother jumped on and I saw how he did it and I took a jump after him and I made it all right, but just then my clarinet fell out. I was wearing these braces and I had my clarinet inside one of the straps where it would stay, and what do you know but a button had come off, and there'd gone my clarinet. Well, my brother had seen what it was and he shouted to me to stay on, to never mind the clarinet. 'Don't jump,' he shouted, 'you can get hurt.' But I wasn't listening at all and I jumped off. I had just got to have that clarinet.

Well, I got off all right and I picked myself up and I went back to about where I thought it was and right off I saw the case between two bushes and I picked it up and looked at it and was some relieved to find nothing wrong with. I was just closing the case when my brother came along. He grabbed my arm and ran me out of there fast before some detective would come busting along and he got me out of the yard and gave me a long talking too about such damn' foolishness. But he's seen already that I've never really hoboed it, that I wasn't so all experienced, because someone, if they're travelling that way, the only thing important is to catch that train and stay on it. Like my brother says, you can't live forever anyhow, but any man that gets to jumping off a train almost as soon's he's caught it just won't live to catch many another train.

He got me out of that yard and he explained everything how it had to be. Then we got back toward the yard, and, not wanting to be seen, we got under one of those handcars while we waited for another freight. We waited some long time and it looked like there was just no freight going. Then all of a sudden it started to rain. It seems like the rain had hardly started before I was soaked just about through and beginning to shiver like a tree.

Then my brother decided I'd best go passenger. He'd got just about enough money for one passenger ticket, and he took me to the station. He figured it was better to put me on the passenger train than worry about it. Once he'd sent me on, he said, he could look out for himself all right. So he bought me this ticket and we waited around in the station two or three hours trying to get dry near the stove while we waited for this train. Then he put me on it and said good-bye.

And that's how it was I got back to New Orleans the first time after I left my brother at Galveston. Only I hadn't even got out of the train at New Orleans before I saw my brother waiting for me. There's this place on a passenger train up between the baggage car and the coal tender and when somebody jumps up in that place he's said to be going blind baggage. That's how my brother had done: he'd ridden all the way into New Orleans with me on the same train.

7. The Road North

It was all so much a pleasure being back in New Orleans after all that had happened to me the first time I left. I was at Pete Lala's at that time. I was playing there with good musicianers, knowing where I was to sleep that night, hearing real music. It was so different from all that had been happening to me when I took off to play on those stores.

There was this club, too, that we played at, the Twenty-Five Club. That was about 1912, 1913; and all the time we played there, people were talking about Freddie Keppard. Freddie, he had left New Orleans with his band and he was travelling all over the country playing towns on the Orpheum Circuit. At that time, you know, that was something new and Freddie kept sending back all these clippings from what all the newspapermen and the critics and all was writing up about him, about his music, about his band. And all these clippings were asking the same thing: where did it come from? It seems like everyone along the circuit was coming up to Freddie to ask about this ragtime. Especially when his show, the Original Creole Band, got to the Winter Gardens in New York—that was the time they was asking it most. Where did it come from? And back at the Twenty-Five these friends of Freddie's kept coming around and showing these clippings, wanting to know what it was all about. It was a new thing then.

Freddie took his Original Creole Band out of New Orleans early in 1912 and he went to San Francisco, California. That's where the act was first put together for the Orpheum Circuit. It was made and rehearsed out there. But it wasn't really until they got to New York that all this public and critics and what-not, they really stopped and demanded to know about this ragtime. No one knew what to do when they heard this music. They never heard anything like it in their lives; they didn't know if it was for dance or sing or listen.

Well, going off that way, playing all around the Orpheum Circuit, that's a business thing. You hear lots of talk about that, about the way business can't mix with the music. But there's no reason for saying a thing like that. Freddie, he was playing the music; he wasn't really caring about the business thing. He was playing the music from the inside.

Three or four times while he was up there his band was engaged to make records. The directors from the recording company, they come to them, wanting to engage them. But they never made those records. There was all kinds of reasons given. These writers since then who been writing books about Jazz, they all had a reason to give; they was all sure they had an idea why Freddie never made those records. But all that writing, it was just writing from hearsay. There was only one real reason: Freddie just didn't care to, that was all.

Someone had it that Freddie was hiding something, some secret about the music. He used to play with a handkerchief over his trumpet so you couldn't see his fingers, and so this writer had it figured out Freddie was afraid to make records. Well, you couldn't see that in hearing it. Freddie just did that joke like, he was having his fun. Any musicianer knows you don't learn from seeing someone's fingers. You learn by hearing; there's no other way—not if you're a real musicianer. You can't find the notes by watching them, not if you're going to feel them to play what you got to play.

Freddie never said it just that way, but many times we've spoken of that recording session business, and from his answer it's the only conclusion I've come to: that these people who was coming to make records, they was going to turn it into a regular business, and after that it wouldn't be pleasure music. That's the way Freddie was.

What Freddie asked of a musicianer, was that he keep on playing like he always played. If you were sick, well, there was no pain big enough to keep you from playing; you could be sick after. If he saw a musicianer not playing right, he'd practically get right up there in that horn or clarinet and want to show him. He wouldn't play with no one that had no heart for what he was doing. Sometimes Freddie could be kind of arrogant in a way, but it was the right way; the one thing he couldn't stand was bad music. He left many a band because he didn't like the way they played. He'd walk right off the bandstand and never come back. One time he was playing with the Tennessee Ten and they was doing really well moneywise. But Freddie couldn't stay in it, he couldn't find any heart in the music the way they played it, and he just up and left. Freddie really understood music; he had a feeling for it. He wouldn't give away any part of the music, and he wouldn't stand for its being played wrong. Freddie, he was a real musicianer. And he had a feeling about that recording thing; he had a feeling that every Tom, Dick, or Harry who could ever blow a note would be making records soon. It would get so the music wasn't where it belonged. It was going to be taken away.

And that's true, you know. Pretty soon every fellow who ever heard a piece of music in his life was showing up with a recording. He'd gone out and bought himself a pretty instrument, and soon they was recording the fellow who had the fanciest instrument and the nicest case. And these companies got to adding all sorts of instruments. They began adding saxophone in bands: there'd never been a saxophone when we played. About 1921 they even took out the clarinet. And they began having three, four saxophones. And they got arrangers to arrange all these pieces for things like that. Oh, we had arrangers back in New Orleans; but you don't play just because there's an arranger. He isn't going to be able to show you how to play . . . not if you know inside yourself where it is the music has to go.

I had a feeling about all this changing. I had a feeling the clarinet would come back. I was playing saxophone by then, but it wasn't alto like everyone was going out to buy. I played my soprano sax and clarinet, the two both. And the time came when the clarinet did get back.

And about the time they were making all these changes, some of the white musicianers had taken our style as best they could. They played things that were really our numbers. But, you understand, it wasn't our music. It wasn't us. I don't care what you say, it's awful hard for a man who isn't black to play a melody that's come deep out of black people. It's a question of feeling.

But these musicianers, they all showed up in New York. The record companies sent for them to come and make their records. The people had come wild about this music and the companies were giving what they had closest to it. They couldn't call it New Orleans; it just wasn't New Orleans. But they had to have a name for it, so they called it Dixieland. And that was the Original Dixieland Orchestra. Larry Shields, he was one of those musicianers.

They made a lot of those records. There was *Livery Stable Blues, Dixieland One Step, Tiger Rag.* Those were all numbers they had learned from playing opposite us back in New Orleans. But the way it was . . . after they made a record, it was finished. Those are numbers you've got to *do* something with . . . you've got to make them original. All these Dixieland musicianers could do was play what they learned from us, and after that there wasn't anything more for them to do. They had played all they knew, and it wasn't any longer a question of them adding something to the music so it could grow; they never had it to add. It was all arranged and you played it the way it was written and that was all.

And in a way, you know, once you had a thing arranged and down like that, you got to owning it. You could put your name on it and almost believe it really was yours. But you can't own a thing like that unless you understand a lot more about it than just repeating what's written down. Take a number like *Livery Stable Blues.* We'd played that before they could remember; it was something we knew about a long way back. But theirs, it was a burlesque of the blues. There wasn't nothing serious in it any more. And there was *Teasing Rag*: that became the *Dixieland One Step*. Or you take *Tiger Rag* for instance. It had come originally from different parts of a quadrille put in different tempos. But when Northern arrangers got hold of it, they felt there was enough numbers like that, so they started to build up the timing and they took the pieces of the number and they began to arrange them different. They were damn' good arrangements, that you can't deny. But it's a pity the thing couldn't continue to be played the way it was meant, advancing on its own instead of having all those instruments added to it and all those parts written down. Because all that writing down, all those notes on paper, they was only trying to write down the atmosphere we were in when we were adding parts spontaneous.

But the main thing is, after those fellows made these arrangements, the music had to go back where it came from. Those Dixielanders had played all they had learned and the thing just dropped. But we kept on. And the music, it was staying popular; there was still all the excitement for what was happening to it.

But to go back a bit, around that time I was talking about they was building a railroad up to Chicago. Back in New Orleans people were hearing a lot of excitement about what was happening up North, and I had this idea in my head that I was to see other places. I wanted to go North and see Chicago and I wanted to see New York. I guess I just about wanted to see all there was. But back there in New Orleans I played with Joe Oliver in cabarets, like Pete Lala's. Then finally Freddie Keppard left. He'd been playing with the Olympia Band, and Billy Marera, he was the manager of it. And Joe Oliver, he played with the Magnolia Band. But when Freddie Keppard took off, Joe Oliver moved over to the Olympia and he and Billy Marera kept the band together. It was at that time that I joined them, and I took the place of Louis 'Big Eye' Nelson. Well, we played like this around a year or more, and then I left Joe and went to play at the theatre on Claiborne Street. I played at Lala's Theatre, and it wasn't so long before Joe Oliver, he left too and went to form a band

115

with Kid Ory. They wanted me to come with the band; they were going to have two clarinets, me and Johnny Dodds. He went, but for some reason I wanted to stay with the theatre.

But after a while more with the theatre I guess I still wanted to see places, so I joined up with the Bruce and Bruce Stock Company and we set off on a very big tour. We went to the South first. That's where we picked up Louis Wade again on the piano, and then in Birmingham, Alabama, we picked up a little drummer by the name of Johnny Sawyer. That was a very good company. We played comedy and dramas. Sometimes I played on the stage myself, with solos and things. Well, we went on up to Chicago and played at the Mardi Gras Theatre, that was on 35th and State Street.

And it was right around this time, and a bit before— I'd be talking, I'd say, about 1917—that a whole lot of music- ianers started to leave New Orleans for up North, mostly for Chicago. There was the Royal Garden, the Deluxe, the Dreamland—that's where they went. Some of those men was real musicianers. There was Lawrence Duhé, Sugar Johnny, Roy Palmer, Tubby Garland, Wellman Braud, Minor Hall, Tubby Hall, Herbert Lindsay . . . they was all playing at the Deluxe and they was all writing back to New Orleans that work was plentiful, telling the New Orleans musicianers to come up. That's how Freddie Keppard, Bill Johnson, George Baquet, Kid Ory, Mutt Carey, Tig Chambers all come up from New Orleans. Oh, there were others too; it was a real excitement there.

Then the show that I was with, the Bruce and Bruce Company, left town. But I stayed on, and I went over to the Deluxe cabaret with Sugar Johnny, who played cornet; with us we had Roy Palmer on trombone, Lil Hardin on piano, Minor Hall drums, Wellman Braud on bass, and Lawrence Dewey playing clarinet with me—they were all there. And while we were together, it was really something. It was the real music. There was Darnell Howard, he was the only man who wasn't out of New Orleans who played with us, who we let in. He was from Chicago; he played violin, a hell of a good violin, and he was learning trumpet—he played trumpet some

116

with us. And there was his mother, too; she played a real fine piano. But then Sugar Johnny died, and Freddie Keppard took his place. And other bands began taking our men. But that was a hell of a band while it was all together.

Then Bill Bottom, who owned the Dreamland, sent for Joe Oliver down in New Orleans, and Joe came up and we got a band together. There was Joe and Lawrence Dewey and me, and Lottie Williams, she played piano. I played with them a while and then I left and went back to the Deluxe.

About that time I took another job, too, at the Pekin, sort of after hours—about one to four—with Tony Jackson, who was playing there at that time. Tony was a wonderful entertainer, a wonderful composer, and a wonderful piano player; he was the onliest man I know who could entertain an audience for two hours by himself alone. We'd played together at the Deluxe, and then he had this band at the Pekin and asked me to join him there. Oh, I really went with Tony. He wrote several songs—you remember *Pretty Baby, Some Sweet Day* and *Such a Pretty Thing*; he certainly was a great entertainer. But when I was all booked to go to London with Will Marion Cook, like I'll tell you in a minute, I couldn't figure why Will wouldn't take Tony along with him. I was a young fellow, you know, and he just wouldn't say; but finally he told me, because Tony had some kind of venereal disease and had sores back of his neck, and so that's why the old man didn't want to take him. And then in 1921 when I was playing at the Hammersmith Palais de Danse in London I read in the paper Tony was dead.

That was the time you began to hear a lot about Chicago Style. You pick up a book by some writer and he's talking about Chicago Style. And everytime he says Chicago Style he's talking about *Royal Garden*; the way they talk, you'd think a musicianer has to be playing nothing but that one number if he's playing real Jazz. Well, I'll tell you how it was. I'm not a person who's saying we ought to have horse and buggy today. You can have anything you like. You can have a car or you can have an airplane. But whatever it is, you've always got the wheels. No matter what kind of thing you've got, it's the wheel you start from; it's the foundation. Once you got those wheels under you, you can turn this way, and you can turn that way, or you can take off and fly. But you got to have the wheels.

It's the same with Chicago Style, New York Style, Kansas City Style—any style you want to talk about; you're turning one way or you're turning another. But New Orleans, it's the wheels; it's the foundation.

There's no mystery about Chicago style; it's not some romance how they got it. It was just that when they got to something they couldn't do, they substituted their own feeling. The rhythm, the story, the roots—they were all there and they were all the same; but it was like they couldn't hear New Orleans. It wasn't no different tempo. It wasn't really anything new. They were just hearing different. They were remembering different because mostly they didn't have the same things to remember.

You take a man. If he's doing something—say he pats his head and rubs his stomach: if he concentrates on what he's doing, he can do it. It isn't so easy, but if he knows what he's about it's like he was doing just one simple thing. He's knowing both things; they're there; but he's doing them like it was one. It's like that with the music; there's listening to it and there's playing it. It's two things that's being done with no difference. And even that's only a beginning. There's so much more that's got to be done. You got to beautify it. It's got to be moulded. The two things have to become one thing. But if the musicianer's only doing one thing, he's losing out before he's even worrying about it being beautiful. If he's only patting his head and watching you rub your stomach, that isn't much music.

Oh, it's a hell of a thing, but it happened in New Orleans.

Freddie Keppard, he wasn't all serious—he was a hell of a go-round man . . . they just don't come any better. Freddie and I used to hang out together a lot when we was in Chicago. After we finished playing we'd go through a whole lot of saloons, and sometimes we'd find we'd gone and left our

Bill Reinhardt and Sidney Bechet at Chicago's Blue Note, 1948

Haus Vaterland, Berlin, 1929, 1931

Sidney Bechet and Tommy Ladnier, 1938

Sidney Bechet and Sammy Price at Jimmy Ryan's, New York, 1949

instruments somewheres in one of them. Well, the next day we'd go back over all those different saloons we'd been in. We'd try to time it so the same bartender would be on duty as the one who was there when we had been carousing and all. We wouldn't know where we'd left them, but we'd walk into a place and we'd tell the bartender, 'Get us our instruments, will you, we're in an awful hurry.' And then we'd put our heads down and look at one another and laugh like hell because the way we was asking, they couldn't just make up something; they *had* to know if the instruments was there or not. So if they went and looked and couldn't find nothing, we'd pass on over to some other place we'd been and pull the same thing all over again: 'Get us our instruments, man,' just like we knew for sure they was there. And the bartenders never figured on anything else; and some place the instruments was bound to be there, so sooner or later some bartender would answer right away and go off into his back room knowing he had them there, and we'd look at one another and laugh like hell. 'So *that's* where they are!' we'd say. Oh, we had some times. We weren't for selling out any part of the music. We was sincere musicianers. But we had some real times, too; there was ways of laughing.

Armand Piron played in the old Olympia Orchestra that Freddie Keppard made up, and he published a piece of music that became really well known. That was *I Wish I Could Shimmy Like My Sister Kate*. Piron published it, but the music for that piece came from Louis Armstrong. Whether Piron bought it from Louis or not I don't know, but I do know that Louis composed the music and then later Piron got the rights to it.

Around 1913 Piron had a partnership with Clarence Williams down in New Orleans for publishing songs. They were doing real fine, too. Piron was playing and publishing his songs and being liked by all; he was a man who got a lot of respect from people.

Clarence, though, was seeing big chances. He wanted to go North; he saw that was going to be the place where a whole lot of opportunities were going to open up, and it wasn't long after this song came out that Clarence saw his chance. He left for Chicago but he didn't stay there long before he went on to New York and opened his own publishing house there. And right off he published *Sister Kate* in New York. Well, the way it was in those days, when a man published a song, it was almost like it was *his* song. The writer of it, his name didn't even have to be on it, and I don't even know if Piron knew at first how well *Sister Kate* was selling. But after some while when Piron heard about the publication, he went up to New York to collect for his advance royalty which was bringing him seven or eight hundred dollars. Clarence gave it to him, and Piron, as soon as he got it, went right back to New Orleans.

Then a few years later—this was about '20, '21—he was back again in New York, and this time he brought his band. While he was there he got his band together and recorded some numbers, like *Mama Gone, Goodby, Ghost of the Blues*. Those were great records too: he had some real fine musicianers with him; there was men like 'Steve Lewis on piano, Peter Beaucart violin, Pete's brother on guitar, Degaston playing bass, Lorenzo Tio on clarinet, Louis Warnock alto, and Louis Cotrelle and Johnny Lindsay playing clarinet and trombone. And about this time too he took his band into the Cotton Club and the Roseland so that a lot of people were hearing the music for the first time. That's one reason why Fletcher Henderson, when he come along later, could be so popular; in some ways Piron had made it possible. It was Armand who was responsible for Fletcher Henderson even being able to come into the Roseland in later years.

Off and on at this same time, Piron was around Clarence's office helping to boost his own songs. That's all pretty natural, the way it is: if you're writing songs and a publishing company's been publishing them, you just naturally work a bit for that music publishing office. In a way it's just no more than scratching your own back.

Piron didn't have his worries then. He had his health and he had enough money and he had things to look forward to. *Sister Kate* was doing well and it wasn't giving him any concern. But even that didn't seem like enough reason for staying on in New York; it wasn't his natural place. So he packed up and went back to New Orleans. Staying in New York wasn't the same for him as it was for someone like Clarence; it just wasn't Piron's way. New Orleans was more personal to him, more natural like; he was more used to the New Orleans way of doing.

But there's something else that has got to be explained here to really understand Armand J. Piron and what happened to him. It's about this ASCAP. It's supposed to be, you know, if anyone composes some numbers and one of those numbers becomes popular, it's quite easy for him to be admitted as a member of this ASCAP. Anyone what has written a piece that becomes popular, they *can* become a member. When that happens, there's a rating made up to show how popular the number becomes, and ASCAP pays you money according to that rating. Well, Armand had written more than one number, and now that he was back in New Orleans and he was getting along in age and had fallen ill somewhat, he wanted to see something setting him up so he wouldn't have any worries. Those last ten or thirteen years, they'd really made a big difference in his life . . . changed so many things—his health, his way of feeling things.

So he began writing up to Clarence that he wanted to become this member, that *Sister Kate* wasn't bringing him any more royalties, and that he was needing some security like what would come to him when he was made a member of ASCAP. And just at that time when Piron was writing to Clarence, hoping for some money, there was a meeting going on in New York and it seemed ASCAP were meeting on giving *Clarence* a higher rating, wanting to advance *him* to being a higher officer, and a lot of the reason for this was because of how popular *Sister Kate* was becoming. Because *Sister Kate*, you know, was really responsible for a many, many people's success who played it or sang it. It really had a hold on the public. Every two or three years it was coming out all over again in some different kind of issuing.

Clarence knew that it was Armand who should really be a member, and he didn't let him down. He really worked for him. That meeting, it was almost convention-like . . . all the ASCAP officers getting together with a whole lot of business, and before the meetings ended, Clarence brought Piron up from New Orleans, and he finally saw to it that Armand was admitted as a member.

Piron, he was really happy when he got back to New Orleans. He was thinking he hadn't any more troubles now. But he hadn't been back long when a trouble did come upon him; a family thing and it was serious. It was something money would help, too . . . the kind of a situation that could all be changed if he had some money. Well, it got Piron worried bad. He fell really ill. He hadn't got his health any more.

But still he was sure all his troubles were going to be over by his becoming this member in ASCAP. You don't know why he hadn't been one sooner, but there are all sorts of things in what happens to a man . . . you just don't know all the reasons what are behind something. Right now, Piron, he was sure he could live in New Orleans peaceful-like and his family would be able to work out of their difficulty; they'd all be looked after. And the only thing he'd got that was going to bring this around—he wasn't playing any more at this time and he didn't see much people—the only thing he'd got was *Sister Kate*. And he really believed that, being a member, he was going to get royalties amounting to between $5,000·00, near $10,000·00. He didn't know that the first cheque that's sent to any member of ASCAP is usually for $5·00 or $10·00, and after, *after* that, the regular amount is sent.

Well, he got this cheque for $5·00 or $10·00, and looked at it and turned it over once or twice. And that was the end of it. He went completely out of his mind. He just looked at it, turned it over, and he couldn't believe it. And that was the end of Piron.

That's what I know of this one man. He had all those troubles, and he had his music. His music is what he had for explaining himself, for making his troubles over so they would

122

have a pride to them. It was his way of being a man that could stand up to himself.

Some people hear how you've got to smoke reefers, be hopped up before you can play. How you've got to have a woman or a bottle coaxing you on from the side. But that's not it. That's not it at all. You might be able to play—it's possible—if you've had all this dope stuff or if you've got some woman standing near feeling every note you play . . . or not feeling it even, but wanting to get some of the thrill from it if you're in the limelight. You can get yourself drunk up to most anything . . . drunk up, or womanned up, or thrilled up with a lot of dope. You can do that. There's a many who think you *have* to do that.

But the real reason you play . . . it's just because you're *able* to play, that's all,

Inspiration, that's another thing. The world has to give you that, the way you live in it, what you find in your living. The world gives it to you if you're ready. But it's not just given . . . it has to be put inside you and you have to be ready to have it put there. All that happens to you makes a feeling out of your life and you play that feeling. But there's more than that. There's the feeling inside the music too. And the final thing, it's the way those two feelings come together. I don't care where that life-feeling comes from in you . . . even if you start playing a number from a love-feeling, it has to become something else before you're through. That love-feeling has to find the music-feeling. And then the music can learn how to get along with itself.

But drinking and reefers and all that stuff, most times they just mess up all the feeling you got inside yourself and all the feeling the music's got inside *it*self. When a man goes at the music that way, it's just a sign that there's a lot inside himself he don't know how to answer. He's not knowing which way he needs to go. He's not going anywhere at all.

Buddy Bolden, maybe it was all his women and all that drinking that did him in. Or maybe it was something back of the women and the drinking . . . something the same thing that made him carry on so, something that hadn't anything to do with the music. And Perez . . . his was different . . . a kind of growing tired maybe, a kind of not being able to stand up to himself any more. But that could happen to anyone, not just to a musicianer.

And still there was so many of them . . . a man like Piron . . . a man like Perez . . . all those musicianers going that way . . . so many of them. God, I just don't know. But it's a thing that has to find its answer yet. Maybe a musicianer, he finds too much in his music . . . too much of what he wants to find, of what he needs to find. And then when he turns away from the music, when he's through playing, it's not there. It's not there, and he needs it so desperate bad. Maybe it's like all the life there is to him is in the music. But he can't play all the time. Whether he's got to stop for the night or whether he's got to stop for old age . . . whatever it is, he's got to stop some time. And then maybe he just can't bear to have it stopped.

My answer—all I can say of it—it's just to be giving, giving all your life, finding the music and giving it away. God maybe punishes a man for wanting too much, but He don't punish a man for giving. Maybe He even fixes it so that what you give away, it's the mostest thing you've got.

And maybe there's another thing why so many of these musicianers ended up so bad. Maybe they didn't know how to keep up with all this commercializing that was happening to ragtime. If it could have stayed where it started and not had to take account of the business it was becoming—all that making contracts and signing options and buying and selling rights— maybe without that it might have been different. If you start taking what's pure in a man and you start putting it on a bill of sale, somehow you can't help destroying it. In a way, all that business makes it so a man don't have anything left to give.

I got a feeling inside me, a kind of memory that wants to sing itself . . . I can give you that. I can send it out to where it can be taken, maybe, if you want it. I can *try* to give it to you. But if all I've got is a contract, I've got nothing to give. How'm I going to give you a contract?

8. First Sight of Europe

I was playing in the Deluxe at Chicago after I left playing with Joe Oliver about 1918, and Will Marion Cook came there one night. He sat around and listened to the music and after we had finished playing he asked me, did I want to go to New York to play with him.

He was a fine man and a good musicianer, Will Marion Cook. When he was young he played violin and he used to give concerts, classical music. And when he was around sixteen, I think it was he told me, some teacher came up to him and said it was a pity that he hadn't learned the violin proper, because if he had he would have been a wonderful violinist. So from then on he thought he would come to Europe to take lessons, and he went to Dvořák. And Dvořák listened to him play and then said, 'Listen, I'm awfully sorry. I like you very much, but I have boys here in my class eleven and twelve years old. And if you wanted to take lessons from me you would have to start way back with the twelve-year-olds.' So Will accepted that and came back to America. When he got home he went in for a contest, for a scholarship, playing violin. And when it was over one of the judges said to him that if he hadn't been coloured he would have won the scholarship for sure. Well, that burned him up, and he broke his violin and never played no more. He just composed and conducted. He wrote some very good numbers—*The Rain Song, My Lady's Lips, Mammie of Mine* and things like that. He wrote an awful lot of numbers, and he never wrote a bad one. I wonder why they are hardly played now.

When I got to New York I showed up to play, and Will knew I couldn't read notes. I could look at the page and tell where the music was going, but I never had learned things note by note—I couldn't play it that way. The music, it's almost like it don't want any parts: it wants to be all of itself. Leastways, you gotta *feel* it like it was all at once.

Will knew about this, so he got me aside and told me: 'Son, I want you to listen to the band a couple of times and I'll let you know when to rehearse.' I told him I didn't need a rehearsal and he looked at me and said, 'If you got the nerve, go ahead.' That was all he said, and that's all there was to it. All the band needed was to go over a few of my pieces to learn my solo parts. That was mostly for numbers like blues. The *Characteristic Blues*, that was one I played. That's how it was put together and we went on at the Metropolitan.

But Will had some kind of trouble over contracts and things, and we all broke up for a while till he could get it all straightened out. So to fill in time I went and played with Tim Bryen on Coney Island. We all wore very fancy uniforms and the pay was good. Tim had a regular clarinet player, named Kincaid; and this Kincaid, he had a curved soprano saxophone. I liked the tone of this saxophone very much, so full and rich. I'd tried one in Chicago when I was playing at the Pekin but I hadn't liked it, and I think there must have been something wrong with it. Well, I liked this one Kincaid had, and from that time I got more and more interested in the soprano saxophone.

After a while Will got round all the trouble, and he decided to take this band, the Southern Syncopated Orchestra, to London. He asked me if I wanted to go along and I told him yes. But while I was getting packed up someone told me there was a terrible soap shortage in Europe, and particularly in England, on account of the war. So the next time I saw Will I said I'd still come along, but I must have $500·00 advance. He was a bit surprised, but he gave me the money, and when we sailed most of my baggage was made up of four vast crates of soap.

We sailed in a cattle boat; the trip took fifteen days and we

were all as sick as dogs. We got there in June of 1919 and
we played at the Royal Philharmonic Hall. That's where I
met that Swiss conductor, Ernest Ansermet. He used to
come every performance. He'd sit there in his box and after
it was over he used to go on backstage and talk to Will.
Many a time he'd come over to where I was and he'd ask me
all about how I was playing, what it was I was doing, was
I singing into my instrument to make it sound that way?
We talked a whole lot about the music. This man, he was
trained for classical, but he had a real interest in our music.
There was just no end to the questions he could think to ask
about it. I don't think he missed a performance all the time he
was there. And then he wrote a piece about us and he said—
I've still got it by me now—he said, 'The first thing that strikes
one about the Southern Syncopated Orchestra is the aston-
ishing perfection, the superb taste, and the fervour of its
playing.' And then he went on, 'There is in the Southern
Syncopated Orchestra an extraordinary clarinet virtuoso who
is, so it seems, the first of his race to have composed perfectly
formed blues on the clarinet. . . . I wish to set down the name
of this artist of genius, as for myself, I shall never forget it—it
is Sidney Bechet.' Well, I don't know about this genius
business; like I said, I've always played the music I know the
way I feel it, and I was mighty glad at the way Ernest
Ansermet understood right off what we were doing.

And another thing I did when I got to London was to buy
a *straight* soprano saxophone. I was walking around with
Arthur Briggs when I saw one in the window of an instrument
maker. We went in, and I ran through *Whispering* on it: this
was the first number I played on it. I liked this saxophone as
soon as that London instrument maker gave it to me, and Will
Marion Cook, he liked it too. So he had some special arrangements made so I could play this; *Song of Songs* one of them was
called. This was a piece of good luck for me because it wasn't
long after this before people started saying they didn't want
clarinets in their bands no more. And there was I all set with
my saxophone.

We played there at this Philharmonic Hall about a month.

This orchestra, you know, it was big: there was thirty-six pieces all together. It had twenty singers, it had violins—the whole thing. And we had a business manager, George Lattimore. It was really a show. Then one day Will came up to me—that was in August of 1919—and very quiet-like told me there was to be a special performance at Buckingham Palace, a Command Performance, that's what you call it. And I had to perform, he told me. He was going to take a quarter of the band and feature a quartet around me. Well, I didn't know what to say to a thing like that, walking right into a King's palace. I didn't know what to expect, but the way it turned out, it was just bigger than another place; it was like Grand Central Station with a lot of carpets and things on the walls. Only it had more doors. By the time we got to play I was thinking I'd gone through enough doors to do me for a month. There was this butler all dressed up and he led us through all these doors and finally he showed us out into the garden where we was to play, and after that it was like any other. Once we got started we had the whole royal family tapping their feet. There was over a thousand people there. And Will told me later that he'd asked them what it was they'd enjoyed most, and the King said it was that blues, the *Characteristic Blues*.

But there was a funny thing I was thinking there between numbers when I was looking at the King. It was the first time I ever got to recognize somebody from having seen his picture on my money. After that, every time I bought me a gin I'd look at the money. He wasn't on all of it. There'd been these other kings, and there'd been this King's grandmother, and they'd left some money with *their* pictures. But this King, it was George V, he had his picture on a lot of this money, and when I bought something I'd take a look at it. It was a funny thing looking at your money and seeing somebody you'd know.

Well, after that we had an engagement for three or four months at the Philharmonic Hall in London and then for a week at the Coliseum. We should have gone over to Paris then, but things didn't work out and the orchestra sort of broke up and all changed around. There was a lot of legal trouble, too, and it wasn't good. Benny Peyton, the drummer, he formed a little band from some of the men in Will's orchestra; the Jazz Kings, he called it. There was Benny, Henry Sapiro on banjo, George Smith violin, Pierre de Cayo piano, Fred Coxito on alto saxophone, and me. We played at the Embassy Club, a smart place where we had to wear white tie and tails. And it was then, too, that I first took part in a recording. We recorded for the Columbia Company; but they made a mess of it and overcut the waxes so the records were never issued. Then the big orchestra got reorganized; Will Marion Cook had left by then, during all these disagreements; Lattimore was running it, and the conductor was a man called E. E. Thompson, who used to play trumpet a bit too. Then we did go over to Paris. That was my first time in Paris. We played for a couple of months at the Apollo Theatre in Montmartre in 1920. It was only just in 1950 that I played there again. It was a funny thing coming back to that same place after all that thirty years.

A thing like that—you come in the same door and you're in the same place and nothing seems to be changed. It could be that other time thirty years ago all over again. You could try to forget and then you could pretend it was the same time. But all the time you know how much has changed. You're not trying to kid yourself. You don't believe you can go back. What you're doing when you pretend, that's a way of feeling how much change there's been. It's a way of realizing, like. But that's getting ahead. That's another time. When we got through there we went back to London, and we played through the summer at the Kingsway Hall, and again at the Philharmonic. That's where I had me a lot of trouble. The way it ended, I was deported from England. That was a hell of a thing.

There was this fellow I knew, his name was Clapham. He was a classic piano player. One night when I got through playing I walked out and I ran into him, and we got to talking. 'Sidney,' he told me, 'where are you going? You're not going to turn in yet. Let's go out someplace and have some fun.'

Well, we walked along a ways thinking to stop off somewheres for a gin maybe and on the way we met two girls. Two tarts they were; 'tarts', that's what they call them in England. These were two we knew from having been around there. One of them I'd been with before a time or two.

We all got to talking and after a while we went up to this Clapham's apartment and we got to fooling around. Clapham, he played the piano and we all of us had a few drinks playing around at this and that, just the way it is when you're having this kind of a party. After a while Clapham stopped playing the piano and he wanted his girl to go with him into the next room, but she wouldn't go, she just didn't want to. Well, I was with my girl and we'd been talking and kissing some, just fooling around, and *I'm* wanting to make things more serious, but *she* didn't want to. Well, the way it goes sometimes, one thing leads to another and all at once she bit my hand and I slapped her. I didn't slap her hard. We were just messing around together and all at once I felt this bite and I just made a natural move like, what you call a reflex. It wasn't anything big: after all, we'd been with one another before. The only thing about it was there'd been this little argument.

But she was a little drunk and she got excited and started to holler. The way people are, when you're liquored up like that, even if it's not really drunk; it seems like things just get to happening their own way. There's nobody doing any thinking. My girl, she started out to holler and her girl friend jumped up and began to scream, and the landlady ran out and called the police. And the first thing you knew there were people all over the place. It seemed like no matter where you looked there were fifteen people coming at you from that direction.

So the next thing, we were in jail and I was just sitting there picking my teeth and waiting. I didn't think I needed a lawyer . . . I hadn't no intention of raping her. What did I have to do that for? I hadn't done nothing at all. We'd just had a silly man-woman kind of dispute. My hand, it was bit first.

The police, though, got to this girl. They got to her, threatened her, made her say there was this rape business. They told her they'd pick her up and bring her in any time they saw her.

Well, she didn't want any of this business. As soon as she'd slept off what liquor she'd had she didn't want anything to do with it. But there wasn't much she could do. They knew she was a whore. She just didn't have any way to protect herself. But that's something I've learned: it can be a bobby or it can be a policeman or it can be a gendarme, but I don't care what language it is—a cop is nothing but a cop, and he's bound to do things his way. Whatever it is he gets in his head, that's the way he'll have it be.

I didn't know about all this till after the next morning. That's when this case came up, and I was hauled into court; I kept trying to explain but all I could hear was rape, rape, rape. It seemed like there was no court at all for listening to what *I* had got to tell.

The members of the band had come around and they wanted to go bail for me, but it seemed the court wouldn't let me have bail. They got all kinds of charges and reasons and words why they wouldn't do it, but after a whole lot of talk they finally let me out. Oh, they had all kinds of reasons. They said I was going to be in on a deportation charge; and assault and battery they had that too. The judge said there was no point in letting me out as they'd have the case cleared in a couple of weeks and then I'd be up for deportation. Finally, though, it was fixed up for an appeal and I was finally clear to go until that came up.

When the appeal came up, I had a fine lawyer and I won the case in no time at all. They couldn't even say this was the first time I'd been with the girl. So there was no charges against me, but the judge who was doing the case, he wouldn't clear the deportation charge. That judge, he was one of those men—I've seen plenty like him—he could know exactly how a thing was, he could know altogether different in a way, objective-like, but when it came down to him and his court, all he could see was that police authority that practically makes it like it's *his* authority. And, you know, there's a pride a man's got for a thing like that. It takes him.

And there was another thing happened too. While I was there in that court, the judge was asking me all kinds of

181

questions and I was trying to answer, but I didn't understand all it was they'd made it up to look like. What do I know about all these legal ways? Then at one point the judge, he told me, 'Why don't you explain yourself?' and I said, 'Your Honour, I'm all balled up.' That's what I said. All balled up. But my God, you should have seen the judge. Later, it was explained to me: in England, *all balled up*, that's a bad expression, it's a hell of a thing to say, you just don't use it. Well, my lawyer he got to the judge and explained to him how in America, all balled up is just something confused, it's being like a ball of twine that's wound up around itself. He told him it was an expression anybody could use in America. But the judge, he'd heard it his own way, and he was remembering it his way.

And at that time too, back there in the early 'twenties, England was having all this trouble with foreigners and agitators and one thing and another; they were doing all they could to get foreigners out of the country. And that's how it was. I was told I was being deported, and I was handed over to this uniform and to that uniform, and after I've been kept around a while, there's some more uniforms and then I'm taken to the train and I'm put on a boat, and that's how I got back to New York.

But there was one thing. One of those things you just don't forget. When we got off the train there was some delay and I was walked around a bit by this officer-like that's delivering me over and we pass a pub and I invite him in for a drink. He says he don't mind, so we go inside, and I order up a couple of gins and when they're brought to us I put this coin on the table, this half-crown and there's this king's picture on it lying there on the table, like I could look at a snapshot and say, 'Why, I know this feller.' In a memory way, I could still see him sitting there tapping his feet while we was playing. But I'm feeling now that it's nothing I care for. Just leaving that half-crown, it's too much of a tip for two gins, but I don't want it. I just leave it there on the table. And when I'm on the boat I look through my pockets for all the English money I've got, all the coins, and I just chuck them overboard.

Maybe that's some kind of foolishness. But after I'd done it, somehow I was happier in myself. A coin, that's something with two sides, and I'd seen both of them. You put a lion in back of a king, that's a big thing, but you look behind the lion, *if* you could look behind the lion, there's nothing to see but cops, and I'd seen all the cops and judges I'd been wanting to see. So there I was on a boat going back to America. And in spite of all the trouble I'd had, I was lucky in one way. For not long after that, in October 1921, the band was all going over to play in Ireland when the ship they were travelling in got hit and sunk. And eight of the band got drowned, and they lost all their instruments. It was a terrible thing. If I hadn't been back in America, God knows, I might have gone on too with those poor boys who were drowned.

9. Bessie and Duke

When I got back to America from England, right away I met up with an old friend of mine, Donald Haywood. He was a wonderful composer and a piano player. He was interested in having me make some records. But meantime he was concerned then with a show called *How Come* and he fixed for me to join it and he worked in quite a few spots for me.

Gloria Harven was playing the lead in this *How Come*. She had a very deep voice, and had sung with a lot of drummers. In one scene she was singing *Pagliacci*, and I was coming on after her doing a solo.

When we got to Washington the show had a fine success, and we stopped off there for some time. And, well, you know the way things are—there's always some retired entertainer who's got a home in some big town. Or there's some special place in the town you're playing, like some home for retired entertainers, some place that's offering hospitality. It gets to be a kind of meeting place. There's three, four or five people living there, and they're cooking for four or five more and there's friends coming by and there's always some party going on. One of these places where people drop in for the evening and the talk, and the first thing they know, they're being given a toothbrush the next morning. Virginia Liston, she had a place like that in Washington. Virginia, she was a singer, and she made an awful lot of records with Clarence Williams, sometimes just him on piano and sometimes with a band; I played on a lot of these with her. And it was at her home that I first met Bessie Smith.

I was around there one night and some person told me this Bessie, she was a damnest singer and I asked her to sing, and that's how it started. Just as soon as she started out I knew her voice was something that would really have the public going. I thought she should be in the show, and I was all eager to arrange for it; and the way it turned out I had no trouble at all getting her in. Gloria Harven, she was a fine singer, but Bessie had even her beat.

Bessie was a hell of a fine woman. A fine farmer too; she had a place of her own in New Jersey and was doing well growing things. Another thing about Bessie, she could be plenty tough; she could really handle her own. She always drank plenty and she could hold it, but sometimes, after she'd been drinking a while, she'd get like there was no pleasing her. There were times you had to know just how to handle her right.

After that we toured together. That show, it went all over: Cleveland, Cincinnati, Chicago—we made them all. And everywhere we went, we stopped the show; people tore the house down. I was playing the part of a Chinaman—How Come, that was my name. That wasn't the lead, but that's the way the show was written and named. I had a Chinese laundry, and Bessie would come on and she wouldn't have enough money for her laundry and she'd start singing. She'd go off into *St. Louis Blues*. And by the time she got started, I'd be off from the stage out of sight, but soloing there with Bessie out a ways singing, and the way that act would go, man, that was a real thing, that was a pleasure. Most of the times before we was even through, people would be clapping and yelling. They'd just never heard anything like that before; there just was nothing better of that kind that *could* be given to them.

But a little after that the show was finally to come into New York, and somebody decided it had to be dressed up; it had to be all changed and fancied for New York. So they changed that act, and right there all that fine naturalness we had in doing it our way was all taken out. They gave Bessie some number to sing that were no good for her, and that killed it. The show didn't last long after all those changes.

But there was something else too, and it did as much to kill our numbers as all that changing. Bessie and I, we'd been going with one another. After a while we had some falling out. It was just one thing and another . . . the way people get. Sometimes we got to fighting real bad. I don't know what it was—misunderstanding, some kind of jealousy—we just weren't being good for one another. It seemed after a while like Bessie was feuding with me, and from that she got to feuding with the music. We weren't doing the act together any more. I was still there playing and she was still there singing; but the being together that we had to have, that understanding there had to be inside the music, it wasn't there any more.

After that show closed I didn't see Bessie for a long time. She was away touring, singing and making records. I'd taken her over to Okeh to make a test record. *I Wish I Could Shimmy Like My Sister Kate*—that's what we made and that was the first record Bessie ever made. I had a contract with Okeh and I brought her over. But they had so many blues singers recording for them—Virginia Liston, Sarah Martin, Laura Smith, Mamie Smith, they had all those—and they had so many of them around wanting to be signed up, that Okeh figured it just didn't want any more. So they didn't keep Bessie; and that first record was never released, and now no one can't even find the master. Then Williams, who'd played piano with us on that first test, brought her over to Columbia. So I wasn't seeing her at the show any more, and I wasn't seeing her at Okeh, and we just got being apart. It's the way things are; I was away travelling a lot with another show called *Seven Eleven*; she had her contract at Columbia and her own things to do. . . .

But some time after that I did run into her in Clarence Williams's office, and there's a story about that. It's just to show the way Bessie could be sometimes. I walked into Clarence Williams's office and there were a few people around and there was Bessie. Well, I hadn't seen her in a long time; I went up to her, put my arms around her, hugging her, just glad to see her.

'Baby,' I told her, 'how are you? What've you been doing?'

But that Bessie, she hauled back and she just about swore. She nodded at some man standing over to one side there, and she said, 'That's my husband.'

Well, there wasn't much I *could* answer. 'Oh,' that's what I said. But Bessie, it seemed like she wanted to hit me with something if she could have. That man she'd married—I found this out later—he was some kind of policeman. He was a mean man, really a mean man. She'd had a hard time with him; she'd quit singing for a while and I found out that she was drinking pretty heavy.

I guess she never did stop that drinking. The next time I heard about her, she was starring in some show, and she'd been drinking so heavy all the time, they used to have to prop her up on the stage and she'd just sing that way, standing still, almost about to fall over. But the people didn't seem to know the difference. The only ones that knew about that, it was the ones that were around with her when she was doing her drinking or buying them *their* drinks. And whoever it was who was managing her, they put her on the stage with maybe a chair to hold on to and they'd let her sing and then they'd pull the curtain and get her off: that's what I heard.

Then some time after that I was with my wife one night— I had got married by then—and I ran into Bessie again. My wife and I were in a club in Philadelphia and Bessie just showed up and came over to our table and sat down. She'd been drinking and she wasn't too careful about how she'd do things. She just came over and sat down and starting fooling around with me, talking in a way that could lead on to things.

My wife was one of those real pretty girls and she wasn't having any of this. The way it was, Bessie must have known how much my wife had been hearing about me and Bessie, all what people had been telling her about our going together; 'Bessie this and Bessie that' whenever old friends meet. Bessie must have known that pretty well; it was the kind of woman-knowing she'd been born with. And she started in deliberate-like, needling my wife. Only my wife got to needling right back and it seemed like she was a little better at it because before long I could see Bessie was ready to haul off and pull hair. She wasn't one to stand for anything, Bessie. She was really a hell of a woman.

Lucky though, before anything really happened, the woman who owned the place, who liked my wife, came over and got Bessie to go with her. She brought her into the back of the club and got her calmed down.

And all that needle-talking and that fooling around was Bessie's way of getting back at me for the time I hugged her in Clarence Williams's office. That's all that ever it was. Bessie, she was that kind of a woman, especially when she'd been drinking. It's like I was saying about that coin: Bessie had that side to her.

That night at the club, it was the last time. That woman led Bessie away to the back of the club and I never saw her again. Later I heard she was off touring somewhere, and then I heard she was killed. It was somewheres down in the South: she'd been touring with some outfit—that was 1937—and gotten into an accident. She'd hurt her arm real bad, but they hadn't cared for her right away and when they finally got her to a hospital they'd made her wait. She died of losing all that amount of blood. She was *too* far in the South. I was told the doctors, they hadn't too much concern for getting to her quick . . . she was just another that could wait. That's all, I guess; that was the end of it. That's all there was finally to Bessie Smith. Someways, you could almost have said before-hand that there was some kind of an accident, some bad hurt coming to her. It was like she had that hurt inside her all the time, and she was just bound to find it. It was like so many of the musicianers: whatever troubles they had from the world outside, they had more trouble from themselves, of their own making.

But the other side of the coin, that was Bessie too. Bessie, she was a great singer. People come up to me and ask me: 'Who's the most important? Was Bessie Smith the most important blues singer?' Well, it's a hard thing, you understand what I mean, to say who's ever the most important of something. So many people go at themselves like they was some book: they look back through themselves, they see this so and so chapter, they remember this one thing or another, but they don't go through the pages one after the other really finding out what they're about and who they are and where they are. They never count their whole story together. And if you take someone—a blues singer—take her all the way back; she's bound to be something at one time that's got herself from a whole lot of influences. It's people, or it's music, or something that came Natural to her—her own feelings of not being wanted or of being mad or of being happy. It's all those things, and it's all of them put together. The great person, he's the one who takes those influences, gives them what he's got inside him, and he expresses that. It's like he's reading that book, and he's reading all of it. He knows where it started and he knows what it has been before it got to him, and he's been doing his own thinking about it, adding to the understanding.

Most people, they think they make themselves. Well, in a way they do. But they don't give enough credit to all the things around them, the things they take from somebody else when they're doing something and creating it . . . things like what it is you remember, or how you feel, or what you're going to do. Things like being a kid and waiting in a field for the late afternoon to be night, like standing by a river, like remembering the first time you heard the music, who it was was playing it. Things like that, they're just life.

Bessie had that. She had this trouble in her, this thing that wouldn't let her rest sometimes, a meanness that came and took her over. But what she had was alive; she'd been through the whole book. And you can say that one way and you can say it another. If you understand it, it's there, and if you don't understand it, it's not for you. Bessie, she was great. She was the greatest.

It don't seem to matter where you go, there's always some musicianer who has something inside him, something driving him to some meanness, something driving him against himself. Bessie, she just wouldn't let herself be; it seemed like she *couldn't* let herself be. And she was the greatest. But you don't *have* to have that to be great. There was always some musicianer who knew how to smile right from inside himself and still be great. Duke Ellington, he's one like that.

I met Duke in Washington the time that I was there in *How Come*. He was hanging around the stage door then, coming in all the time when we were doing our rehearsals and asking to play the piano. He played it James P. Johnson fashion then. At that time, 1922, he and Elmer Snowden had a band together called the Washingtonians, and we hung out some; we were good buddies for hanging out together. Duke was a fine man to be with, an easy man in himself. I'll come back to him.

The *Seven Eleven* show finished after a year or so and I was in New York. I joined James P. Johnson and we played at the Old Kentucky Club over on Eighth Avenue off Broadway. This was one of the times when this feuding thing gets all mixed up in the feelings you like to remember. James P. wanted to make it more orchestrational Jazz, and I was playing New Orleans, playing foundation in the numbers, but ad libbing and giving my improvisation to it. And there was trouble because of the attention I was getting, because people wanted New Orleans. That spirit was what they were coming to the Club for, it was what they wanted to hear. But one day the manager came up to James P. and there was some trouble. That's what James P. said; he said the manager wanted some changes made. So James P. came up to me all man to man honest-like and said, 'Sidney, that's the way it is. You gotta go, man. I'm sorry.' So I was out. All I could say was, 'Yes, James P. Good-bye, James P.'

With James P. it was another of those things between musicianers. Things get to happening the way they never should. The musicianers, they're so busy worrying about the arrangements they forget about the music—they almost forget about being musicianers. That's not music any more. James P. was trying to make it almost like one of those big swing bands

—hit parade stuff. He was all for making these big arrange-ments, adding musicianers, adding instruments—all that business that leaves a musicianer with nothing to say and no way to say it. Arrangements for ragtime, they're understood between the men, between one another. What you miss in a whole lot of pages, parts all written up for you, you make that up in working together. If you know in advance every note you're going to play and just the way you're going to play it, there's no need to have feelings. Like that, if you've got a feeling, you just can't use it; you can't even stay interested. Music like that, you could almost make a machine play it for you.

But the funny thing was that after it was supposed to be New Orleans that was responsible for the band's drawbacks, and after James P. had got me out on account of that, he went and got himself fired. And the band which took his place was Duke and me.

Duke had come up to New York. He remembered me from Washington and he wanted to make up a band together, so we did that. And that was a fine time, playing with Duke in 1924. He had his feelings inside the music where they belonged, and none of any kind of meanness outside the music. When we played, we were playing together, doing what the music wanted done with none of this personal *me me* feuding through what we were doing. That music was just liking itself because we let it *be* itself. That's the thing about ragtime. It's no arrangement for two juke boxes. It ain't a writing down where you just play what it says on the paper in front of you, and so long as you do that the arranger, he's taken care of every-thing else. When you're really playing *ragtime*, you're feeling it out, you're playing to the other parts, you're waiting to understand what the other man's doing, and then you're going with his feeling, adding what you have of your feeling. You're not trying to steal anything and you're not trying to fight anything. Duke has right feelings; he wasn't as good a piano player as he is now, but he had right feelings, and he let the music come first. That was a good time in that Kentucky Club. We made some records, too, while we were together, but for some reason I don't know, they were never released. I feel real sad about that because they were good records, and now there is no trace of them.

That's why when Duke and I went in there, we had this big success. We were working around each other. We were using our feelings, and the people listening *had* to feel because *we* were feeling it. There was none of this trying to give a name to Jazz, Orchestrational Jazz, Concert Jazz, Fancy-Arrangement Jazz—there wasn't any of that kind of pushing from Duke.

But after a time, even then, I was still having trouble with two fellows in the band—that feuding business you find so much if you're a musicianer from New Orleans or South somewhere. It's like a man, instead of playing along with you, he wants to trip you up. Like instead of carrying your feeling and adding his, he's fighting your feeling. These two, they were Bubber Miley and Charlie Irvis, the trumpet and trombone. A musicianer should be too busy for figuring out things like that. His profession has got more respect than that. A man can't be with the music and fighting it at the same time. When I first joined the band Bubber Miley was in jail over some trouble concerning a girl. And the first money that was put up for him, the pool that was started for having him put on bail so he could come join the band, it was from me. But still, just as soon as we were all working in the band, I could see Bubber and Charlie still had this trouble going. There was still this talking aside business in the music. There was a competition for the wrong things at the wrong time: all this tugging when they should be carrying, and sulking when they should be following, and this refusing to be with the music when they should be leading.

Everyone in the band could feel that. There was a fellow with us, Otto Hardwick was his name, who played clarinet and alto saxophone. He was my friend and he tried to talk to them, tell them what was the sense, they'd be hurting themselves. But no, they went right on making it hard.

At that time Otto, Duke and myself used to go over to Duke's place evenings to fool around on the piano, talk how we were going to build this thing with all the band. Duke, he'd be making arrangements for the band—not this kind of hit-parade arrangements I been saying about, but a kind of dividing of the piece, placing its parts. What we were after, it was to get the *feeling* for the band, playing it together. That way the music is working for itself. From hearing Otto play to me, me playing to Otto—playing *for* each other—we were making up what the band was to be, how it was to feel itself. The arrangements, they came out of that. And that was good times there in Duke's apartment. That was real music. But still, I could see those were just evenings after a fashion—there wasn't going to be much to it. That Bubber Miley and Charlie, they had it all too uncomfortable.

So I had some money coming to me from some records I'd made, and I thought I'd like to open my own cabaret. So that's just the way of it. There's some is real fine and there's others you just can't get along with, others that can't even seem to get along with themselves. I think back to all these things and, you know, what makes me happy is that it seems like no matter how much you run up against that one kind you can't get along with, you're just never far from the other kind. It just takes both.

But that Duke—I've seen him off and on all these years. There's no limit to what I can say about Duke. He's a man with a life in him. And some of the things he's done are really great; he's a real musicianer. Duke, he belongs to the music, and the music belongs to him.

10. From Harlem to Europe

When I was in London in 1921 there was a fellow by the name of George, and we used to go around a lot of those pubs there together. And back in America he used to remember those good times we had together; and I met him again when I was still with Duke at the Kentucky Club. One day he said that he'd like to open a cabaret with me. Well, with this discomfort like I said, I had been thinking anyway, so I said, 'All right, George. Let's see about it, if we can find a good place.'

So we went out all ways looking around, and we ran across a cabaret that was closed called the Hermit's End that was on 155th Street and 7th Avenue. And we went to look at the place and it was all right, so we took it and we got the decorators in. I had some money due to me from some records, and I sent Wellman Braud over to the Kentucky Club to get it. The owner of the Club, Bernstein, he was a hell of a grand fellow; he sent Braud over to get me to come over as he wanted to talk to me. So we was talking, and I told him I was fixing to leave as I had a place of my own. And he wanted to know if it was on account of those two fellows; but I didn't want to tell him the real reason, so I just said no, I just had this money and it was my idea to have this cabaret. Then he shook hands with me. 'Any time you ever want to come back, there's always a place for you,' he said. 'Bring in your own band if you want; you know there's no asking even. Now where is it you're going to have your place?'

So I told him, and he said, 'I'll be there your opening night when you start,' and he was.

When the decorators were all through we were about ready to open; we called the place the Club Basha. We had a lot of liquor because George made it; he was a bootlegger, you know. So we had a lot of gin, and we had the band playing. But in those days it was hard to get people in cabarets unless you were very well known; so for the first three nights we just had a few people in there, a few friends, and we had the hell of a time. And like I said, Bernstein was there and he sat at my table with me the whole evening. But around the fourth night, I'm telling you the truth—we really didn't have place enough for the people that came downstairs for the cabaret. So we had a swell time.

Just after we opened up, too, I worked a short while as a staff writer for Fred Fisher. I wrote several numbers at that time, like *Do That Thing*, and *Pleasure Mad*, and *Here It Is Daddy, Just Like You Left It—No Hands Have Touched It But Mine*. And another one was *Street Department Papa, Mama Wants Her Ashes Hauled Today*. I had a fellow with me who wrote songs and lyrics too, and we did all this at the Fred Fisher place.

At this time Will Marion Cook wanted to write a show with Jimmy Johnson, and he wanted me as well. We used to meet every day to get this show going. It was called *Negro Nuances* and it was a wonderful thing, but we just couldn't get it started. I had done quite a few numbers there with Will Marion Cook, but nothing happened, so I had to stop.

And I was making a whole lot of records around this time, with all sorts of bands and using all sorts of names. Like I said, in those days people, musicianers and singers would have a contract to record with one company and maybe there was a band coming together to play a date for another company and you just called yourself something else and everybody was satisfied. Like at this time Louis Armstrong and I made a lot of records with Clarence Williams, the Blue Five, and these were made for the Okeh Company. And Alberta Hunter, she was under contract with the Paramount Company. But at

145

this time, this would be getting on late in 1924, the Gennet people said how they would like her to record some numbers for them; so she did—*Nobody Knows the Way I Feel This Mornin'*, that was one of them—and she used her sister's name of Josephine Beatty, and Louis and Lil Armstrong and I, we played with her and called ourselves the Red Onion Jazz Babies. Louis and I played some other numbers, too, under that name through 1925. But we made more records as Clarence Williams's Blue Five than any other, and we played with a lot of singers, too, like Virginia Liston, Margaret Johnson, Sippie Wallace and Eva Taylor. But the trouble with Clarence was that he would never give any of us credit on a date. I spoke to him about it and in the end he put my name on two dates: one of them I never played on at all, and the other—that was a date with Virginia Liston—he put down I played guitar! That's the reason why I left him in the end; and Louis, he had the same trouble and he left too.

After a while we started to have trouble in the cabaret. We had a girl named Bessie Desacheux there, and she was sort of floating around with George. So I told George, I said, 'Look, the girl likes to dance for some people, and there's some people she doesn't like to dance for. And if she's working in a cabaret she should dance with everybody.' So he said, 'Sidney, what do you want me to do?' So I said, 'Well, if you don't want to talk to her, I will.' So we always seemed to be having a discussion about this girl.

Then one night she had been out with a friend of mine, a fellow by the name of Terry Preston that owned a cabaret. So the following night Terry came to our cabaret and he wanted Bessie to dance, and she wouldn't. So that was really tough, and I wouldn't stand it. So I went to George and said to him that we would have to get rid of her. But George didn't want to, and it almost came to blows. And this guy George, he had some friends in there who were in the bootlegging with him. But I had some friends too, and one of them, Jack Diamond's brother, was a very good friend of mine. He knew all about the story, and he said to me, 'You go ahead. I'll clean the whole joint out if you want.' So I said, 'No, no;

don't do nothing like that, because he's my partner. When you take a man as a partner, naturally you must like him, or care something about him, or have confidence in him, otherwise you really wouldn't take him into partnership.' So that just ran on.

So the next thing George did, he opened up a numbers racket in the place. And one of the badest men in New York hit the numbers. His name was Bob Ewley. He really hit the numbers, and George couldn't get the money up; it was something like eight or nine thousand dollars which at that time was a whole lot of money. Bob Ewley was a friend of mine also, and when his fellows came to break the place up I went and spoke to him and told him about it. He said, 'Listen, you better get rid of that guy.' But I said, 'Well, I think I am the one who's going to go.' So I engaged a lawyer, a brother of George Lattimore he was; I got him to run the place and see that all the debts were paid up. And that was the end of it for me.

It was the summer of 1925 by now, and Spencer Williams and Louis Douglas they were getting together a show that was to come to Europe with Josephine Baker in it. Josephine Baker, she was an understudy then at the Plantation Club and this was her first real break. Spencer Williams wrote the numbers, and Claude Hopkins's band was along. And we all sailed in the old *Berengaria* mid-September and opened the *Revue Nègre* soon after at the Théâtre des Champs Elysées. The show was a great success. Josephine and Louis, I remember, danced the Charleston and nobody in Europe had seen that dance before, and that really started something. That show really had Paris going. All the critics and all the papers were writing it up, and the house was full every night.

After we'd had this great success in Paris we took the whole show on to Brussels, and then to the Nelson Theatre in Berlin. It was while we were there that Josephine Baker got an offer to go to the Folies Bergères, so she left to go back to Paris and was replaced by Maude de Forest. And not long after that I left too, and went to Russia.

There was a number of musicianers going to Russia at that

time, and that's when I first met Tommy Ladnier. The way it came about was like this. I had a projector but something had happened and I didn't have no camera. So I was inquiring about how I could get me a camera and some friend of mine said, 'Do you know this orchestra of Sammy Wooding?' And I said, 'Sure, I know Sammy Wooding very well.' 'So he's got a trumpet player named Tommy Ladnier who's got a camera to sell.' I said, 'Well, I know of Tommy Ladnier; I'd like to meet him.' So when I got to Tommy we had a lot of fun. Tommy reminded me that in Chicago he used to go and see me playing pool with different people and he wanted to speak to me but he was afraid. I said, 'Why were you afraid?' 'Well, I wasn't playing so good at that time,' he answered, and I said, 'Well, that's funny. You don't have to play good or wonderful to speak to somebody.' But he said, 'Well, I just felt that way.' Right away we got to know one another, and I bought that camera. We've always been close. It was always good.

11. Trouble in Paris

Some of what came to me, there was a good feeling to it, and some, it was poor. When I was playing at Chez Florence the second time, after Noble Sissle had gone back to America, I got myself into real trouble on account of bad feeling. I got into a gunfight and I went to jail for it.

In those days it was really something the way things went on. Times just aren't like that any more. Any time you walked down the street you'd run into four or five people you knew—performers, entertainers, all kinds of people who had a real talent to them. Everywhere you'd go you'd run into them; you couldn't help yourself. And everybody had a kind of excitement about him. Everyone, they was crazy to be *doing*. Well, you'd start to go home, and you'd just never get there. There was always some singer to hear or someone who was playing. You'd run into some friends and they were off to hear this or to do that and you just went along. It seemed like you just *couldn't* get home before ten or eleven in the morning.

It was almost like Prohibition up there in Montmartre in those days. It was almost like back in the days when you'd get a bottle of essence of garden gin and some seed alcohol and some distilled water and pour it into your bathtub. You'd start out with four people waiting in the other room and when you looked out again there be ten or a dozen. One of them, he'd come into the bathroom. 'Here let's taste some of that,' he'd say. Then first thing you'd know you'd have a consultation. 'No, it's not right yet,' somebody would say when he'd tasted

149

it. 'Not enough gin.' And there'd go some more of the Gardens. Somebody else, he'd try it, and he'd decide it needed some. There'd go the rest of the Gardens. By that time you were gone too. When you come out of the bathroom with a jug of that stuff, there wouldn't be more than room enough to stand up for the crowd, everybody playing the piano, talking, drinking, fooling around, everybody full of a kind of excitement, a kind of waiting for something big to happen.

That's the way it was in Montmartre in 1928, except that there wasn't any need to be making your own gin. And just like there was the Prohibition mobs in New York, there was that kind of mob around Montmartre, too. There were always men there who had rackets. They were making a lot of money by getting paid off by the owners of the clubs and cabarets, just so they could stay open. It was a kind of protective association they called it, but it was really just a shakedown. And to run a racket like that, you need a certain kind of person, a thug like. There were a lot like that around in those days and sometimes when one of them got drunk, it wasn't safe around them. So what happened as a result of things like that, nearly everybody, he carried a gun. You could be surer if you had a gun on you. There was tough times back there.

We musicianers, the ones I knew the most about, we'd meet when we were off work. We had regular places where we could expect to find one another. Mostly it was in one little café off rue Fontaine. We'd sit in the back room of this café and we'd joke, play a few cards, or someone would take out his instrument, or we'd just talk. Pretty soon you'd begin to see those saucers piling up.

One night a fellow named Mike McKendrick was there. He was the one I had the trouble with, and the trouble was really brought on by a fellow who was supposed to be his friend, Glover Compton. Glover was a piano player. He was from Chicago and he was always talking about being a Northerner. He really liked to talk big; whatever he had to say, he talked like he expected everyone else to listen and be mighty ready to shake in their boots while they was doing it. It was like he was looking for a reputation as a bad man, as someone really evil. He wasn't no one in any big-time way, but he was trying to cut in as much as he could. He was always acting like he wanted to stir up trouble, like he wanted to be known as a place where trouble started.

For some time before this night he'd been getting after Mike, telling him this and that about me, getting to see if he could start an argument between us, get some kind of a feud going. Mike was just a kid then. He was playing banjo somewhere in one of those cabarets. I don't know nothing about his wanting to be any trouble-maker; but this night he started coming at me with a lot of stories he told me this Glover had passed on to him, and I wasn't in any mood for that kind of thing. So finally we had an argument. It didn't really amount to anything right then, and we both had to leave to go to work after a while; but all the same there had been this argument.

The same night—it was morning by then—I was walking home from work and I passed this cabaret. I was about to go inside, but just as I got to the door I saw Glover. He had a whole party with him and I knew if I went in there he'd be only too happy to start some more trouble, so I stayed out. I just turned around and started to walk off, but Glover had seen me and he sent Mike out after me. That was his way, that Glover . . . he wasn't the kind to do anything himself if he could get someone else to do it for him, especially when it was trouble he was wanting.

So Mike came hurrying up after me and he said, 'Sidney, come on inside. My friend wants to see you.' Well I knew better than that; that was only a ruse like. If I went in there and sat down at their table, there'd be a whole lot of baiting and there was only one way that could end up. So I said, 'You tell your friend I'm not special about seeing him.' But Mike started insisting. He'd drunk some—quite a bit, in fact—and he wouldn't listen to anyone saying 'No'. Finally I just told him, why didn't he smarten up some? 'What you doing getting mixed up in something like that Glover?' I said. 'Don't you have anything better to do?'

Right away he started in talking like this Glover. Mike, he was from Chicago, too, and he'd picked up these big ideas

151

about being a Northerner. 'I don't think I like you,' he said. 'I don't think I like the way you look, Dixie-boy. You want to see what we do to people like you in Chicago?'

Well, it's one of those things I know something about. I'd heard that all before. Northern musicianers, they start themselves going sometimes. There's something jealous-like about them when another musicianer, he's from the South. So now this one, he's going to show me some of Chicago!

I didn't want to mess with him. I didn't want any trouble and just so long as he didn't go too far I didn't want anything at all to do with him. So I turned to go on, and just as soon as I turned my back he began to shout out, all excited. Maybe it was just that he was waiting for me. 'My friend won't like that,' he said, and he pulled out a gun and fired two shots at me. I pulled out my own gun then—he hadn't hit me—and my first bullet grazed his forehead. Then Glover heard the shots and he came running out, and one of my bullets got him in the leg, and another hit a girl, and one ricochetted off a lamp-post and, what's really unfortunate, hit some Frenchwoman who was passing on the other side of the street on her way to work.

It was something, the way it happened . . . something hard to make it clear. It's like there's somebody else inside a man, somebody that's not really that man, and when a thing happens, an anger like I had then, that other person takes over. That's not to make excuses. I know well enough it's me all the time. That's just to try to tell you what feeling there was to it, standing there on the street, not even giving a goddamn' how many shots they're sending back at me, not even seeming to know whether or not they're shooting at all, just standing there pumping my gun and wanting to see everyone of them dead in front of me.

And all the time, I don't like it. There's a kind of disgust to it. I'm not for covering up any part of what's true: I can be mean. It takes a awful lot; someone's got to do a lot to me. But when I do get mean, I can be powerful mean. That's the way I was right then on the street outside that cabaret. I'm busting mean. If someone was to change the world into glass and throw it up in front of me, I was in a mood then to just smash it right there. I would have smashed any damn' thing.

And then, after it was over, the mood was gone from me. All I'd got left was disgust. I started walking away then. I was on my way over to the police, to give myself up and explain to them what had happened. But before I no more than got started, I was identified by some bystanders who pointed me out to a policeman who came up from behind me. He wanted to know what the trouble was. He told me the people had pointed me out. Right off I told him I wasn't denying any part of it; I told him exactly what had gone on. I wasn't afraid of anything serious happening. I'd had nothing to do with starting it; all I did, I was acting in self-defence. There was that girl who had been with Glover, she'd gotten a scratch, but I didn't give a damn about her; and at that time I didn't know about the Frenchwoman. But it was right there that the real trouble started. That Frenchwoman had had to go to hospital, and just the fact that she *was* a Frenchwoman and I a foreigner and I had sent her to the hospital—that put it into a whole new jurisdiction like.

The police took me and Mike McKendrick in, and right away our friends started raising some money for us. Mike had got some very influential friends who got him a lawyer, and a lot of people pooled some money together and got a lawyer for me. Gene Boulard put out a lot of money to help me. Gene was a real man about Paris; he had a way. He was a man—well, the only way I can say it, he was what Glover Compton would have liked to have been in regards to making a name for himself. Except Gene had no meanness in him. If someone needed help, he did more than any Salvation Army could do with a whole army; and what he wanted to do for himself, he could do in a smooth, smart way. He'd made himself the kind of man people around Paris had a need for. The cabarets, the clubs, the musicianers—when there was some trouble they couldn't straighten out by themselves, they called on Gene. He was a man you could count on.

Gene could almost have fixed this. It would have been just a fight among musicianers. But this Frenchwoman who was hit, that took it out of the law of being simply something that

Americans were involved in. Gene just couldn't get it quieted down and Mike and I both had terms to serve; we both got sentenced.

So there we were off to prison together, and when we got to the prison they put us in the detention cell while they're fixing up our regulations, making out papers for what cells we're to have, and all that official business. We were locked up together there for a while. Mike kept coming over to tell me how sorry he was. 'I wish it had never happened,' he told me. 'I'm sorry for the whole business, Sidney. If it hadn't been for that Glover it never *would* have happened. He's the one who told me to get after you. If I hadn't listened to him. . . .'

He went on like that all the time we were together. What could I answer? You know what you'd think. There's only one thing you can answer: it's happened and it's too late. There's nothing left for it but just to forget the whole thing.

But that Glover, he *still* wasn't ready to forget it. It was in 1928 I went to prison. I was in jail for eleven months, and when I came out I had no rights, it wasn't even legal for me to stay in France. And yet even then, I found out later, this fellow Glover was working at his lawyer, planning some way he could arrange for me to have more time to serve, some action he could bring. The day I was coming out of prison, he was still trying to get up an action to keep me there, trying to get his lawyer to put out a warrant for me, urging him to figure out some case he could bring against me. When I ran into him later, I told him he'd better watch out for that other leg; I was tired of the whole thing, and I wasn't fixing to take any more of what he was giving out. I was really close to getting God-almighty sick of it all and of him too. But this Gene Boulard, he could see there was maybe trouble coming. He took this Glover aside. 'You stay away,' he told him, 'you really better stay away.' And he made him do it. I never had any bother from Glover after that.

That was all a long time ago, but it's not a thing a man can forget. Twenty, twenty-one years later, I was in Paris at the Préfecture, getting my visa arranged, and the Commissioner started talking about it. 'That wasn't your fault,' he said. 'If

154

that had been your fault, you couldn't have come back to France. That was self-defence; it was your right.'

I couldn't very well tell him it was a little late for figuring that out, but that trial I got was a hell of a thing. Even that eleven months I spent in a French jail made less impression on my mind than what I kept thinking about that trial. I had that inside me for a long time.

There was two things about it. The first, it was that Frenchwoman. That part of it, it's still the same today: I don't care who you are, if you go to France and you get into some trouble where there's a Frenchman mixed up in it, that court don't care what's right, it don't care what's wrong. If there's a Frenchman and a foreigner mixed up in it together, the foreigner, he's in the wrong. Whether it's justice or injustice don't matter: the Frenchman, he's the one that counts.

But there was another thing, too. I sat there in that court watching my lawyer, watching the judge, watching the people. My lawyer was supposed to be representing me, but after a while you'd have got the impression that it was not a man that was being represented, but his money. It really came right down to that: there wasn't enough money. A deal had to be made.

Like I said, my lawyer was supposed to be representing me, but he was so busy working with Mike's lawyer, it's as if I've just been forgotten. To save themselves trouble, those lawyers decided they'd make it easier on *both* of us by kind of sharing the guilt. They had it all figured out: it was just a couple of foreigners mixed up in this thing and somebody had got to pay for hurting a Frenchwoman, so they'd work it for both of us to pay up some time and that way it would all be cleared up. No question of right or wrong or who shot first or who shot in self-defence: just a question of a couple of foreigners. The easy way was to treat them all alike.

So they got together and they told us to say what they had prepared. We were to tell the court it was just an argument that had got started somehow, that we were very sorry about it all but we had been drinking and we hadn't known what we was doing. All that kind of talk. Instead of having me cleared and one of us going free, they fixed it so that both of us should serve time, and that way Mike would get less and neither one of us would get a whole lot, and the whole business would be cleared up.

The day they had that all fixed, my lawyer got up and began saying that to the jury. 'Here's a man,' he says, 'who admits to doing wrong. You who are in the jury, you can feel how that is; give this man your understanding. He knows he's done wrong. He recognizes his mistake and asks for sympathy. . . .' There was a whole lot like that.

And all of a sudden Gene understood what they were doing, and he jumped up right there in court where he was with the spectators. He called out from where he was and then he came hurrying up before the court and he told them no, that wasn't the way it had happened. He explained all he could . . . what he knew about it, what the witnesses had said.

Well, it was like he'd gone crazy. It was like the whole court had gone crazy. There was one lawyer shouting one thing and another lawyer shouting something else, and this court official pounding here and that court official pounding there and before anybody understood what-all was going on, the court got recessed.

After that Gene, my lawyer and me talked for hours about what was to be done, and what it all came down to was that Gene and me, we just couldn't raise the money. It would cost a certain amount more to present the case the way it should have been, and we just couldn't get that much money together.

That's the thing. Not being able to stand up the way you are to have the right to say what's the fair thing, what's the real thing that happened. That was the wrong.

12. Back in New York

Well, I put in my eleven months, and when I got out I wasn't allowed to stay in France; so I went back to Germany and played at Haus Vaterland in Berlin where I'd been before, back to that Wild West Bar. While I was there Noble Sissle, who was touring America with his orchestra, wired me to come and join up with his band. And that's how I came back to America. It was late 1929, and that stock market crash had happened by then.

I went back to America and I played with Noble Sissle, but I didn't stay long. We came over to Europe in the summer. Tommy Ladnier, he'd been with Sissle too, and we quit together, in Paris. So I went back to Berlin to Haus Vaterland for three months in the summer of 1931. But I was back with Noble in America during that winter and we played various theatres in New York until I had a disagreement over a salary question. Then, a bit later, in 1932, Tommy and I had a band together. We had our own eight-piece outfit, opening at the Saratoga Club in Harlem. We were only there a few weeks, and then we played three gigs a week in Jersey City and some in White Plains, New York. But in the fall we took a six-piece band into the Savoy in New York City. That was really *the* band. That was the best band. The people liked the band; it was small and we were all musicians that had a feeling and we understood what Jazz music really meant. We didn't have to make any arrangements or anything like that; we just followed the old school, and just recorded, and we were feeling just that way. We had a fellow named Wilson Myers with us then. He'd played a lot of instruments in his time—clarinet, trombone, drums, banjo and guitar. But around the time Tommy and I were getting that band together, he'd started in to play bass, and he played with us and he certainly played fine bass.

It didn't last too long—we played through till the spring—but while it was still on we had one recording date. We played six numbers that day—*Sweetie Dear, I've Found a New Baby*, Scott Joplin's great number *Maple Leaf Rag*, and the last we cut was *Shag*. I guess by the time we got around to that one we were feeling pretty good because we felt we'd played good and had had a good day; anyway we made it a fine finish up. We were very happy and it was the last piece. That was a fine band, and besides Tommy and me there was Teddy Nixon on trombone, Hank Duncan on piano, Wilson Myers on bass like I said, and Morris Moreland drums.

After my band with Ladnier broke up, I played for a while with Lorenzo Tio at the Nest. Of course, I'd known Lorenzo since I was in short pants. He was a great musicianer, and was a good bit older than me. Well, he came up to New York, and I fixed a number of gigs for him. Then when Tommy and I had finished at the Savoy I had this chance to take a band into the Nest with Lorenzo, and I went because there was a chance to build a band a little bit bigger than the band I'd had at the Savoy. And it was pretty good. Roy Eldridge, he used to come there every day. He was working at Small's, but he came every night to play with the band because we got to working rather late—around five, six, seven in the morning. It was Roy's pleasure to come and sit in with the band. There was a trombonist, too, by the name of Harry White, he played with Cab Calloway's orchestra and the Blue Rhythm Boys; and he worked, too, with Roy at Small's Cabaret. And he also used to come, and he had a lot of fun with us. Well, we stayed there a long while, I guess for about five or six months. That wasn't the last time that he played in New York, because after we had finished our engagement we parted, and he went on and played some place else; then he disappeared. I saw him one time more. I got word from his wife she wanted to see me, you know, and when I went to see her she said that Lorenzo was very ill, and she tried to prove that I owed him some money or something. But I didn't owe him a thing; he was paid just like anyone else. And after that I saw him and related to him what his wife had told me; but he knew—she was just thinking things. I guess she was worried because he was so ill, and she had to do everything she could think of. And that was the last time that I saw Lorenzo, because it wasn't long after that he died right there in New York.

Well, by then things was pretty bad, and for a while there Tommy and I had a tailor shop there up around St. Nicholas Avenue. It wasn't any shop for making suits—just a pressing and repairing place and we called it the Southern Tailor Shop. Tommy, he used to help out shining shoes. We were pretty easy going with the money part of that business, but we got along. A lot of musicianers who didn't have jobs and some who did used to come around and we'd have our sessions right there in back of the shop. That was a good time. It was real enjoyable.

Then around 1934 Noble wired for me to come join the band again, and I went. I tried to talk Tommy into coming with me, but it wasn't what he wanted to do. He had some reason for not wanting to go. He wasn't saying what it was, but I got to see pretty clear that he wouldn't, so I said no more.

I went on out and joined Noble at the French Casino, in Chicago. And then we toured all over for about four years in all. I didn't know the whole story at the time, but it wasn't long before I got the idea, why Tommy wouldn't come with me. Noble hadn't been special about having me, but the man who had the contract for where Noble was working came up to him at one time when I wasn't with the band and said, 'Where's Bechet? This isn't the band I made a contract for. Where's Sidney?' So Noble had to send for me. He was strange in some ways. It wasn't just about me, but about music. He liked music right enough, but that wasn't all of it. Sometimes it was like he was more interested in having his own band than he was in the music.

Well, right away there was trouble for me. It was no time at all before I notice there's this feeling in the reed section; it's feuding with me. One fellow who was there—he played tenor sax—he went up to Noble and said, 'How come Sidney's here?' He didn't want me playing with the band. Noble told him: 'Look, that's all right. You wouldn't be here today if Sidney wasn't playing; you wouldn't have a job.' Then he explained how the man wouldn't give them the contract unless I join up.

But the feuding still went on. That fellow had friends who all the time were fixing numbers that I was supposed to have, giving me hard feature numbers with hardly nothing to them, numbers a man couldn't do nothing with. The reed section there was James Tolliver, Harvey Boone, Ramon Usera and myself. But that Usera and Boone, instead of concentrating on how the music should be played, they were all het up in this jealousy business. But I wouldn't do things that way: I'd seen too much of that. Even after they give me those bad numbers, even when they'd picked out my feature pieces without any regard for my taste about how they should be, I still refused to fight them back. I took what numbers I got and toned them up the best I could. But it's a hell of a thing. There's just no sense to a thing like that: it don't help anyone at all and it just raises hell with the music until there's no enjoyment left to it.

But that James Tolliver, he was my friend; but I didn't know that until later. This group—Usera, Boone, and some others—they got up a meeting in Noble's office and Usera began by complaining how he didn't want to handle my numbers. He was opposed to working on features for me. Usera was doing the arranging for the band and that gave him a power: it got to the point where he'd almost got me out of the band. But just at that time James Tolliver spoke up. 'If you won't arrange for Sidney,' he said, 'I will.' And that's the way it turned out. Tolliver was trying to get away from the bad support and all those off-runs they've been giving me. He really proved to be a friend. The way things were, he'd still have to go back to them sometimes, but now I could begin to feel that the music had a chance of going some.

But the way it worked out, even then it wasn't much good. You can stand a whole lot of double talk for something you really care about, but after a while you can see it spoiled too easy and it isn't worth that. I'd had enough of all that bad feeling; I wasn't looking for any more of that.

There was another thing, too, about being with the band. Touring like that, you're always in a new town. You don't know what place to stay at so you pick the nicest. It comes time to eat—you don't know any of the restaurants so you walk down the street and you pick out the cleanest place you see. That way you're sure you won't be finding last week's menu on your plate. Well, it doesn't take long when you're doing that way—the first thing you know, all your money's gone. And after a little of that, you get fed up. It's just no fun having to scramble all the time and then seeing that nickle disappear and thinking to yourself, 'Had I kept that nickle and the one before it I'd have had me a dime now.' The hell with that. Noble was making the money, and as far as I was concerned he could keep it. It was bad enough just feuding with those others in the band. I quit.

I went back to New York then and it wasn't long before Noble brought the band there too. And just about that time Billy Rose came up to Noble and wanted him to audition for something that Billy was getting together. Right off Noble came after me, begging and pleading. He wanted me to audition with them and after a while I said I would. So we all auditioned, but I was still not with the band and when they went back after the audition, which had been successful and all, Billy said, 'Where's Sidney?'

'He's out of town,' Noble told him.

Well, I wasn't out of town and Noble knew it. What I'd told him was that I wanted more money if I was to play. But he wouldn't say that; there wasn't anything at all said about me in a money way. It was Perry Bradford who told me. He dropped by the hotel where I was staying; he was on his way to visit someone else there and he ran right into me. He was surprised. 'What are you doing here?' he told me. 'I thought you left town.' And that's how it all came out that he

161

told me about the conversation between Noble and Billy in Billy's office.

But a thing like that, that's nothing I take a big accounting of. There's some who are your friends and there's some who are only for themselves and I guess there will always be some of both in this world. What I figure is I got nothing to complain of; I haven't had it bad. I guess I've always been a rolling stone, but there was always somewheres I could stop. There was always something else I could be doing. I told you about that time Tommy Ladnier and I had that tailor shop: that was just one thing, but there'd always be something I could pick up if I had to.

What you really miss, being a rolling stone, it's the things most other people, they have natural. You're always looking for a home somewhere. You're always concerned that you're losing what's the important thing. But that's not the whole story. There's still a thing as big as all of it put together, and that's the music. Having that inside me, I got a lot. No matter what else is happening, the music is the thing to hold to, and it's all mine in a way of speaking: I can be off alone somewhere, I can be sitting here and I can be sad and lonely, but all I got to do is think of some melody and I'm feeling better right off. It's like you could slice up a piece of apple and then you put in a piece of pear, but it doesn't matter about the pear: you still know there's the apple there; you can taste it. That's the way it is with me. I can mix in anything I've got in my life and I've still got the music. I can be damn' near broke but I'm still like the song says—'I'm as rich as Rockefeller in a way of speaking'. There's some people, they're able to be happy watching their money pile up. Well, that's all a matter of your trade, you can say—it's a way you can take your life, if you wish to. What I've wished for, I got. It's the music. There's always those melodies inside me. I can pick and choose them, hear them in my own mind, or put them together—pieces of them—the way Omar used to do when he was making up his feeling, trying to find out what his feeling was. If I've got a trouble, I can answer it right out of my own head. . . . But people are always out to make their judgment about the music from the wrong things. Too many of them, they're more interested in how a musicianer carries on *after* the music. Personality stuff, that's how it is. It's still the way it was back there in New Orleans with Buddy Bolden. People there, they loved that music. And *still* it seemed like they cared more for all those other things Buddy Bolden was doing, all those women he had, all his carrying on. It was something they could point to as if *that* was as much as the music. Even the musicianers themselves get carried away by it. Either they get to feuding for a name for themselves or they get to thinking up some personality thing which has nothing to do with the music.

That's one of the things that make it why a musicianer, if he's real serious about the music, has to have this place inside himself. You've got to say that to yourself. 'I won't have it; I've got the music and I don't give a damn for the rest. Rich or poor, the music is there and that's what I'm for.'

And if you can say that to yourself, if you can say that and mean it, then it doesn't matter so much about whether you're working here or working there; you can fill in some way or another. You're not needing favours from somebody who cares more for a big sign with his name on it than what he cares about the music.

It's like I say: the important thing is to stay with the music, to be honest with it. So when I left Noble Sissle's —that was back around 1937—I wasn't worrying. I wasn't owing any favours, I wasn't missing any meals, and I had the music. I was all right.

So I played here and there, and after a while Herman Rosenberg, he was a good friend of mine, he brought me around to the Hickory House. Joe Marsala was working there; he played clarinet. He had a brother Marty who was there too; Marty played trumpet. And there was Joe Bushkin on piano. I wasn't working then and Herman wanted to bring me around; he was sure they'd be wanting to hire me after they finished hearing me. So I used to work there nights sometimes, but mostly it was Sunday evenings from around four to eight; that was when they had their jam sessions. My pay was mostly from those sessions on Sundays. I wasn't making much in a money way, but the music was real fine. And that's just an example of what I was saying. There's one way or there's another, but if a man really cares for the music, there's always *some* way.

And then one night Herman, he told me to come with him to Nick's. If Nick was to hear me, he said, he was sure to want me. So I went there. They had Bobby Hackett's band at Nick's then: there was Pee Wee Russell on clarinet, Brad Gowans on trombone and sometimes on clarinet too, Eddie Condon on guitar, and Ernie Caceres on baritone. And a friend of mine, Zutty Singleton, he was playing there as a feature. The night I went down there I brought my soprano, and the boys in that band, they were really good, we made it real fine together. Nick, he came in and listened and when we was all through he hired me. After that I was working there for quite a while.

There was some real musicianers there at Nick's. It was something real fine. Eddie Condon was there, and Eddie, he was one of the best. Eddie, he didn't have his own band yet. I could always see, though, that he had the idea. He wanted to do something really sincere to advance Jazz. He had a lot of feeling about how it should be presented, under what conditions. He used to talk to me a lot about that, about how a band should be made up. It was his idea that when you're doing the presenting right you're not giving a name or a colour to a musicianer. What you're doing, you're putting him together with others so that one man in the band helps another find the music, one man working with another. Eddie was always telling me how he'd do if he had a place of his own, and how much he wanted me with him if he had his own band. And ever since that time, if there's been something for the radio or a concert or a job, he's always thought of me and been very happy to see me work with him.

Eddie's a big man now, but he's gotten big in the right way. His interest was always for the music. Even back there at Nick's he was always managing to get work for us between times, helping us get along together. The way he'd say it, helping one is helping another and that way the music, it's helping itself. When he helped me, he saw it as my music he was helping. He saw what I was doing by how I was playing. And it's not been only me: Fats Waller, Louis Armstrong, Lips Page—he got so much pleasure out of working with them that he did them a lot of good.

Aside from being a real good musicianer, Eddie was a fine manager. And the way things were, somebody like Eddie was needed real bad to help Jazz, to help it get away from all this other business where a man was judged more by how he looked or what he did than by how he played. And there was a need for what he was doing. His work, it was real strong for helping Jazz.

One time I remember I was going to do something with Jelly Roll Morton who was going to make a show, and some fellow who handled the money for it said to Jelly, 'Sidney? Why him, he's an old man! We don't want anybody as old as he is. Just look at him!' But Jelly, he just told that man that if he didn't take me there wouldn't be any outfit. That's the way it happened to Jazz back there. What a man's got in his soul, that's got to be dressed up to meet the public. If he's got white hair you don't allow him a soul.

A man like Eddie Condon, though, what he looked for was the music. He had that inside him and he had the ability to manage things, and that way he did just about the most for helping Jazz to be itself in the way it got to be presented. There's nobody done more than Eddie.

13. Blues for Tommy

I tried one time to get a real New Orleans band together, that was in 1938. It was with Tommy Ladnier. I wanted him to come with me and start a band where we could play how we wanted to play, composing our own numbers and all. I wanted to play things the way they really had been played back in New Orleans, not doing a whole lot of unnecessary numbers that's like putting on a switch for a lamp when there's already plenty daylight. It was my idea that we'd just play how we felt.

Tommy, he was all enthused; but right away his wife, she began to get after him. She tells him, why don't he get a band of his own? 'This way Sidney, he'll get all the credit.' She says, 'You ought to watch out for yourself. You'll never get anywhere on that.'

Well, it's all the things a wife can say to her husband. I had nothing to say against her; she was doing how a wife does, it was her right. But she didn't really understand about the music. And another thing—she couldn't see the present. She was seeing what we could be, how we could go over. She was having pictures of one of those 'it's going to be wonderful, it can't come soon enough, but look at it now' things. She was seeing what a woman wants to see, all how she would have a lot of fine things. Only her trouble was she saw them too soon; they weren't there yet.

I tried to talk to Tommy. I told him it could be *his* band; it didn't matter to me. 'It can be any so-and-so's band,' I

166

told him. 'You can be manager or we can hire us a manager. You can have it any way you please. But it's the music—we'll be getting together, the both of us. We can do what we really know about, what we really feel.' But it didn't work out. That's how it would be and that's how it was. It was an idea I had, but nothing would come of it.

Then in late 1938 we played together again and made some records for the French critic, Mr. Panassié. We made *Really the Blues, When You and I Were Young, Maggie* and a couple of other numbers—*Ja Da* and *Weary Blues*. When we recorded *Really the Blues*, it really hit. That was a sensation. All of a sudden people were asking, 'Who's playing that? What's happening? I haven't heard anything like that.' My God, from the way they were talking you'd think we never played a note before in our lives.

This was when I had trouble with Mezzrow about my money. I said to myself, 'Well, I better go and get my money.' So I went up to Mezzrow's house, knocked at the door and rang the bell. He came to the door, but he put the chain on, you see. So I said, 'Well, listen, I come for my money.' He replied, 'Panassié, he hasn't come back from downtown. He has been downtown doing some business.' I said, 'Listen, I want my money, I must have my money.' Then he said, 'Well, I tell you. Panassié, he said you should give Tommy a little of the money, because after all Tommy he is the leader, he was working as the leader for that date. He should have leader's money.' I said, 'Yes, but I was working as the artist. Tommy is my friend, but that has nothing to do with the agreement that we made. You see, you are supposed to pay me a certain amount of money and I want it.' And at that time I pulled the chain and I pulled out my knife. So he said, 'Wait a minute, wait a minute, wait a minute,' and he went back in his room. I said to myself, 'Well, I don't know, maybe he is going for something. I'll throw that knife at him when he comes out again.' But he came back and gave me my money, and he said, 'I'll never make no record with you.' I said, 'Well, I don't give a damn. Good-bye.' Years later his wife came over to Paris, about 1953 or 1954, and was relating to me about this happening, you know. So I said: 'What did pass?' She said: 'You know what he come and ask me? He came and told me that you had pulled out a knife for him and you wanted your money. And he asked me what he should do. So I told him: "Me, in your place I would pay the money." ' So that is how he gave me my money, but I never did get the whole of that story until after she came to Paris.

Right after that *Really the Blues* session Panassié arranged another record date, and he was going to try to make something even better. The men were supposed to be there pretty early in the morning. But something had got going the night before and when they showed up at the studio they were really out; they'd been drinking all night. That was a session I wasn't scheduled to be at, but I heard about it quick enough. Tommy, he showed up dead drunk. James P. Johnson, he just stretched himself on the piano and passed out. Some of the musicianers didn't know how many fingers they'd got on each hand. But they went ahead and recorded somehow. And after it had all been cut Tommy knew the records weren't what they could have been and he wanted to say something to appease Panassié, who was sitting in the corner holding his head—something he thinks will fit the occasion. So he pulled himself up and called out '*Vive la France!*' and then almost fell flat on his face.

After that was when I talked to Tommy for the second time about the New Orleans band. I had a real hope for it. Tommy, he was a man who had feelings; he could have made it so good. But we never did get that band together, for this time it was Mezz Mezzrow who got into it and spoiled it.

Mezzrow, he'd had this rage of being King of Harlem for a while and that was wearing out some. He began to see that something different would have to be tried. I'm not saying Mezzrow is all that bad a player. He's played some nice things and he's put out some good records—he played, for example, on the date when we made *Really the Blues*, and he and I were to put out some records together later which were good. You see, he had a feeling for what he was doing; he had a way of working *around* what was being done. But still, when a man is trying so hard to be something he isn't, when he's trying to be some name he makes up for himself instead of just being what he is, some of that will show in his music, the idea of it will be wrong.

Mezz had some idea for what he wanted to do, and he wanted Tommy so bad to play with him so that he could keep what he thought he had. So he promised him everything. Tommy was in some trouble with his union card and Mezz was going to have that fixed up so he could get Tommy work. And Tommy was to stay at his place and have anything he wanted. He would get him a new trumpet; he was going to do everything for him. And all the time he was telling Tommy, what did he want to play under me for. 'Give yourself something, boy,' he told him. 'Sidney, he's all right; he'll take care of himself.'

Then Tommy would come to see me. 'I don't know,' he'd say. 'You know how it is, man. Mezzrow, he's been nice to me. I owe him kind of something. I've been staying over at his place. I don't know what to do. I'd like to play with you, Sidney, but . . .'

Well, there was a lot of buts, but it was always the same one. I could see right away it was the final end of my idea for the New Orleans band. At that time I didn't have room for Tommy at home; my mother-in-law was staying with me, and Tommy, he'd been living with Mezzrow. I don't know what it was with his wife about then, but I know he was living at Mezzrow's.

All the same I used to go looking for Tommy, watching out for him. He was drinking a lot too much. And he had trouble with hardening of the arteries; he had to have a doctor give him shots all the time. It was a serious thing. And then after one night when I'd been looking for him all over, I heard he'd died. How I heard it, he'd needed one of these shots bad; he'd been at Mezzrow's and there was nobody home, and when they found him he was dead.

That was an awful thing. Tommy could be alive today—Mezzrow, he's told me that. There was a doctor living right downstairs in the apartment building, and if Mezzrow had been home he could have gone down to him for a shot and kept Tommy going. Mezzrow, he couldn't be home all the time. It's just the luck of it . . . if it had just happened somebody had been there. But there wasn't anybody, and that's all about it.

It was four days after Tommy died I had a recording date with the Blue Note Company which was starting around that time. I had Frank Newton, J. C. Higginbotham, Meade Lux Lewis, Teddy Bunn, Johnny Williams and Sidney Catlett. We played *Summertime*, which I've always liked, and then we played *Blues for Tommy*. We felt very sad, and that was about all the tribute we could pay to a man we'd all liked, a man who really had the feeling.

With Tommy gone, I tried once more to get up a real New Orleans band, to get together an outfit that would really do the real thing. We'd be in New York, but we'd get a sort of reunion like; we'd bring New Orleans ragtime right out in front of the people. This was around the early 'forties.

It was something that could be really important and I got a lot of help and encouragement from people. There was Rudi Blesh—I told him about it and he was all enthused; he wrote about it in his paper and that there was to be a grouping again of some of the old New Orleans people who was going to play the music that has started the whole Jazz, and that Bunk Johnson was coming up from New Orleans to play with us. Bunk, he was to be featured in what I was playing. I wanted Bunk Johnson as I used to play with him before—he was the first one to take me out to play. So I really wanted Bunk.

John Reid was another one who was interested in what I had planned. I want to say this about John: he's fine. He's done some awful nice things for me; we've got together many times for recording sessions, contracts, things like that, and we used to have a lot of fun choosing the numbers to be played. He knew how to handle all that kind of business thing, but he had a fine feeling for the music too. And when I told him about this plan I had and about bringing Bunk up to New York, John right away made some arrangements with Victor to have us record.

As soon as that was arranged I wrote to Bunk and Victor sent him some money. Bunk, he'd been having some trouble with his teeth that made it hard for him to play, but I wrote to my brother Leonard in New Orleans and asked him to see Bunk; and my brother made a set of teeth for Bunk which enabled him to begin playing his trumpet again. And I asked him to tell Bunk he should come up and make these recordings with Victor. So John and me, we'd worked this all out and we'd decided that none of us was to say nothing to no one about this recording. So I wrote *that* to Bunk, telling him it was to be kept quiet. And Bunk, he wrote right back that he was coming up. He was really happy.

A little after that I went down to a big Jazz Festival in New Orleans, and I went down and saw Bunk and we made all the arrangements. But then, the way it happened, Louis Armstrong, he was there too, and after I left he went down to New Iberia to see Bunk. Louis, he was like a son to Bunk. He'd taught Louis some, and Louis used to practice with Bunk. Well, they had a long talk. Louis said to Bunk how he was going to get him a new trumpet. It was a real reunion like, and what with one thing and another, Bunk spilled the whole thing about his coming to New York and the recording he was going to do. Well, I guess Louis didn't understand how it was important to keep it secret; he thought he'd do Bunk a favour and get the whole thing some publicity, so he told this music magazine, *The Baton,* and they came out with a big story. Well, I saw this story and I was some surprised, but I was thinking that what's done is done and there was no real harm to it. I didn't think it would make much difference whether it was known or it wasn't known that Bunk would be making these recordings. But Victor, they got in touch with me right away and it was all called off. They told me to tell Bunk that if he'd spent the money, all right he could forget it, but that if he hadn't not to go ahead because the cheque had to be cancelled.

Then right on top of that Bunk went and recorded with somebody else. That was something I didn't learn about until later. The way it happened, these two fellows, Gene Williams and Bill Russell, they went down to New Iberia and they talked to Bunk. Gene, he'd had some kind of Jazz magazine—*Jazz Information* it was called or something like that—but it had folded, and right after that he'd been left some money from some society to do a big research on Jazz, and he was really going out in a big way. So he got down there and talked to Bunk. Bunk, he told me all about it later. Gene, he'd got down there with this Bill Russell, and Bunk had told them he couldn't record because he was coming up to New York with me and *we* had something planned. But, the way Bunk told me, they talked and talked and they got him pretty drunk—and so Bunk, he recorded, and that was it. That was what came of all the big come-back we'd planned for him.

Bunk, he did finally show up in New York, and I couldn't figure out what was going on. I'd known this Gene some, just here and there; I'd never seen too much of him. Then all at once he was always around. I didn't get to know why then, but it all came out later. Gene had recorded Bunk, but there was some trouble; he couldn't release the records because Bunk had been teaching at the time and that would bring some mix-up with the union, some technicality about how the contract had been signed between Bunk and Gene.

That's what he had in his mind, though I didn't know about it at the time, and that's why he just wouldn't more than let Bunk out of his sight. I had an apartment at the time and Bunk was staying with me, but this Gene wanted Bunk to stay with him. I had no idea that what he was really planning, it was to keep Bunk away from me so *we* couldn't record. If Bunk didn't make any recordings with me, this Gene's records, when he got them issued, they'd be really hot.

This Gene, he came right over to the apartment and asked Bunk to move over with him. Old Bunk, though, he was a funny one. He was the damnest fellow for mimicking; he could act anybody on out. And there was something real shrewd about him that dug out in a way what it was a person was after, and if there was the slightest thing he could mimic, that person, he was gone. So Bunk stood there listening to this Gene talking and talking, and when he'd finished, Bunk he pulled his mouth sort of funny and stuttered kind of, something the way this Gene had been talking, and he said, 'Well, you'll have to move out then to make room for Sidney, Gene; I'm here with him.'

But this Gene, he was really worried that Bunk and I would make some records without his knowing about it. I wasn't all sure of this at the time, but I began to see some of what he was doing, there was something funny about the way he went about things; kept trying different ways to get us apart. He wasn't through yet, even though Bunk had refused to move out of my apartment. From time to time Bunk would tell me how this Gene was always getting after him to leave. I was supposed to be bossing Bunk around, making him come and go the way I wanted—that's what Gene was telling him. 'Why don't you get out on your own? Be your own boss? Why do you want to play under him?' Bunk, he told me that.

There was another thing, too: this Gene, he was feeding Bunk too much liquor. Bunk, he was a gone man for liquor. When he didn't have liquor turning him Bunk played *so* fine: I think he was about the best blues player I ever heard. But when he was drunk, there was nothing you could do with him, he just went all to hell. A man like that, you've got to watch him close. But this Gene was always taking him out and getting him drunk.

One night, Bunk was playing at Jimmy Ryan's, and Gene came after him with a girl, let's call her Lorraine. Bunk had a girl he was going around with, but Gene brought this Lorraine around and they took him across the street to a drinking place. Gene paid for everything; they got Bunk plenty full of liquor and he was really going. And Gene kept telling him he should go home with this girl Lorraine.

The way it happened though, Bunk had his own girl there. Well, we sat around a long time and I was trying to get Bunk home, but it wasn't any use. After a while he came rolling over to me and he said, 'Sidney, you don't have to wait around any. I'll see you after a while. I'll be home later.' And he went off with his girl.

Then Lorraine came up to me and she wanted to know what

we were talking about. What did Bunk say to me? Where was he going?

Well, I told her he'd said he'd be home later and that was all I knew. I asked her if she wanted to come back with me and wait for him: sooner or later he'd show up, he was bound to. This Lorraine, she agreed and we went off back to my place and we got to fooling around there, talking, and I played the piano some. So you know how it is, we got to saying this and that, and we got to touching around one another, and pretty soon I was right there. But she stayed around afterwards, still waiting for Bunk.

Well, it's funny how things happen. After that night, Lorraine and I, we were going around together pretty steady. That Gene, he was still hanging around, and still telling Bunk that I was just using him, that he should break off from me and go out on his own. And he was still keeping Bunk full of liquor. And that way we never did get to make the records we'd planned.

Well, right after that I had a sort of a summer job at the Log Cabin in Fonda, New York. I had a little four-piece band, a quartet; I had Kenny Clarke with me on drums, Ernest Myers on bass, Sonny White on the piano and myself with the clarinet. I could come to New York and make records if I had a date, and every year I'd go there and play about three or four months. And I was making a lot of records around this time, and in between, too, I was playing with the band I had at Nick's Tavern in Greenwich Village with Charlie Howard added on guitar. There used to be jam sessions there on Sundays run by Harry Lim, and I conducted a number of them in the winter.

Like I said, I was making a lot of records—some in Chicago, most in New York—and some of them came out real good and some not so good, like the way it is with everything. You know, when a thing happens bad, it seems like it's always something I've known about before; and when a thing happens good, that's like finding a new way of being yourself. The time I remember that could have come closest to playing with someone where I didn't have all the worrying business, some-

174

one where I could just relax and go with the music, that was with Louis Armstrong for some recordings we made in 1940. And when I went to make those recordings I was remembering how we'd put out some records together back in the middle 'twenties. Some of these we were going to make now, they were going to be the same numbers. I remembered how we'd worked together then, and it was exciting to me to think about it because here was a chance again. Here's where we could make a real feeling. Louis's wife, she was doing the arranging. She came to me and she told me, 'Sidney, go ahead just like you want. Play the way you want, like we've been waiting to hear you. You're with Louis; you'll both be together and you'll both be really able to play.' Because she knew how Louis and I can do it.

So we rehearsed, and the rehearsals were fine. And when we came to record we were going along fine, and then something happened. Louis's wife had written down the important things I was to do, and I played them that way. And they'd been written down the same way for Louis, but when it came time to actually record Louis done nothing like what was written for him; it was like he was a little hungrier; he began to take his runs different from how we had arranged. I don't mind that. He can change his mind. What I don't understand is why he didn't come to me first and tell me he wasn't going to go along with how the parts had been written. Because I know he was as anxious as me to have those records turn out to be really something; and he knew the only way that could happen, it was if both of us got there working together. But he didn't *play* as if he wanted it; that's what I still can't understand. The man who was recording the numbers, he told him, 'Louis, take it easy. Just *play* Louis. Play natural. Don't worry about what Sidney's doing.'

Anyhow, those records were spoiled because he'd talked at the end, so that had to be cut out and we got set to start it over again. John Reid was there and he came up to me; he could get an idea that the old feeling wasn't there and he said to me, 'Sidney, that's all right. You were fine. They'll really get them this time.'

So we cut them again, and I still went on playing the way I had. But Louis, it seemed like he was wanting to make it a kind of thing where we were supposed to be bucking each other, competing instead of working together for that real feeling that would let the music come new and strong. And the funny thing is that I can remember Louis years ago when he was so timid you'd have to urge him to get up and play when there was some *regular* bucking kind of session going on, one of those sessions where they were out special to do just that, to play *at* one another.

That's why anyone who knows about Jazz music can feel those records weren't what they should have been. You can have every tub on its own bottom all right, but that don't make real music. What I know is, those other records we'd made back in the 'twenties were talked about much more than those we made at this session in 'forty. The *2.19 Blues*, we'd put that out again, and *Down in Honky Tonk Town*. But there was nothing missing from those first ones; they were something you could listen to and not have to do any waiting for the music to arrive, because it *was* arriving. They had that feeling right there. In the old days there wasn't no one so anxious to take someone else's run. We were working together. Each person, he was the other person's music: you could feel that really running through the band, making itself up and coming out so new and strong. We played as a group then.

And what's changed, you know, it's that hunger. A man now, he's not just a musicianer any more. He's got himself a name and he's got to perform up to that name. It's a demand upon him. His own reputation demands that he become a performer as well as a musicianer. He's got to be a personality. It's what I said at the very beginning when I was talking about Buddy Bolden. If a man can really play where the music is, he's entitled to all the personality they'll give him: but if the personality gets to come first, that's bad for the music. The music, that's for a group to play; the musicianers, they need to be playing together. It's like you could hitch yourself up a fine team of horses. You could get yourself a big carriage and hitch yourself six horses to it. But you let the harness loose or you drop the reins, and that team don't know where it's going. That's where the music is today. It's like that team of horses. And it's a sad thing, but it's the truth.

A man, I guess he can get used to anything. But getting used to a thing, that's no joy. Maybe it's a way of growing; or maybe it's a way of learning. Maybe even that's all the learning there is—coming to know that whatever happens, after a while it's always some part of the same thing happening again. Or maybe that's just the bad things. Maybe there's just this certain way for things to go bad; and if a thing *is* to go bad it has to be pretty much in the same way. The good things, that's something different. The good things come new—the way of having a friend what proves true, of finding a person you care for, or of feeling the music come out right. That's always a kind of discovering, in its way. The place where a musicianer is lucky is in having the music. That's where he can always make it come good and true. If he's a good musicianer and if he really cares about the music he can stay with it long enough until it begins to come. He can find it. But most of all that don't happen real well in the music unless you're playing with the right people. A man can make a whole lot of music to himself, but what growing the music does, what arriving and what becoming arises from it, that only happens when musicianers play together—really play together with a feeling for one another, giving to one another, reaching out to one another and helping the music advance from what they're doing together.

I guess just about the loneliest a musicianer can be is in not being able to find someone he can really play with that way. Sometimes it gets to seem most awful long since I've had someone who could really do for the music. That was really the reason I'd wanted to get that band together with Tommy, and why I felt sad at the way those records went with Louis in 1940. And the thing is, Louis knew it too. It's like I say: we'd done it before back there. He knew how good those records could have been.

I just don't understand it. I don't even blame Louis. The onliest thing, it's not being able to understand what it was.

I've said a lot about this because it shows what I mean about remembering how we'd worked together way back, and the excitement of having the chance again. But I don't blame Louis. And I want to say this. Louis is a fine musicianer. Like I said, I've known him and I've played with him since he had his first cornet; he's stayed with the music, while some of them have gone off every which way with all that personality and performing business. But Louis, he's a fine and sincere musicianer.

There's one thing more I must say about 1940, because it goes back a long way. In the first part of the year, I was playing a good deal in Philadelphia, at dances and parties, like. And one time I led a jam session at the Hot Club down there. Well, who should have a band in Philadelphia at that time but George Baquet, and they asked him to come around, and I had the very real pleasure of introducing him to all these people. And there we were playing together again nearly forty years after that first time when I was a kid and Freddie Keppard's band came to our house for my brother's birthday. That was something. That was a happy day.

14. One Man's Band

I told you about this friend of mine, John Reid. Well, I was up at his house one day, around 1941 it must have been, and he had an idea. There was a symphony orchestra that had recorded a piece, and when they heard the play-back there was something, there was a hole in it for about a second. And they couldn't figure what was wrong, so they called the conductor, called him up for to listen. He listened to it and then he got the score and found out that it was the oboe player who hadn't played his part. So rather than make the whole record over again, they made a trick record. They played the record beside another recording record and the oboe player sat there with a pair of earphones on. So he listened and when he got to the part he played his oboe, and the recording record had recorded *him* with the oboe and the record with the symphony orchestra, and this way it was complete. So this gave John Reid the idea for me to make a one-man-band record.

I had a couple of instruments up there at his house, my saxophone and a tenor, and he had a piano. So I played the piano first and he recorded that and then he recorded that again with my soprano, and that worked all right so he said I should make the record. I was kind of afraid of the thing because it got on my nerves. But finally I said O.K. and he made the date.

So I started out; I played *The Sheik of Araby* and I played the whole six instruments. I started first with the piano, and then I got the drums and my soprano. I meant to play all the rhythm instruments first, you know, but I got all mixed up and I grabbed hold of the bass and then I got the tenor, and I had these earphones on as the company did for this oboe player, and finally I recorded with the six instruments. And then I played a blues, but I was really outdone and I couldn't do more than four instruments on that other side. Oh, it was a great story for the newspaper men, and they raised so much hell that the union made the company pay me for seven men, and it was forbidden to do it again! But the funny part was right after that I met Fats Waller going into the theatre; he was playing at the Polo. So he said to me, 'Bechet, I'm telling you, boy, you certainly did make that one man band record!' And I said, 'It would have been all right if we would have had a rehearsal before,' meaning the engineer and myself, you know. But Fats, he laughed and said, 'Man, how the hell you going to have a rehearsal with yourself?'

Well, it wasn't so long after that there wasn't no cause to be rehearsing, for the union called that stoppage and for a good part of a couple of years and we didn't do no recording no place.

But in 1943 things started up again and I made some of the V-Discs that a number of musicianers were making for the G.I.s. And it was around this time too that Eddie Condon started his concerts at the Town Hall in New York and I played with him, and I toured around with him too.

And about that time I got to know a whole lot about this kind of personality trouble. 'Personality hell,' I wanted to say, 'me, I'm a musicianer.' I didn't want them to look at me for a beauty prize; all I wanted was for them to listen to me play. It was getting on to 1944, 1945 and by this time I was no chicken any more. By the time it was half-way into the nineteen-forties I was pushing fifty and I began to have one trouble and another. I'd got some white hairs by then, and that was part of the trouble. To hear people talk then, you'd think Sidney Bechet was too old and weak to pick up his instrument and hold it to his mouth.

180

But that was only part of it. The way a man plays—*that* shows how old he is; and there was still enough people who cared about the music itself, so I got along.

It wasn't even so much the fact that I was just getting along. But there are so many people who've got a big mouth that's always wide open. Nothing enough will ever pass into it to satisfy all that hunger, this greed I guess you'd call it, to have a thing for themselves.

Well, I began to collect royalties which were heavy then, about 1945, and I bought a house in Brooklyn because I sort of intended to take life easy and get away from all this hunger, this greed like I said. In January of that year I was invited to play in a concert with Louis Armstrong in New Orleans. That was done by the *Esquire* magazine, and it was to give Louis this gold award that he had won and Higginbotham also. It was a lot of the old musicianers, Bunk Johnson and Mr. Allen too—that's Red Allen's father. I recall father and son, they went together in a street parade, and that must have been a fine day for the both of them. Well, they wanted me to join the boys, and I had a lot of pleasure playing with Louis again, and this concert in the Municipal Auditorium was a very big success. At this time I was with my friend John Reid, he was the one who introduced me to the R.C.A. Victor Recording Company.

So I had an idea again to make a band to bring back to New York; I had the opportunity to work in Boston—at the Savoy Ballroom, that is, and make a tour. So I thought once more I would try to get one of those seven-piece bands like we had in New Orleans. And I wanted Bunk to come along, and I spoke to my brother Leonard about it. But Leonard thought I was doing a mistake because there were a lot of fellows had been recording Bunk and they had been mixing him up a whole lot, you know; and he thought it would be hard for me to control Bunk after all these people putting different things which were not true in his head about what he could do in New York. Because there were fellows that would take Bunk and have him stay at their house and just play for their own pleasure. Naturally, if they had a job for him, they would try to get a job, but it was more so to have Bunk near them; and I wanted Bunk to be playing.

Anyway, Bunk, he came on up to New York and when he first arrived we made some records together. We recorded for Blue Note with Albert Nicholas on clarinet, Pops Foster on bass, Cliff Jackson on piano. We recorded with two different bands we made up. In one of them it was Art Hodes played piano. I remember those numbers. One of them was *Days Beyond Recall*—that was real fine. *Blame it on the Blues*, that was another. And *Weary Way Blues*, that was one. And *Up in Sidney's Flat*. We made some real good recordings there.

And right after that I had this offer to play at the Savoy in Boston. So I got together a quintet—that was Bunk and myself, with Hank Duncan playing piano, Fred Moore on drums and Pops Foster. We made all the arrangements, bought the tickets, and we were all set to go. Then we got to the train and someone hadn't shown up; we were a man short. I was plenty tired by then. The night before Bunk hadn't come home and I had gone out looking for him all over the place. I'd finally found him and we were all set to go and then this other fellow didn't show up. So there was nothing for it; I sent Bunk on ahead with the rest of the band and I went back to look for this other fellow. And while I was looking for him this girl, this Lorraine I spoke about, she showed up again and wanted me to go along to a party with her; she offered to pay for the expense of taking a plane so we'd all arrive about the same time. Well, that made an impression on me. 'This gal, she's all right', I thought to myself, 'isn't she straight?' But the way it turned out I finally found this other fellow and we went off by train, though with all the delays he made getting sober enough so he could move it was the next day when we got to Boston.

I got to Boston and the first thing I learn this Gene fellow, he's there. Right then I know that Bunk, he's been drunk. I called up the Savoy and they told me, 'Sidney, Bunk's been here.' 'Yes,' I told them, 'I know all about it.' When Bunk was that way he just stopped being a musicianer. He'd been up on

The *Revue Nègre,* Paris, 1925. Sidney Bechet is immediately behind Josephine Baker (above) who is doing the splits

Marriage, Juan-les-Pins, 1951

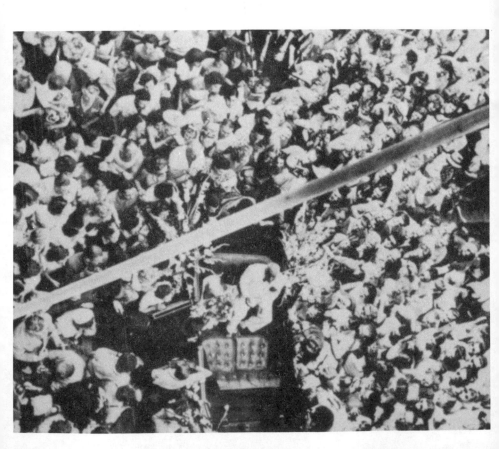

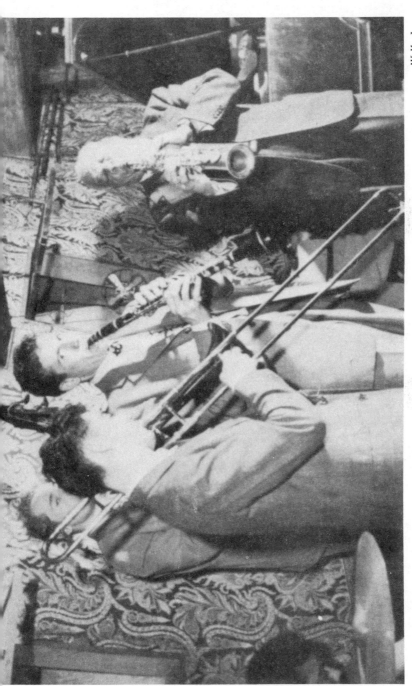

Wolfsohn

Sidney Bechet and the Claude Luter band, Vieux Colombier, Paris, 1950

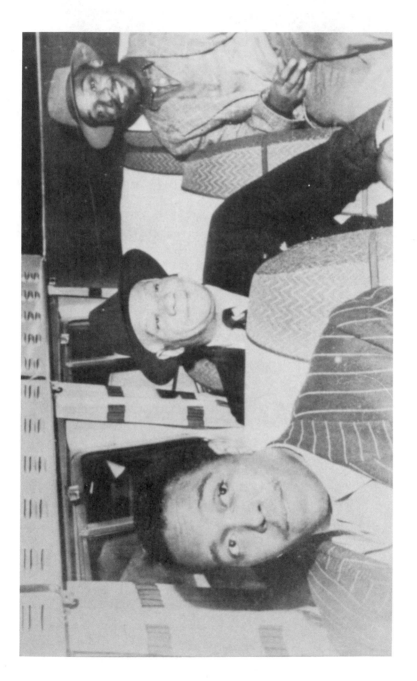

Charlie Parker, Sidney Bechet, and Kenny Clarke en route to the Paris Jazz Festival, 1949

that stage making jokes, bowing, going through pantomine, speeches, everything. He'd really had that place. There'd been no music *that* night.

And it went on that way all the time we were in Boston. That Gene kept Bunk full of liquor all the time. And Bunk, he got really bad on my hands. There was just no music to be gotten out of him anyway; he didn't want to stick to the proper way of playing. And what was worse, up there at the Savoy, we couldn't play music for dancing. There's no dance floor there. Had we been able to have taken just any number and done something to it, they wouldn't have cared, just so it had a good rhythm to dance to. That way we could have been more freer in the numbers. But what it was at the Savoy there, it was more for an attraction-like and we had to stick to the *Royal Garden* kind of thing. Well, that's another thing; there's no faking you can do to that kind of a number, and with Bunk the way he was, it got us down. People, they was paying to hear certain things, and hell, we had to give them to them; we had to get us some pay to get back home on. But whatever it was we were playing that time, it wasn't nothing to what it could have been. We done the best we could, patching up this and that, but it just wasn't so good. All we managed to do, we pulled through one way and another and got our pay, and I was plenty glad to leave. I guess the *Esquire* magazine summed it up about right when they said: 'This group might easily have developed into a fine outfit featuring New Orleans music had it not been for the unfortunate temperamental gymnastics of the oldest member of the band.' Well, that's about all there was to it. I had to let Bunk go, and for a while I had Pete Bocage in his place. He wasn't playing regular then but had some business in New Orleans; my brother Leonard asked him if he'd come up and join me, and he did.

Then later, when we got back to New York, Lorraine, she told me all what it was. She broke down; she didn't want this secret any more. This Gene, he'd made an arrangement with her; she had been hired to stand up in front of Bunk in a way of speaking, show herself off for Bunk, persuade him to leave me and go with Gene. And Gene, all this time, he'd been working the same way, trying to get Bunk drunk enough so he'd leave me. Lorraine, she was up in my apartment one day, and she told me all there was about it. That was really the day; that was something. All this that had been going on, all this plotting and arranging: that was about enough to tell me the whole business of living right there. It makes you think, you know: you get to asking how can the music ever come out and be itself with all this going on around it, blocking it, taking away the real concern from where it should be and just trying to swallow something for itself. Just that big mouth that's wanting everything it can swallow for itself.

After we got back from the Savoy, Bunk wasn't happy and he went back to New Iberia, back to Louisiana. I put him on the train and I had a feeling . . . I hated to see him go. Things, they have a way sometimes . . . you can hardly understand why. Why is it they got to have that reason buried inside them so that all you get is trouble, a whole lot of suffering? I don't know what it is I could have done different; Bunk, he didn't know how to be any different, and in a real deep way we were friends, we could understand part of something. But when you put the whole of it together, we were both knowing one thing: something had happened that was hard to get right, something that just wasn't *going* to get right.

So Bunk, he went back, and this Gene, he went out to California and had some kind of nightclub. He'd spent about the last cent of this money he'd been given to support Jazz and he'd fixed this place down to the last nail on the wall, and then he found out that he couldn't have the coloured musicians he'd been thinking of putting in there—I don't know what it was. So he came racing back to New York. He had some scheme for saving everything. He wanted me to get hold of Bunk, get him back, tell him to go along with this scheme.

I told him no. 'Bunk, he's gone back,' I told him. 'He's done it his way. I can't change that.'

And the way it turned out, if you was telling a story thing this wouldn't be believed, but it's how it was—a week after that, this Gene, he committed suicide. And just about a month after that—not much longer—Bunk died.

Well, after that I settled down in this house I had in Brooklyn. And in these years me and my brother Leonard became closer and closer. So once in a while he'd take a trip over to New York and he would stay with me a couple of months and then go back to New Orleans. Oh, we had such a lovely time together. I was fixing to have him come and live with me, but he got ill in New Orleans and had to stay there a while.

Like I said, I sort of intended to take life easy. I said I wouldn't take out of town engagements except one-night stands. I said to myself I'd just give lessons. And I had quite a few scholars, you know; they were all taking lessons. And that's when I had Bob Wilber.

Bob was about seventeen years old then. I'd come in contact with him first a year or two back when I was touring around doing these concerts with Eddie Condon. And then I began giving him lessons. His parents lived in Scarsdale, New York, and I had a commission from them to look after him. You see, Bobbie, he could read very good, but it was the instrument he didn't know. He didn't know the instrument. He wanted to play but he couldn't. So mostly that's what I taught him, you know, and how to make different tones and growls. They said to me, 'You're driving that poor boy too hard.' But he come back. I had to tell him a lie—I said, 'That's it, Bobbie, that's it. Now you're coming.' I had to tell him a lie, but he come back and he said, 'You told me lots of lies, Pops, or you'd never have seen me again.'

'Yes, I did,' I said, 'but you come back.'

This boy, when he first come to me, he thought this old clarinet would blow itself. He said, 'I can't play all that without breathing!' But I gave him a little sherry to build himself up. He was a bit anaemic then, you know. And they said, 'You take it easy—he shouldn't be taking that stuff. You're rushing him too hard.' But I said, 'I got to build him up or he'll never blow.'

Well, he kept coming back and within a couple of years, Bobbie was very good. He could really blow then; man, he could blow. But the trouble was, Bobbie didn't know whether

185

he wanted to be a Jazz, or modern or classic clarinettist. He really could; he had the ability, he was very good at it. And that is very embarrassing and troublesome to you when you really can't find yourself, you know. He would have liked to have played Jazz. But he played so close to me that it began to annoy him, because people used to say, 'Oh, that boy, he plays just like Bechet. It's just Bechet playing.' Like when we made some records together in 1947—that was when I played with Bob's Wildcats—someone said, 'The two clarinet parts sound more like Sidney Bechet playing a duet with himself than anything on the one-man band record!' Well, it sort of gets on your nerves a bit, you know, because there you get to a certain point where you are on a switch. You see, you want something of your own, and it's a pretty tough proposition to get something of your own in America. But we made some records together, in 1947, like I said, and again in 1949, and then he went out on his own. He had a band of his own from that Scarsdale High School where he was, and they played at Jimmy Ryans and, man, they played good. I haven't seen him in a good while now, and I hope he's doing all right because he was a fine boy and a good musicianer.

While I was there in Brooklyn giving these lessons, Mezzrow came to me. He wanted to open a recording studio and he called it *King Jazz*. And he wanted me to be a partner or have shares in the company, and that was a thing your heart and soul could be set on. The idea of this company, it was to make some good records that didn't need a lot of building up, all this promotion. They could go on their own name. They would have the standard of good musicianers playing good numbers, something that was bound to get a lot of people interested when they learned what we were doing. It was none of this pleasure music, but the real thing. This idea, it could make a lot of good musicianers known, help them to get jobs after the records were out. We'd have the best men you could find and we'd really get them together in a company that would be just for them. That company, it was as good as having that New Orleans band I wanted.

Well, the new label really got under way and started

recording like crazy. On the first session in August 1945 we did *Gone Away Blues, Out of the Gallion, De Luxe Stomp, Bowin' the Blues* and some others; we had Fitz Weston piano, Pops Foster and Kaiser Marshall. They were records you could feel proud of. Then we made some records with a septet, adding Hot Lips Page on trumpet and Danny Barker on guitar. And then we did a long record of *Really the Blues* with a quintet again—Mezz, myself, Wellman Braud, Sox Wilson and Baby Dodds. The last lot of records I made for *King Jazz* was in December 1947, when there was union trouble and Petrillo had said that musicianers weren't to make no records. But we didn't take any notice of that, and it was just as well. Because we had Kaiser Marshall on drums that day, with Sammy Price on piano and Pops Foster. And the day after the recording Kaiser was taken ill with pneumonia and a week later he was dead. So we'd made about ten records that day and one was a new tune which we hadn't given a name yet, so we called it *Kaiser's Last Break*.

Aside from the *King Jazz* label I also made some records that year with Joe Sullivan. We'd played together before, of course, but this was the first time we had ever made any records. We put out an album; some of it was Joe's piano solos, but on the others we played *Panama, Sister Kate* and a tune of mine called *Got It and Gone* with Pops Foster and George Wettling. That fall, too, I appeared in a play at the Playhouse Theatre on Broadway. It was a play about Jazz musicianers, written by Orin Jannings. It was called *The Trumpet Leads* at one time, but by the time we got around to production the title had changed to *Hear That Trumpet*. It was all about Jazz musicianers and a lot about racial prejudice which was beginning to bother people a lot around that time. Coloured and white musicianers had been making records together for years, but it seemed like the managers didn't think the public would want to actually see these musicianers playing together, and these mixed bands like were very slow in coming along the way they should have. Well, that was in people's minds and that was something of what this play was about. Bobby Sherwood was in it: he was a guy who played trumpet, sang a bit, played guitar and had been most anything in the entertainment business except an actor, so this was his first time. There was Ray Mayer, a piano player, and Marty Marsala who played drums in the little band the play was about. I don't know really that it was all that good a play, but it had ideas, and anyway we started off on Broadway; but it didn't run too long.

Then in 1947 I took a trio into Jimmy Ryan's on 52nd Street, when 52nd Street still was a street; it's sad to think now that the whole place is pretty well torn down and Jimmy Ryan's is standing there next to a vacant parking lot, I guess about ready to go. Sometimes a man can move a place and start all over some place else, but it's too often that once the doors are closed they just shut up a piece of life, the life we've known, away with them. I've played there on 52nd Street a good many times, and several times since what I'm talking about in 1947. I'm not one for thinking that everything's got to stay just the same, but even as little as ten years ago there weren't all those number of places where we could play the music we wanted to, and 52nd Street was right there with all those small places where real musicianers could get jobs and that's something. I was there most of the year. I was ill in the summer and missed some time; but I went back to Jimmy Ryan's at the end of 1947. And I took a band down to play at Penn State College in December, with Art Hodes on piano. They certainly had the feeling there. The hall was packed and they really liked the music.

After our fine start, there was trouble about Mezzrow's company a bit and he wasn't making any records. We had stopped for a while. So I had a proposition to make some records for Columbia. Well, I had to get permission from Mezzrow, naturally, as I had a contract with the company. And Mezz agreed, but he wanted to take these numbers into the *King Jazz* company. And that's what I didn't want, because I wanted the numbers to stay in the Columbia list, and actually I would get my royalties from Columbia, you see. And anyway it all worked out pretty good, and we were still not making any records—I don't know whether it was artists were scarce or what. But I was getting letters from Chicago, because I had been there to play a concert, and Bill and Ruth Rinehart were just fixing to open up a place there and they wanted me to play when they were ready to open up. They called it 'Jazz Ltd.' But, like I said, it was the summer of 1947 and I was ill at the time and couldn't go.

But in the next year I accepted the job and went out to Chicago to play—I guess it was the last weeks of 1948. So I played there awhile, three months or so. And that was quite an excitement, because it was the first time that I'd played in Chicago in thirty years. I was still with *King Jazz*, you see, and Mezzrow, he got an agreement to come to Nice to play in a Jazz festival they were getting together. So he wanted to take me with him. I had had trouble in France, like I said earlier, but all the papers had been gone into and fixed that I could return back to France to play the Festival. But I told him I was sorry, I didn't think I would be able to make it. And I told him, I said, 'Why not take Bob Wilber in my place?' So he said, 'Listen, put Ruth Rinehart on the phone, I want to speak to her.' So he spoke to Ruth, but nothing— she wouldn't give permission, so I had to stay. So Bob and Mezzrow, they went along to play the Festival of Europe.

Well, that was really the end of the *King Jazz* company. The company, it was just starting up and it could have done so much; but Mezzrow, he left for Europe. And when Mezzrow came back, I wanted to go and see the fight between Joe Louis and Jersey Joe Walcott for the heavy-weight championship at the Garden. So I was all set to see this fight, and I guess I wanted some money. So I said to myself, I said, 'I'll go and see how the company's going.' But the company had moved; there wasn't no company there no more. So, boy, I finally found Mezzrow and the company. And Mezz, he said, 'Don't worry, don't worry. We ain't moved up the street yet. Let's distribute the records all over Europe and everywhere.' So I said O.K., but I saw him less and less. And that was the end of it, the company. I don't know why Mezzrow let it go that way. That's his secret.

And that's one other time the music, it stayed home. It

could really have got up and gone then. We could have picked the best and made the best. But it's like I was saying about experience: it seems like there's nothing new to happen, not to you and not to the music. All that ever happens to it, it's always the same thing happening in another way. I won't say I understand this. All I say is, that's how it seems to be.

So I moved back to Jazz Ltd. and continued to work. And in the spring of 1949, that's when I had another opportunity to come to Europe, to Paris, to another Jazz Festival. But this time I was coming on my own. Charles Delaunay, he was fixing it. I wouldn't be with Mezzrow or with anybody; I would be alone, you see. I would work with somebody, but I wasn't being shown with anybody. So I asked Mrs. Rinehart, could I go to Europe for these two weeks. She told me she was sorry, that I wouldn't be able to go. So I said, 'I don't see why not. It's only two weeks.' She said, 'You had permission about three months ago and we let you go. Now you've come back and now I want you to stay.' 'Well,' I said, 'I want to go. I want to go to Europe.' So she said, 'I am sorry, you have to stay here.'

I went over to the union the next day, and I explained the whole fix and how I had an opportunity to do this Jazz Festival. They said, 'You've got a contract, a musical contract,' and there it was. So I said, 'I am very sorry. I must just take my own responsibility, and I'm going.' So I left, and that's how I came to the Paris Festival in 1949.

15. Closer to Africa

I arrived in Paris for this Jazz Festival in May 1949. It was got together by the Hot Club of Paris, and it was in the Salle Pleyel. There was a lot of musicianers come over from America—Lips Page, Charlie Parker, Tadd Dameron and a lot more, and there were musicianers from all over Europe. There very nearly wasn't a festival at all because on the Saturday— the festival started on a Sunday—there was a fire in the Salle Pleyel. Suddenly it was all filled with smoke, but it didn't stop the people who were there buying tickets.

I was playing with Pierre Braslavsky's band on the Sunday night; we played *Texas Moaner, Muskrat Ramble* and *Summertime* and I was going on to *Sweet Georgia Brown,* but the people, they liked *Summertime* so much that when we could get them to quiet down a bit I decided to give them *High Society* to finish up instead. On the third day of the festival, Tuesday, I played a lot of numbers, fifteen altogether, with three bands. I played first with Pierre, and we started in an uproar. It seems that another band which had filled the first spot hadn't played too well and the people hadn't liked it much; but they were good people and they were having a good time, so when the compère made some snide remarks about this other band, they weren't having that and they nearly tore that Salle Pleyel down. So I started playing anyway, and at first I couldn't hear myself, but soon it was going fine. Then I played with Claude Luter's band, and last with Lips Page, Russell Moore and a French rhythm section. Well, I don't want to say anything against anyone, but those people there, they certainly showed they liked the music the way we'd always played it.

After the festival was over I went back to America, but I promised to come back to France in the fall. When I got back from Europe I found America gone Jazz crazy all at once. I came back, and it was just like watching some child who's thrown his toy away and seen somebody else pick it up and now he wants it real bad. America had just about forgotten there *was* Jazz until Europe went all crazy for it and all at once it just *had* to have it. Everywhere I went it was a-Jazz-a-this, a-Jazz-a-that. All the damn' jockeys on the radios was playing Jazz numbers, answering all kinds of requests, making all kinds of expert explanations all wrong. Everybody was excited, but no Jazz musicianer had a job except to make records. In a way of speaking, Jazz music had no part of it outside of making the records that were playing every day on the radio.

A little before the time, Rudi Blesh had had an idea and he'd come to me. He was set to have a concert like: there was to be a Bop Band and a Jazz Band to show themselves, and he would kind of explain what they are. Well, they hired this big hall, the Rialto up on Fifth Avenue and 59th Street, and this contest was given. I've still got the clippings about it, how the Bop musicianers came on and played, and the people didn't even move, they didn't move a hand for them. There was nothing for the Bop musicianers; Bop was dead. And then we came on and we hadn't finished the first number before we had them going. They really moved. They were demanding it, they wanted more.

Well, that started a whole lot more excitement about Jazz. People were real Jazz perturbed, they were excited for it. Some promoters came up to me and they wanted to do the same kind of show in Birdland and then at Bop City. They was to have a Bop Band and a New Orleans Band. It was getting to be a real fad, that kind of contest. Louis Armstrong, he'd been to one of these contests at Bop City before then and he'd been there for weeks. He'd really broken it up. He'd topped all receipts they'd ever had. They told him he could stay just as long as he wanted.

So these people wanted me to do the same thing. Well, I had the men I wanted then; I'd picked my own musicianers. I had Buster Bailey, Wilbur de Paris, Sidney de Paris, Kansas Fields, Ralph Smith, Charlie Shavers. And we played our own numbers our own way. That was a real band.

But right away when I was to go into this contest, these people who'd come to me, they were doing the choosing of the musicianers and the numbers. I wasn't to have my own men. Every time I mentioned the men I'd played with at the first contest, they tell me the budget wouldn't permit it. So I'd try to pick some others. I told them I wanted Vic Dickenson for trombone, Jonah Jones or Lips Page for trumpet, Kenny Kersey for piano, Joe Jones for drums, Walter Page for bass and Buster Bailey. I wanted these men with me if we were to play right, but all these promoters had to say was *budget*. Every one of these men, they wanted a decent salary, but what they were asking was nothing you'd have to build a real tall ladder to reach. They didn't want any million dollars. But all I hear is *budget*. *Budget*, that got to be the biggest and the oftenest damn' word I ever did hear in those days.

So I refused. I could afford to refuse at that time. I had this contract in Chicago which would bring me enough salary to get by on. If I was to get up this band, I told them, I wouldn't have anyone else do the selecting and I wouldn't have anyone else picking the numbers. And the most important reason I had for refusing, it was that I didn't want to have ragtime music go on being deceived that way. These promoters, they could take their ads and put up their signs in front of the hall and do a great big promotion, make a real spectacle of what they were having, but there was to be no music to it. There wasn't to be any of that heart the music has got to it when it's speaking to you to let it have its own voice. None of that quality you got from the music back there in New Orleans when the music was home, being itself, free and easy and natural as the air it was being played into.

So I refused, and I went on out to Chicago. And I said to

Mrs. Rinehart, I said, 'Here, Mrs. Rinehart, here is $500; I think you take out what I owe you.' So she took $200 and called the union and explained what I had done, and she gave me a receipt and said she didn't want no trouble with me or anybody else. 'But,' she said, 'when you come back to Chicago, you will have to work here.' I said, 'Sure, but if somebody else offers me work, will you give me the same money they offer me?' At that time she didn't think that I would get any large sums of money, so she said, 'Oh, very well; you let me know.' So I said O.K. and I returned back to New York, to Jimmy Ryan's where I played happily for some months. And one fellow, a friend of mine, he came home and said, 'Sidney, there's a job waiting for you; there's a job to go to the Blue Note in Chicago. And if I'm not mistaken the job's worth $500.' So I said, 'O.K., I'll go and see him in the morning,' and I called Ruth up right away and I told her about it and I asked if she would pay me $500 a week; but she said, 'No, I'm sorry, that's too much for me.' And I said I was sorry too. Well, the other job, as it turned out, didn't want to pay much more than $300, and I didn't see how I could really go out to Chicago to either of them, and I think that's about all I'd like to say about that because Mrs. Rinehart wasn't happy and there's some matters still under discussion between us which had best be left that way just now.

So I went on working at Jimmy Ryan's; but I'd been corresponding with Charles Delaunay seeking for some work for a longer period, you know, probably six months or a year some place. And he arranged it, and that's how I came back to Paris in the fall of 1949. I had a look round those Jazz clubs in St-Germain-des-Prés, and in the end I settled with Claude Luter's band; and I settled in Paris, too, for that's been my home since that time.

In October of that year I was recording with Claude, and we made a record which had a great success—*Les Oignons*. Like I said at the beginning, I felt when I settled in France that it was nearer to Africa, and I suppose too that being there is nearer to all my family and brings back something that I remember of Omar and my father too. So I started to record some lovely Creole tunes that I remembered from when I was young and some I made myself out of the same remembering. And the same month—I think it was October—there was a lot of American musicianers in Paris at that time and I got them together and we had ourselves a time recording a few numbers; there was Bill Coleman on trumpet (he lives in Paris too), and Kenny Clarke on drums; we made around half a dozen numbers, among them *Mon Homme* and *Klook's Blues*—'Klook' being what Kenny Clarke was often called.

Well, in November I had the chance to go to England. It was thirty years since I'd been there, and I was still remembering that head on the coins like I talked about. So I wanted to go over there because I'd heard, too, that there was a real interest in the music that I'd always played. So I went on over to London, but when I got there I found that we'd run right away into union trouble. At that time the American musicianers' union didn't want to let any British bands go over there and play, figuring there wasn't too much work for their own members without people coming from across the ocean. And the result was that the British union, it just said the same, that they wouldn't have no American musicianers playing around the place. Of course, I suppose they all had their members' best interests at heart, but when you think of it the music's bigger than that—you can't really just talk about unions and who's to play here and who's to play there.

But like I said, at this time they were all standing on their dignity when I came to London. The idea was that I should play with Humphrey Lyttelton's band. Well, I arrived all right and the arguments had got themselves from the union to the British Ministry of Labour, which gives these permits like. Well, I went to London, to the Jazz Club where Humphrey was playing, the first night I was there, and I was certainly happy with what I heard; those boys were blowing and they were really making music. Besides Humphrey I want to say that I really admired Wally Fawkes playing on clarinet —he's a real musicianer and I'll remember his playing a long time. But they were planning this concert at the Winter

Garden Theatre for Sunday night, and still the union and the Ministry were stalling. Well, I was having a fine time, but no music. So in the end the Ministry came out with a flat No, so there we were. But they asked me to go along to the concert on the Sunday night anyway, and I sat in one of the boxes at this theatre where they were going to do this 'Humphrey Lyttelton Show'. And I was listening quietly, enjoying myself like, when the compère—that was Rex Harris I think—suddenly said that I was there and they turned the lights on me. Well, it was one of the loveliest things you could imagine; all those people, filling that theatre, they shouted and they stamped and they cried 'Play for us, Sidney'; so I got down out of the box and I went up there on the stage as a guest and I played with Humphrey and his band. And we played *Summertime*, *Careless Love*, the *Weary Blues* and a lot of numbers, and it was a wonderful evening and that was one of the most sincere audiences I have ever played to.

Well, anyway, the union didn't mind me making some records while I was in London and I recorded six numbers with Humphrey before I went on back to Paris.

I think I'd made up my mind then that Europe was to be my home for what time there was left to me; I wanted to play my music as long as I could, and that's what I'll always want to do. But I went back to America again in 1950 to play at Jimmy Ryan's in New York, and in Chicago too. But I came back to Paris, and it was around this time that my brother Leonard died. I said how he used to come up from New Orleans to see me, and after I came to Europe we kept corresponding together. I wanted him to come to Europe, and I was always on to him about it but he never made up his mind. Then, about two or three o'clock one morning, I received a telephone call to tell me my brother Leonard, he was dead; and that was the end of him, poor fellow.

Leonard, he never made up his mind. He never just wanted to play trombone, and it was a sort of hobby for him, you see. But in later years we had a feeling that he really wanted to leave the dentistry alone and just play Jazz music. That was his intention, but, I guess, time caught up with him, and he had to leave us. He died right there in the hospital in New Orleans. He was around twelve or fifteen years older than me, and he was the member of my family who had always been nearest to me—right from the days when he started that Silver Bells Band—and whom I loved best.

Well, I went on back to France, and in 1950 I was touring with Claude Luter and went on down to Algiers; and it was here that I met my wife. We decided to get married, and that was in 1951 at Antibes. You see, M. Badel down there, he was remembering how in New Orleans every year we have a Mardi Gras and we have this Zulu parade. And it is the ambition of every big guy in New Orleans to be the King of the Zulus. So Louis Armstrong, he happened to be the King a year or two before, and it was in *Time* magazine and everywhere. So M. Badel, he asked me, 'Would you like to be King for a day?' So I accepted it. I phoned my fiancée up and we accepted it. And it was one of the biggest things that's ever been seen since Aly Khan's marriage. We went right around the town, and there were bands on carts going around just like I remember from way back when I used to be in the second line. It was really something, and I am certainly grateful to all these people and to all those musicianers who made it into a day I won't ever forget.

Well, it wasn't long after this that I was writing to Billy Shaw, and he said he'd like to line up a few dates for me in America if I'd come. So I said, 'Certainly, I'll come.' So he went ahead and one of them was in Chicago, but that's a long story, like I said, which I don't think I ought to tell about here because the end of it hasn't come around yet.

So with all this I went on back to Paris, and played with Claude Luter again. And then two very old friends of mine came to Paris, and we were able to make some records together —Lil Hardin, who'd been Louis's wife way back, and Zutty Singleton who'd been with me on so many recording dates of the last thirty years and is still beating it out as good as they come.

I was back at the Vieux Colombier when there was a gentleman who came to me and he asked me, 'I have a

197

proposition to make. I'm working,' he said, 'on a story for television, for ballet, for this young lady'—and he introduced me to her. And I said, 'I'd like to see the story.' He showed me the story, and I put the music to it as best I felt about it; I always had a desire to do something like that, you know. So when I went to America, my old friend James Tolliver arranged it for me. I came back and everything was fine. Everybody liked it very much. But the young lady that was supposed to dance this ballet, she went to Vienna and she just gave up dancing entirely, and I thought that was the end of the ballet. But that young André Coffrant who wrote the story, he got in touch with some other people, and they wanted to make a film of it. So it was a discussion with this young director and producer. I think that one of them wanted it in colour and the other wanted it in black and white, I don't know: anyway, nothing happened to that. Time passed and it was some years before we really got the ballet going again. We recorded the music in 1953, but it wasn't finally produced until 1955 in Brussels. Then we brought it to Paris, where it was played twice. M. Commann, he conducted the orchestra, and the dancers were Pierre Lacotte, Arthur Bell, Claire Sombert, Irène Bamziger and Guy Laine. The title of the ballet is *The Night is a Witch*, and it is about a fellow that walks in his sleep, and his parents, they are frightened because when he walks in his sleep he goes up on the roof and walks along the beams. And they are awfully frightened about it, you know, and the father makes up his mind that he is going to try and stop him if possible. So the father, the mother and the sweetheart, they all wait up for him; they see him going upstairs and they wait for him. And when he comes up to the roof the father tries to speak to him; and he is throwing darts, you know, at one of these dart boards, and he finally hits his father purposely with the dart and kills him. And then he kills his mother; she tries to be with him like she was when he was a child by making tricks with a string on her hands—you know, cat's cradle—so he takes the string and he strangles her with it, and he kills his fiancée too. And every time he kills somebody a spirit, which is his servant, a Negro boy that dances, is the one that makes him do these things in his sleep. And he thinks this servant is really his servant, but it is this servant who is making him do all that—because finally when he has no one else to kill he tries to do the tricks and he sees that he cannot do them any more. So the coloured boy does everything for him and he walks into space to do away with himself.

So this ballet was done in Brussels and in Paris, and it was recorded. I hope that it will be done in London one day, too.

I've told how I was on the stage in several shows more than thirty years ago, and I guess that I've always had some pleasure from that. Anyway, in 1955, right after the ballet had finally made its début, I made two films in Paris. One was called *Série Noire*, and I played a bandleader up in Montmartre, and that great actor Eric von Stroheim was in it. The other was called just *Blues* and it featured Viviane Romance. Both were what you'd call, I suppose, 'thrillers'. I suppose they weren't the best films ever made, but in both of them I got to play some music the way I like, and I don't care how the hell it comes about—that's what I'm there for and that's what I want to do.

Well, the story of the ballet carried me on a bit. I'd been playing with Claude Luter, but in September 1951 I played for for the first time with a band got together by André Rewéliotty, which was then an amateur outfit. But shortly after that they became professionals, and I've played with them since that time right up till now. Well, I don't know what to say about these last few years. I've been playing the way I've always played. I had a recording date with two old friends, Lil Armstrong and Zutty Singleton, in Paris in 1952, I went back to America for a while in 1953, and that fall I played for the very first time in San Francisco in what they called a Dixieland Jubilee with Bob Scobey. Then I was playing at Storyville in Boston in 1953 when I was taken seriously ill, and the doctor, he said I must be operated on; so I said, if I'm going to have that, I'd rather have it in France. And I went right back and had this operation. I suppose I'm not getting any younger, but I got over that all right all the same. There's only about three things I'd like to mention before I close this story. First, I had a recording date with Joe Jones in Paris in the fall of 1954. And Roy Eldridge was in Paris, too, and we played together. He plays a lovely trumpet, and I know he's changed around and thought about the way the music's going; the fact remains that when he plays in the real way the music wants to be played, he is certainly a musicianer that I'm glad to play with.

Then, the same fall my millionth record was coming up, and Bruno Coquatrix, who owns the Olympia Theatre in Paris, fell in with an idea I had that I should give a concert for free just to celebrate that million. So I played at the Olympia, where I'd played a lot before and since—and I don't know whether I'm glad or sorry that there were terrible scenes outside. The people there were so anxious to get in that the police had to be called and there were scuffles and arrests and everything. I'm sorry that these people who love the music should have got into trouble, but . . . hell, I'll play for them whenever they want me. I'm getting on now, but, like I've said, I've lived for the music; I won't play when it's wrong, but I'll play any place, anywhere, when it's right. It's the music and it's the people that's made what I've got to say in this world worth while. And as long as I'm around and as long as I can get that instrument up to my mouth that's what I want to do.

16. It's the Music and It's the People

I wouldn't tell all this in a story about the music, except that all I been telling, it's part of the music. That man there in the grocery store, the Mexican, the jail—they're all in the music. Whatever kind of thing it was, whenever it happened, the music put it together. That boy having to play for those people to dance there in his own house; that man wanting to scare me down by the railroad tracks, getting a pleasure out of wanting to scare me; and when I was in jail, playing the blues, really finding out about the blues—it was always the music that explained things. What it is that takes you out of being just a kid and thinking it's all adventure, and you find there's a lesson underneath all that adventure—that lesson, it's the music. You come into life alone and you go out of it alone, and you're going to be alone a lot of time when you're on this earth—and what tells it all, it's the music. You tell it to the music and the music tells it to you. And then you know about it. You know what it was happened to you.

I guess all of us in some way or another learn that way when we're young. The only difference is most people don't have something they're travelling along with, that's just going on. They just stop being a kid; that's all they know. They never know why. They just know something's happened.

But with something like the music though, you can be stupid or wise or a kid, or anything at all, but you've always *got* it. And as long as you've got it, you haven't got any time, so to speak. Life isn't just a question of time; it's a way you have of talking back and forth to the music.

You tell it to the music, and the music tells it to you. That's the life there is to a musicianer. I guess I've known about all of them. Some of them was good, and some of them was real good, and some of them was just nothing. But if they was real good, that's what their life was; it was a way of telling, a way of remembering something that has to be remembered.

It was Omar started the song. Or maybe he didn't start it exactly. There was somebody singing and playing the drums and the horns behind Omar, and there was somebody behind that. But it was Omar began the melody of it, the new thing. Behind Omar there was the rhythm and after Omar there was the melody. He started the song and all the good musicianers have been singing that song ever since, changing it some, adding parts, finding the way it has to go. But if you're a musicianer, if you're any good musicianer, it's Omar's song you're singing.

I met many a musicianer in many a place after I struck out from New Orleans, but it was always the same: if they was any good, it was Omar's song they were singing. It was the long song, and the good musicianers, they all heard it behind them. They all had an Omar, somebody like an Omar, somebody that was *their* Omar. It didn't need just recollecting somebody like that: it was the feeling of someone back there —hearing the song like it was coming up from somewhere.

A musicianer could be playing it in New Orleans, or Chicago, or New York; he could be playing it in London, in Tunis, in Paris, in Germany. I heard it played in all those places and a many more. But no matter where it's played, you gotta hear it starting way behind you. There's the drum beating from Congo Square and there's the song starting in a field just over the trees. The good musicianer, he's playing *with* it, and he's playing *after* it. He's finishing something. No matter what he's playing, it's the long song that started back there in the South.

It's the remembering song. There's so much to remember.

There's so much wanting, and there's so much sorrow, and there's so much waiting for the sorrow to end. My people, all they want is a place where they can be people, a place where they can stand up and be part of that place, just being natural to the place without worrying how someone may be coming along to take that place away from them.

There's a pride in it, too. The man singing it, the man playing it, he makes a place. For as long as the song is being played, *that's* the place he's been looking for. And when the piece is all played and he's back, it may be he's feeling good; maybe he's making good money and getting good treatment and he's feeling good—or maybe he starts missing the song. Maybe he starts wanting the place he found while he was playing the song. Or maybe it just troubles back at him. The song, it takes a lot out of a man, and when it's over it can trouble him. Because there's misery in the song too. He can remember the trouble the song was making all that time. And a man, he can get mean when he's troubled.

I met many musicianers and there was none of them hadn't found himself some trouble sometime. Many a one, he just had this trouble stored up inside him, and it was bound to have him. Just like all those old musicianers in New Orleans—Buddy Bolden, Armand J. Piron, Manuel Perez, all those that ended up so bad. I met a many another and there was always that trouble waiting to go bad in them. Some of them, they were strong enough and the trouble didn't take them: they were stronger than the trouble. And some of them, they had the trouble too strong and it took them. But I don't care how strong they were, they all of them had a piece of this trouble in them.

There was all this feuding between musicianers, and there was a whole lot of meanness at times. There was all kinds of bad things. Bessie Smith, she was the best blues singer there was, but that trouble was inside her and it wouldn't let her rest.

But what I mean is that when a musicianer made a bad end, it was never a surprise. Sometimes you got the feeling that a musicianer was *looking* for a bad end like it was something he had to have. So many of them had something inside them and it wouldn't let them rest. It was like there was something in that song deeper than a man could bear, something he could hear calling from the bottom of his dreams so that he'd wake up all in a terrible hurry to get up and go there, but then not knowing where to go. It was that stirring, all that night sound there was at the bottom of the song all that long way back making itself heard.

People come up to me and they say, 'What's Negro music? What is it really being?' I have to tell them there's no straight answer to that. If I could give them a straight answer, just in one sentence like, I wouldn't have to say all this I'm saying. You can't say that just out straight. There's no answer to that question, not just direct. You could come up to me and say, 'What's an American? What's a Frenchman?' How do you answer a thing like that?

But it's coming to an understanding; people are learning it. And when you get so you really hear it, when you can listen to the music being itself—then you don't have to ask that question. The music gives you its own understanding of itself.

But first, you have to like it; you have to be wanting to hear it. I read many a thing written by this critic and that critic, but it all comes to that one thing: if you're interested to hear the music, if it's a pleasure to you, then you can understand it; but if you're only writing to be a critic, to be saying what's a fashionable thing to say, then there's nothing to it.

I talked before about meeting Ernest Ansermet in London. Well, when we were in Paris in 1926 he was there: I ran into him in the street and he reminded me of the first review he'd written back in 1919, and how he had foreseen that the world would swing along this highway. And there it was: it had all come about in seven years. There's a man, you see, a classic musicianer, but his feeling for music could show him what it was going to mean to people. He had felt that right off. And I know what that means, because I can remember back in New

Orleans when people who first heard our music just didn't know what to think. They'd never heard anything like it in their lives; they didn't even know how to dance to it. And in New York later, it was the same thing: people didn't know how to listen to it, they didn't know how to sing to it, they didn't know how to dance to it. But they learned the music, it made itself important enough to them; it made them want to learn.

But that doesn't really say what Negro music is. That's just to illustrate that it can be understood and it can be misunderstood. It's a way of feeling. It's a way of listening too, and that complicates it because there's so much difference that can be listened to. For instance, there's people come up to me, they still think Jazz, it's that whorehouse music. They say, 'What about barrel house? Where's all that vaudeville I hear about being part of the music? What's this about redlight music?' Well, all I can answer is it's like I've already said about Freddie Keppard; it was just that pleasure music. A man, he's got all kinds of things in him and the music wants to talk to all of him. The music is everything that it wants to say to a man. Some of it came up from jokes and some of it came up from sorrow, but all of it has a man's feelings in it. How that came about, that's my real story. The music has come a long way, and it's time for it now to come out from around a corner; it's got to come up and cross the street. If I could believe it would do that, I wouldn't worry. For me, all there is to life aside from the music, it's not the things you'd expect people to say. All I want is to eat, sleep, and don't worry. Don't *worry*, that's the big thing. And that's what's holding back the music from this step it has to take. It's still worried. It's still not sure of itself. It's still in the shade, and it's time it just stood up and crossed the street to the sunny side.

But that's not yet. It won't happen yet. It has a way to go, and I'm not ready to say what that way is. All I say is, it's my people. The worry has to be gotten out of them and *then* it will be gotten out of the music.

I suppose most people would think right away of that show

Porgy and Bess. But what do you call a thing like that—
symphonic Jazz? That's not real Jazz. There's some feeling
there, it's a nice show; but that's about the closest it comes.
There's one or two nice pieces to it: *Summertime*, that's one,
that's nice, in that you get just about the closest to the mood
of Negro music. But listen to it, listen to it real careful—
you get a feeling of *St. Louis Blues* there. It's a borrowed
feeling.

Gershwin, I've got a lot of respect for him. He's a hell of a
fine writer. All his music you can listen to, there's a whole lot
of beauty to it and a whole lot of feeling. It really tells a story
inside itself. But it still isn't Negro music. It still isn't saying
what the black man, he'd say.

There's one thing about Negro music that hasn't really been
put on yet, and that's how hard it can be to get Negro music
performed, the trouble there is to getting it staged and
listened to. Let me tell you about a show once in New York.
Just for an example. This show was called *Shuffle Along*,
and it was put on by coloured people and it was acted by
coloured people. The music was written by Noble Sissle and
Eubie Blake. That show had troubles you wouldn't have in
the regular kind of production. The writers had to be awful
clever about what they wrote because everything had to be
done on what you call a limited budget. There were costumes
they had a hell of a time finding and sets they had to go out
after, God knows where, and there were even things for props
that couldn't be come by. Noble and Eubie had to write
their songs to what they *could*, to the kind of budget they had
for getting them produced. They weren't free to do it how they
wanted: they just had to work it whatever way it was possible.
But they made real numbers of them. It was really music: you
couldn't help it being that. Some of those numbers are still
famous: *I'm Wild About Harry* was one of them; and *Dear Old
Southland*, that was from that show too. But if you could have
seen the trouble they had to go to just to see that the songs
could be produced in any real manner of a show—I don't mean
just the worry of when you're having a show and hoping it
will go over, but just the trouble of getting it together with

just about no budget at all—all that changing that had to be done to save money, all the good things that had to be left out, all the ideas that couldn't be made to work because of expense. If you could have seen some of that, you'd have an understanding of what it is with Negro music, how hard it is to get it really performed.

And that show, it was a really beautiful thing. They could bring it out again right now and you'd still find it was a hell of a fine show. But every Negro show had this same trouble. There was never enough to do it with. It's like having a hundred verses you want to write down and all you can find is one scrap of paper: there's so much of it that gets lost.

I remember another time when I was in England back in the early 'twenties. I'd written a play and I had the music to it, a lot of singing and melody. It had a story too, but nothing complicated, nothing so involved that you couldn't see it for what it was, just a show with music. I called it *Voice of the Slaves*. I've got it with me still. Well, back there in England I took it to this director and he told me, 'It's very beautiful. I'd like to put it on but I don't think the public is interested· enough in coloured people to put out the kind of money it needs for getting produced. That's what he said. I'm not trying to say the white-man-this and conditions-that and change-how: I'm just telling you the story, how the fact of it was, and I'm not saying what interpreting you can find to put around the fact, because I don't know myself for sure. I do know for sure, though, that music—a melody, a story—if it's to be at home on the stage it has to be simple enough to tell you about itself. After that there's no importance in who's written it so long as it's good. I'm trying to say there's so much Negro music *waiting*. It hasn't been heard yet. *Conditions* haven't been right.

Well, conditions can happen to anyone, just like they happened to me. Conditions, they've been happening to many a fine musicianer. And it's a hell of a thing when you got a piece that has a place, a piece that should be heard, but you can't catch up with the place for it. I can tell you about some pieces of music I had once, just for example.

Once you know, I composed a few numbers. Some of them maybe you've heard. There was *Pleasure Mad, Ghost of the Blues, Do That Thing*, and there were several others too. And there was one which was no Jazz number—it was *The Twenty-third Psalm*; I'd composed music for it. So I went to get them published, and all those numbers was placed with the wrong publishers. Conditions had them to be placed wrong. You take a number like *Ghost of the Blues*. Clarence Williams, he published that. The way it was at that time, anything that had 'blues' in the title you published with Clarence Williams. That's how it was, and *Ghost of the Blues* just never got heard. Where it should have been published was someone like Irving Berlin Publishers or Hahns.

Because with music publishing it's all one thing. A publisher gets a number he can push, and the public want to hear it because he's pushing it. I don't care what you say, if a publisher hasn't got in his house what's necessary to back up the piece—if he hasn't got connexions with a sincere singer that's the type for that song, someone really good—then the piece should be sent over to some other house, someone who's got the right connexion with the right person. That way a musicianer will know that the correct thing is being done by his number. That's what I mean by placing them right.

And that's why I didn't let but a few of these pieces get out. The way they was being handled, they wasn't expressing the right thing. Some of them was the best numbers I composed. *The Twenty-third Psalm*, I've got it with me yet: I never have heard it played even. I was told at the time I was trying to place it that Warrock Publishers had some connexion with Fred Warren, and I felt that they would be the right house for placing it. Marion Anderson, Paul Robeson, Fred—anyone of them could do it. Fred could do it beautiful, but still it wouldn't have the right feeling because it might be expressing something that was coloured. He's got the number, but he's never played it. Perhaps to him the number interpreted a feeling that was Negro music, and he didn't want that feeling. That could be the reason he hasn't played it.

And that's the way it is. You wait and you wait . . . there are so many fine numbers that's being kept waiting. And then there's a thing happens inside the musicianer too. He's like any other man; he's all enthused about something, he gets his hopes raised, then he gets tired of all this waiting. 'What's the good of a lot of music just kept in my head?' he tells himself. So he gets out and he gets them placed just wherever he can. And right there *conditions* begin to appear; that piece, there's nothing happens to it, it don't get heard. The conditions, they have to be right, but mostly they're not happening right for Negro music.

That's just an instance of what happened to me; what I know about. But there's so much beautiful music waiting. There's some of Will Marion Cook's pieces. There's *Rain Song*: that piece, it's really something; a feeling it has, it would go right through you, it just lifts its heart. Will was married to Abbie Mitchell and her voice was beautiful to hear. When she sang the *Rain Song*, it was something to take the heart right out of you. And there was another piece Will wrote, *My Lady's Lips*—I wish you could hear it.

There's some of Scott Joplin's numbers, too—they're still waiting. And they're just as beautiful. Scott had a show once, *Treemonisha* it was called. The numbers he had in that were really fine. You could look a long time to find something as fine as that.

And it's all waiting. All these numbers and many more. They're just listened to mostly by themselves, the way you wind up one of those little music boxes once in a while when you step into your own room. If they could be heard, if they could get out of that room, they could really add a whole lot of understanding to what Negro music really is.

But still, you know, there wouldn't ever be any straight answer. Like I said before, you could ask me, 'What's classical music?' I couldn't answer that. It's not a thing that could be answered straight out. You have to tell it the long way. You have to tell about the people who make it, what they have inside them, what they're doing, what they're waiting for. Then you can begin to have an understanding.

Treat It Gentle

This story of what's happening to Jazz, there's a whole lot
to it, a whole lot of changes; but one thing, it's still the same
that it was when the musicianers first began to come North.
Right away then, this *presenting* began to take over the
music. The men who are doing the business part of the
presenting, they won't let the music be. They give the public
what *they* want them to hear. They don't care about the music;
just so it's something different, something a little bit more
novelty like from what's being played the next dial down—
just so long as they can get that, they don't care about
nothing else.

Some band leader gets himself a reputation for being a
personality, and that's it. From there on out it has to be his
personality first and *then* the music. He's busy doing every
kind of thing *but* the music. 'Here's another saxophone,' he
says. Maybe you don't need that extra sax, it doesn't belong,
but that's no matter to him. 'Here, here's another bass,' he
says. Well there's no reason for it, but there it is. And before
you know it, you've got eighteen pieces, you've got a whole
lot of noise, you've got a whole lot of something that hasn't
got any spirit. All you've got, it's something like running
a ball through a pinball machine and watching all the
lights come on. You've got a hell of a lot of lights showing
themselves off.

These personality boys don't ask the musicianer what *he*
thinks is best: they arrange it for him. 'Here,' they say, 'you
play it *this* way.' They've got themselves a great big band.
They've got themselves a kind of machine. And so to make
sense out of whatever it is the machine is doing, they get a
whole lot of composers and arrangers to write it all down,
ju t the way the machine is supposed to run—every note
of it.

And all that freedom, all that feeling a man's got when he's
playing next to you—they take that away. They give you *his*
part to play and they give him your part, and that's how
it's to be: they've got a trumpet taking the clarinet part and a
clarinet taking the trombone part, and every man doing
any damn' thing but the one thing he should be doing if he's

really to find the music. All that closeness of speaking to another instrument, to another man—it's gone. All that waiting to get in for your own chance, freeing yourself, all that holding back, not rushing the next man, not bucking him, holding back for the right time to come out, all that pride and spirit—it's gone. They take away your dignity and they take away your heart and after they've done that there's nothing left.

You know, a lot of musicianers, they drop their playing. 'Well, I'm going to become a clerk,' they say, 'or I'll drive a taxi, or I'll shine shoes.' And they try that for a while. And then pretty soon they're back at their instrument. Lots of times that's a thing I don't understand. Why do they come back? It's not because they love their music, or because they cared too much and dropped the music because they didn't want to see what was happening to it. It's not like going back home when you can't stay away any longer. Because they keep coming back to play *any* old way. Like it doesn't matter at all *what* they're playing so long as they *are* playing. Some of them get their jobs playing again and they get paid less, maybe, than what they were making doing something else. But still they come back and there they are playing without any kind of ideas or soul or respect for the music. They come back and they fit themselves into any kind of a combination that comes along, playing any which way they're told to play.

And that's what I can't understand. I can guess maybe it's how the life is, how they like being in front of people, wearing dress clothes, making the night-time over into day-time, being known as a musicianer. Maybe it's some of all those things. But you put that all together and it's still no music.

And what they're playing . . . well, it *was* New Orleans. A long time ago it had a memory of being that. But what it is today, it's nothing. It's no music. *New Orleans*, well it just stopped back there in New Orleans. These new musicianers, they lack the memory of it. They don't know where the music comes from and they don't know where it's going. So how do you expect someone to know that that foundation, that *real* foundation, is capable of saying sincere things? And if the musicianers don't know that, how can you expect the audience to know it? You say *Jazz*, you say *ragtime* and right away they're thinking, '*Royal Garden Blues*, give me that, that's it.' Or *Maple Leaf Rag*; they'll name that. It's like they believed the music stopped way back there. 'Give me some ⁚⁚ that old-time stuff,' they say. You could take some new piece and play it in that rhythm, you could make a real rendition, but that's not what they'll listen to. *Give me some of that old stuff*: that's all they want. And then they want to know about barrel house and honky-tonks. That's what's supposed to be New Orleans. That's where it's supposed to have been born.

But those things don't exist today. They're gone. But the people won't let them *be* gone. That's what they're wanting, and so a musicianer who knows his music, a man who's had his training, he's always under this necessity to give a spectacle. He gets up there to play, but they won't let him be a music-ianer: they haven't got him up there to be a musicianer, he's an *attraction*. Look at him, they say, he composed *Maple Leaf Rag*, or *Royal Garden*, or any damn' number of that time. Look at him, they say, he's still around: why he can *still* play!

But ragtime, that's no history thing. It's not dead. Ragtime, it's the musicianers. *Rag it up*, we used to say. You take any piece, you make it so people can dance to it, pat their feet, move around. You make it so they can't help themselves from doing that. You make it so they just can't sit still. And that's all there is to it. It's the rhythm there. The rhythm *is* ragtime. That's still there to be done. You could do that to all kinds of numbers still being played, still being composed today.

That rhythm goes all the way back. In the spirituals the people clapped their hands—that was their rhythm. In the blues it was further down; they didn't need the clapping, but they remembered it, it was still there. And both of them, the spirituals and the blues, they was a prayer. One was praying

212

to God and the other was praying to what's human. It's like one was saying, 'Oh, God, let me go,' and the other was saying, 'Oh, Mister, let me be.' And they were both the same thing in a way; they were both my people's way of praying to be themselves, praying to be let alone so they could be human. The spirituals, they had a kind of trance to them, a kind of forgetting. It was like a man closing his eyes so he can see a light inside him. That light, it's far off and you've got to wait to see it. But it's there. It's waiting. The spirituals, they're a way of seeing that light. It's a far off music; it's a going away, but it's a going away that takes you with it. And the blues, they've got that sob inside, that awful lonesome feeling. It's got so much remembering inside it, so many bad things to remember, so many losses.

But both of them, they're based on rhythm. They're both of them leading up to a rhythm. And they're both coming up from a rhythm. It's like they're going and coming at the same time. Going, coming—inside the music that's the same thing, it's the rhythm. And that rhythm and that feeling you put around it, always keeping the melody, that's all there is to it. That's nothing that's dead. That's nothing that could die: 1910, 1923, 1950—there's no difference in that. And to give you what this Jazz is—all you need is a few men who can hear what the man next him is doing at the same time that you know your instrument and how you can say on it what you gotta say to keep the next man going with you, leading one another on to the place the music has to go.

Back in New Orleans when I was young, back there before all this personality stuff, all this radio and contracts and 'attraction'—the music, it was free. It was all different then. We were always having contests—those 'bucking contests'. There were always people out listening to us play. Wherever there was music, a whole lot of people would be there. And those people, they were just natural to the music. The music, it was all they needed. They weren't there to ask for 'attractions'.

And that left the music natural to be itself. It could have a good time; it was free to. And that spirit there was to it, that was a wonderful thing, there was a happiness in it. It was there to be enjoyed, a whole lot of spirit.

The musicianers in those good bands, they could really play; they'd come out of a bucking contest just as sweet as they went in. But what made that possible, in one way at least, it was the people. The people knew what they wanted to hear and the musicianers gave it to them. The musicianers could be sure the people would know what they were hearing. If the music was being played right, the people would know it, and if it was being played wrong, they'd know that too. And because the musicianers knew they were being *listened* to by people who cared for the music, that made it all different. They could want to play then; they could want to have those people cheering them.

In some ways it's like a play. The actors come out on the stage and there's an audience. That audience has a feeling for the play. They want to see it, they have an understanding for it. And those actors feel that; and they play their best; they *want* to give what they can. But you take those same actors and bring them out somewhere with no audience, or with some audience that just don't care. You have them act their play in front of some crowd of people who don't know why they've come. And there's just no performance then; the play it just dies down inside itself.

I saw a movie once about Chopin, and it showed a scene from when he was a young fellow in Poland. There's a lord of this castle who hears there's a good piano player in the town and this lord, he's giving a big dinner party, so nothing will do but Chopin has to come up and play for them while this party is eating. Chopin got there and he played the best he knew, all kinds of numbers. But all the time he's playing, the party at the table they're just chatting along, laughing, small-talking, admiring themselves, congratulating themselves for being who they are, paying no attention to the music. And all at once, Chopin just banged the keyboard and walked out of there. He had to get out of Poland to keep out of trouble then. The lord of this castle, he didn't like what Chopin had

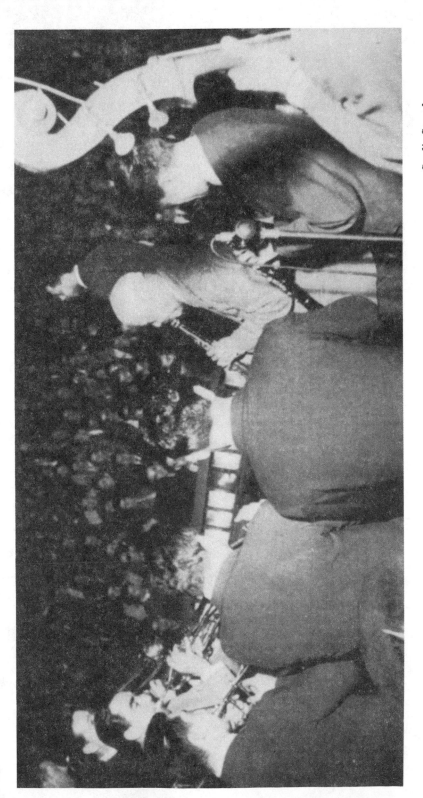

Sidney Bechet at a jam session, Paris, 1952. Claude Luter is immediately behind Sidney Bechet

Andre Nisak

The fingering Georges Baquet did not change

Andre Nisak

Late in life

done. But that's how a musicianer has to be if he cares anything at all for his music. The music, it's something you can only give to those who love it.

Maybe that's one reason why so many musicianers get mean in some ways. A man, he signs a contract and he goes to play somewheres; he wants to make music, but he gets up to play and nobody cares what he plays. That's how it is in some places. Well, pretty soon he starts playing to *insult* the audience. That's all he can do. But that's no music. The music, it's not meant for that; it's for giving. But there has to be someone ready to take it.

New Orleans, that was a place where the music was natural as the air. The people were ready for it like it was sun and rain. A musicianer, when he played in New Orleans, was home; and the music, when he played it, would go right to where he sent it. The people there were waiting for it, they were wanting it.

The bucking contests were one way the people had of coming toward the music, but it never stopped there. The next day there was bound to be some picnic out at Milneberg Lake. There was a big park there with all kinds of walks, a saloon, wharves, open spaces. And there'd be these different camps where the people would be and the musicianers would go there to play. In those days there wasn't anything you could do without music—holidays, funerals, pleasurements, it was all done to music, the music had all that to say.

At these camps there'd be a big square hall with a porch at one end and the sun would be beating on one side. We'd come to play there, but a musicianer, you know, he wouldn't care to be playing in the strong sun, so right off as soon as your band got together, you'd have a big bucking contest with whatever other band there was. And that was the real thing then: we'd play at them until finally we'd beat that other band right out into the sun. The way it was, they'd have to back out or stop playing because they weren't able to play against us.

Labour Day night in New Orleans, that was always a big celebration. The Labour Association had the biggest place at the fairgrounds and that would be their biggest night in the year. The fairground was there on the outskirts of town off

Esplanade Avenue, and they'd have the place all lit up and decorated, and they'd have the best bands they could find in all New Orleans. The people would come from way up the river for that celebration. They'd come for dance or they'd come for listen, but there wouldn't be anybody staying away.

And every year Manuel Perez, he'd be there with the Onward Band. Like I told you, the Onward was a brass band that usually just played for parade music, music for marches. But people would start to listen to the band and pretty soon some of them would go out in the middle of the grounds and start dancing, and then some more would join them, and before long everybody would be dancing. And you could look out past those people dancing and you'd see another band—the Eagle Band maybe. That would be a natural band for dancing; the Eagle, it was an orchestra really. And just beyond the Eagle there'd be another space with people dancing. And you'd look somewheres else and you'd see the same thing. Everywhere you looked there was bands playing and people dancing to them.

But the interesting thing is that Manuel, *he* was playing music for dancing. It's not easy to dance to a brass band, but Manuel had a way of playing different when he came to the fairgrounds. He'd take his brass and he'd really make it danceable. What he'd do is change the arrangement. He'd play it so it wasn't a matter of everybody taking his chorus; the important thing it would be the tempo and the way each player carried the tempo. He'd keep them together and he'd keep them playing with a real swing to it. He'd have twenty, twenty-five brass men playing like one together, no one taking his chorus like they would in regular ragtime, but all the phrases together, just like you've got a really well-trained chorus of people to speak a part for the stage and they're all talking together and stopping together so you don't miss a word. And when you'd hear that it would give you a feeling that would be making you want to dance. It would just take your feet and make them go like it was something inside you.

And all that music, whether it was Manuel Perez or some

other band or orchestra that was really good, it was a music those people could take home with them. Just remembering it they could start all over again dancing and singing. You could walk by a house and hear some of it and it would follow you all the way home. Or you'd leave some place like the fairground after you'd been listening and dancing; you'd leave and start to walk home, and you'd *still* have a feeling in you to make you want to bust out dancing again.

That music, it was like where you lived. It was like waking up in the morning and eating, it was that regular in your life. It was natural to the way you lived and the way you died. Like when the band, it started back from the cemetery; that band, it would change the music. It would start playing something like *Oh, Didn't He Ramble.* They'd play that and it was like saying good-bye for the dead man: that band it would go back all through the town seeing the places where that man had liked to be before he died. The music it was rambling for him one last time. It was seeing the world for him again.

And that's the way I want to remember the music. That's the way I'd like to have it remembered: the way it came back from the man's burying and spoke for him to the world, and spoke the world to him once more.

I've been telling you this story, and maybe you're asking, 'How's it going to end?' There's ways I could make a fiction to give you an ending. But that won't do. What I got to say has to be as natural as the music. There's no fiction to it. What I have to say, it's what the music has been saying to me and what I've been saying to it as far back as I can remember. The music makes a voice, and, no matter what happens, the man that cares to hear that voice, he *can* hear it. I don't mean there's any end to the things that make it hard for the people to hear the real voice the music has got in it. All I mean is the music is still there for any who want it.

Really, all I been saying, it comes down to something as simple as that, something that's just waiting for its own happiness. A way of speaking.

I did a lot of things in my life that I wanted to do and I am quite sure that there is nothing that I would be ashamed of.

If I had to live my life over again, I would do the same that I have done again because some things that people probably say was bad, probably seem bad to them, but in a time when something happens and you know that you have done wrong, you sort of take your own judgment and you try to get out of it the best way you can. Anyway, I am very happy now and I am living a life pretty easy. And I'll always play music as long as I possibly can. All them crotchets, I'll put them down with my clarinet or my saxophone and I'll play as long as I have breath. I think I did the best that I could with my life. I made everybody happy close to me. I had a lot of worries, but now I have decided I have figured that out because I figured the day would come when I'd have to leave here, which everybody does. Nobody lives for a lifetime. I'm not worried about the body. If I didn't do with it what they want, I have used it and it is finished and I am satisfied.

I'm an old man now; I can't keep hanging on. I'm even wanting to go; I'm waiting, longing to hear my peace. And all I've been waiting for is the music. All the beauty that there's ever been, it's moving inside that music. Omar's voice, that's there, and the girl's voice, and the voice the wind had in Africa, and the cries from Congo Square, and the fine shouting that came up from Free Day. The blues, and the spirituals, and the remembering, and the waiting, and the suffering, and the looking at the sky watching the dark come down—that's all inside the music.

And somehow when the music is played right it does an explaining of all those things. Me, I want to explain myself so bad. I want to have myself understood. And the music, it can do that. The music, it's my whole story.

There's all the music that's been played, and there's all the music that hasn't been heard yet. The music of Scott Joplin, things he wrote. So many a piece of Will Marion Cook's. So many men who've spent their lives just making melody and who haven't been heard yet.

I'd like to hear it all one more time. I'd like to sit in a box at some performance and see all I saw years ago and hear all I heard way back to the start. I want to sit there and you could

218

come in and find me in that box and I'd have a smile on my face. What I'd be feeling is 'the music, it has a home'. As long as I got a heart to be filled by it, the music has a place that's natural to it. I could sit there and listen, and I'd smile. And when I've got to go I could go that way. I could remember all the richness there is, and I could go smiling.

A Catalogue of the Recordings of
Sidney Bechet compiled by David Mylne

1. This catalogue contains every title known to have been recorded by Sidney Bechet in as accurate a chronogical order as possible. Accurate data concerning the recording sequence is unavailable for some taped sessions, especially concert recordings
2. All sessions are studio recordings unless otherwise mentioned.
3. The 'style' or band-name etc. for each session is taken from the original label.
4. The catalogue numbers given are those of the original issues by the companies responsible for the sessions.
5. 'Not issued' against a title means that it has never been released by any company: if the list states that a tune has not been issued by the 'parent' company this infers that it has subsequently been issued by another.
6. As many unissued titles have been included as are known to have been recorded, although it is, of course, impossible to have the full facts for concerts recorded on tape.
7. When different matrixes or 'takes' of a tune have been recorded, these are accordingly listed, but only when such alternative versions have been subsequently issued.

KEY TO LABEL ABBREVIATIONS

All companies are of American origin unless otherwise stated below.

Bb=Bluebird
Bld=Baldwin
BN=Blue Note
Br=Brunswick
BSt=Blue Star (France)
B & W=Black & White
Cir=Circle
Cmd=Commodore
Co=Columbia
CSB=Collection Sidney Bechet
  (France)
De=Decca
Disc=Disc
GNP=Gene Norman Presents

Gnt=Gennett
HRS=Hot Record Society
J Ltd=Jazz Limited
KJ=King Jazz
Mldsc=Melodisc (England)
Mnr=Manor (England)
OK=Okeh
Pe=Perfect
Story=Storyville
Sw=Swing (France)
'V'-d='V'-disc
Vic=Victor
Vo=Vocalion
Vog=Vogue (France)

V of A=Voice of America   Vrs=Varsity
Vri=Variety   WS=Wax Shop

—.6.23 **CLARENCE WILLIAMS' BLUE FIVE.**
   Wild Cat Blues   OK 4925
   Kansas City Man Blues   —

(?) mid. 23 **SARA MARTIN AND CLARENCE WILLIAMS' BLUE FIVE.**
   Blind Man Blues   OK 8090
   Atlanta Blues   —

(?) mid. 23 **MAMIE SMITH.**
   Lady Luck Blues   OK 4926
   Kansas City Man Blues   —
   EVA TAYLOR AND CLARENCE WILLIAMS WITH CLARENCE WILLIAMS' BLUE FIVE.
   Oh! Daddy Blues   OK 4927
   I've Got the Yes! We Have No Banana Blues   —

—.10.23 **EVA TAYLOR, acc. by Clarence Williams' Trio.**
   Irresistible Blues   OK 8129
   Jazzin' Babies Blues   —

—.10.23 **CLARENCE WILLIAMS' BLUE FIVE.**
   T'ain't Nobody's Bizness if I Do   OK 4966
   New Orleans Hop Scop Blues   OK 4975
   Oh! Daddy Blues   OK 4993

—.10.23 **ROSETTA CRAWFORD, acc. by King Bechet Trio.**
   Down on the Levee   OK 8096
   Lonesome Woman Blues   —

11.10.23 **SARA MARTIN AND CLARENCE WILLIAMS' HARMONIZING FOUR.**
   Graveyard Dream Blues   OK 8099
   A Green Gal Can't Catch On (Blues)   —

—.10.23 **MARGARET JOHNSON, acc. by Clarence Williams' Blue Five.**
   If I Let You Get Away With it Once You'll Do it All of the Time   OK 8107
   E Flat Blues   —

—.10.23 **EVA TAYLOR—LAWRENCE LOMAX, acc. by Orchestra.**
   Old Fashioned Love   OK 8114
   Open Your Heart   —

—.11.23 **CLARENCE WILLIAMS' BLUE FIVE.**
   Shreveport Blues   OK 40006
   Old Fashioned Love   OK 4993
   House Rent Blues (The Stomp)   OK 8171
   Mean Blues   OK 40006

—.1.24 **VIRGINIA LISTON, guitar acc. by Sidney Bechet.**
   Jailhouse Blues   OK 8122
   MAUREEN ENGLIN.
   Foolin' Me   Pe 12135

17.10.24   **CLARENCE WILLIAMS' BLUE FIVE.**
      Texas Moaner Blues   OK 8171

           VIRGINIA LISTON, acc. by Clarence Williams' Blue Five.
      Early in the Morning   OK 8187
      You've Got the Right Key but the Wrong Keyhole   OK 8173

28.11.24   **SIPPIE WALLACE, acc. by Clarence Williams' Blue Five.**
      Baby, I Can't Use You No More   OK 8212
      Trouble Everywhere I Roam   —

—.12.24   **SIPPIE WALLACE, acc. by Clarence Williams' Trio.**
      I'm So Glad I'm Brownskin   OK 8197
      Off and On Blues   —

6.12.24   **JOSEPHINE BEATTY, acc. by the Red Onion Jazz Babies.**
      Nobody Knows the Way I Feel This Morning   Gnt 3044, 5626
      Early Every Morning   —

           RED ONION JAZZ BABIES.
      Cake Walkin' Babies Back Home   Gnt 5627

17.12.24   **EVA TAYLOR, acc. by Clarence Williams' Blue Five.**
      Mandy, Make Up Your Mind   OK 40260
      I'm a Little Blackbird   —

8.1.25   **MARGARET JOHNSON, acc. by Clarence Williams' Blue Five.**
      Who'll Chop Your Suey (When I'm Gone)   OK 8193
      Done Made a Fool Out of Me   —

           CLARENCE WILLIAMS' BLUE FIVE.
      Cake Walkin' Babies Back Home   OK 40321

           EVA TAYLOR, acc. by Clarence Williams' Blue Five.
      Pickin' on Your Baby   OK 40330
5.4.25   *Cast Away*   OK 40330

           CLARENCE WILLIAMS' BLUE FIVE.
      Papa De Da Da   OK 8215

15.7.25   **GET HAPPY BAND.**
      Junk Bucket Blues   Co 14091
      Harlem's Araby   —

8.10.25   **CLARENCE WILLIAMS' BLUE FIVE.**
      Coal Cart Blues   OK 8245
      Santa Claus Blues   —

24.2.31   **NOBLE SISSLE AND HIS ORCHESTRA.**
      Got the Bench, Got the Park   Br 6073
      In a Café on the Road to Calais   Not issued
      Loveless Love   Br 6073

24.4.31   *Basement Blues*   Br 6129
      What Ja Do To Me   Br 6111
      Roll On Mississippi, Roll On   —

15.9.32	THE NEW ORLEANS FEETWARMERS.	
	Sweetie Dear	*Vic 23360*
	I Want You Tonite	*Vic 23358*
	I've Found a New Baby	*Vic 24150*
	Lay Your Racket	*Vic 23358*
	Maple Leaf Rag	*Vic 23360*
	Shag	*Vic 24150*

15.8.34	NOBLE SISSLE AND HIS INTERNATIONAL ORCHESTRA.	
	Under the Creole Moon	*De 153*
	The Old Ark's a-Moverin'	*De 154*
	Loveless Love	
	Polka Dot Rag	*De 153*

11.3.36	NOBLE SISSLE AND HIS ORCHESTRA.	
	That's What Love Did to Me	*De 778*
	You Can't Live in Harlem	—
	I Wonder Who Made Rhythm	*De 766*
	T'ain't a Fit Night Out	—
	I Take You	*De 847*
	Rhythm of the Broadway Moon	—
14.4.37	*Bandana Days*	*Vri 552*
	I'm Just Wild About Harry	—
	Dear Old Southland	*Not issued*
	St. Louis Blues	—

16.4.37	NOBLE SISSLE'S SWINGSTERS.	
	Okey Doke	*Vri 648*
	Characteristic Blues	

10.2.38	SIDNEY BECHET WITH NOBLE SISSLE'S SWINGSTERS.	
	Viper Mad	*De 3521, 7429*
	Blackstick	*De 2129, 3865*
	When the Sun Sets Down South (retitled *Southern Sunset*)	*De 2129, 3865*
	Sweet Patootie	*De 7429*

26.5.38	TRIXIE SMITH.	
	Lady be Good	*Not issued*
	Freight Train Blues	*De 7489*
	Trixie's Blues	*De 7469*
	My Daddy Rocks Me, Pt. 1	—
	My Daddy Rocks Me, Pt. 2	*De 7617*
	He May be Your Man	*De 7528*
	Jack I'm Mellow	—
	I am a Woman	*Not issued*

	COOT GRANT AND KID 'SOX' WILSON.	
	Uncle Joe	*De 7500*
	Toot It Brother Armstrong	**Not issued*
	Blue Monday Up On Sugar Hill	*De 7500*

*(Although not officially released, a few copies were issued in error on De 7500 labelled 'Uncle Joe'.)

TRIXIE SMITH.
My Unusual Man   *De 7489*

16.11.38   **SIDNEY BECHET AND HIS ORCHESTRA.**
What a Dream   *Vo 4575*
Hold Tight   *Not issued on Vocalion*
Hold Tight   *Vo 4537*
Jungle Drums   —
Chant in the Night   *Vo 4575*

28.11.38   **TOMMY LADNIER AND HIS ORCHESTRA.**
Ja Da   *Bb 10086*
Really the Blues   *Bb 10089*
When You and I Were Young, Maggie   *Bb 10086*
Weary Blues   *Bb 10089*

6.5.39   **THE PORT OF HARLEM SEVEN.**
Blues for Tommy (Ladnier)   *BN 7 (12″)*

8.6.39   **THE SIDNEY BECHET QUINTET.**
Summertime   *BN 6 (12″)*

THE PORT OF THE HARLEM SEVEN.
Pounding Heart Blues   *BN 6 (12″)*

4.9.39   **JELLY ROLL MORTON'S NEW ORLEANS JAZZMEN.**
Oh! Didn't He Ramble   *Bb 10429*
High Society   *Bb 10434*
I Thought I Heard Buddy Bolden Say   —
Winin' Boy Blues   *Bb 10429*

22.11.39.   **WILLIE 'THE LION' SMITH—SIDNEY BECHET ORCHESTRA.**
Magic Island—Méringue   *Vrs 8399*
Mayotte-Méringue   —
Rosa Rumba   *Vrs 8405*
Sous les Palmiers—Méringue   —
Tropical Mood—Rhumba (retitled *Diane*)   *Bld 1013*
Nana (retitled *Baba—Rhumba*)   —
Ti Ralph   *Bld 1012*
Méringue d'Amour   —

5.2.40   **NEW ORLEANS FEETWARMERS.**
Indian Summer   *Bb 10623*
One O'clock Jump   *Vic 27204*
Preachin' Blues   *Bb 10623*
Sidney's Blues   *Bb 8509*

7.3.40   **JOSH WHITE TRIO.**
Careless Love Blues   *BN 23 (12″)*
Milk Cow Blues   —

27.3.40   **SIDNEY BECHET'S BLUE NOTE QUARTET.**
Lonesome Blues   *BN 13 (12″)*
Dear Old Southland   —
Bechet's Steady Rider   *BN 502*
Saturday Night Function   —

28.3.40	BECHET–SPANIER BIG FOUR.	
	Four or Five Times	*HRS 2001 (12")*
	Sweet Lorraine	*HRS 2000 (12")*
	Lazy River	—
	China Boy	*HRS 2001 (12")*
	China Boy	*(10" dividend disc to HRS Members)*
6.4.40	*If I Could be With You*	*HRS 2002 (12")*
	That's a Plenty	*(10" dividend disc to HRS Members)*
	That's a Plenty	*HRS 2002*
	Squeeze Me	*HRS 2003*
	Sweet Sue	—

27.5.40	LOUIS ARMSTRONG AND HIS ORCHESTRA.	
	Perdido Street Blues	*De 18090*
	2.19 Blues	—
	Down in Honky Tonk Town	*De 18091, 25699*
	Down in Honky Tonk Town	*De 18091, 25100*
	Coal Cart Blues	*De 18091, 25100*

4.6.40	NEW ORLEANS FEETWARMERS.	
	Shake It and Break It	*Vic 26640*
	Old Man Blues	*Vic 26663*
	Wild Man Blues	*Vic 26640*
	Nobody Knows the Way I Feel Dis Mornin'	*Vic 26663*

SIDNEY BECHET AND HIS RHYTHM. Chicago

	Make Me a Pallet on the Floor	*Bb 8509*

6.9.40	SIDNEY BECHET AND HIS TRIO.	
	Blues in Thirds	*Vic 27204*

NEW ORLEANS FEETWARMERS.

	Blue for You Johnny	*Vic 26746*
	Ain't Misbehavin'	—
	Save It Pretty Mama	*Vic 26740*
	Stompy Jones	—

11.11.40	PROF. SIDNEY BECHET, with Dr. Henry Levine's Barefooted Dixieland Philharmonic.	
	Muskrat Ramble	*Vic 27302*

8.1.41	NEW ORLEANS FEETWARMERS.	
	Coal Black Shine	*Vic 27386*
	Egyptian Fantasy	*Vic 27337*
	Baby Won't You Please Come Home	*Vic 27386*
	Slippin' and Slidin'	*Vic 27337*

226

18.9.41	SIDNEY BECHET.	
	Sheik of Araby	*Vic 27485*
	Blues of Bechet	—

28.4.41	NEW ORLEANS FEETWARMERS.	
	Swing Parade	*Vic 27574*
	I Know That You Know	—
	When It's Sleepy Time Down South	*Vic 27447*
	I Ain't Gonna Give Nobody None o' My Jelly Roll	—
13.9.41	*I'm Coming Virginia*	*Vic 27904*
	Limehouse Blues	*Vic 27600*
	Georgia Cabin	*Vic 27904*
	Texas Moaner	*Vic 27600*

	SIDNEY BECHET TRIO.	
	Strange Fruit	Not issued on Victor
	You're the Limit	—

14.10.41	SIDNEY BECHET AND HIS NEW ORLEANS FEETWARMERS.	
	Rip Up the Joint	*Vic 27663*
	Suey	*Vic 20-3120*
	Blues in the Air	*Vic 20-1510*
	The Mooche	—
	Laughin' in Rhythm	*Vic 27663*
24.10.41	*Twelfth Street Rag*	*Vic 20-3120*
	Mood Indigo	—
	Rose Room	*Vic 27707*
	Oh! Lady Be Good	—
	What is This Thing Called Love	Not issued on Victor

8.12.43	*Bechet Parades the Blues (St. Louis Blues)*	'V'-d 753 (12")
	After You've Gone	'V'-d 270 (12")
	V-Disc Blues (Bugle Call Rag)	'V'-d 214 (12")

20.12.44	SIDNEY BECHET'S BLUE NOTE JAZZMEN.	
	St. Louis Blues	BN 44 (12")
	Jazz Me Blues	—
	Blue Horizon	BN 43 (12")
	Muskrat Ramble	—

24.12.44	CLIFF JACKSON AND HIS VILLAGE CATS.	
	You've Got Me Walkin' and Talkin' to Myself	B & W 1204 (12")
	Quiet Please	—
	Cliff's Boogie Woogie	B & W 1205 (12")
	Jeepers Creepers	—

27.1.45	SIDNEY BECHET'S BLUE NOTE JAZZMEN.	
	High Society	BN 50 (12")
	Salty Dog	BN 49 (12")
	Weary Blues	—
	Jackass Blues	BN 50 (12")

10.8.45   SIDNEY BECHET AND BUNK JOHNSON.

Days Beyond Recall	BN BLP 7008
Milenberg Joys	—
Lord Let Me in the Lifeboat	—
Up in Sidney's Flat	—
Porto Rico	Not issued
Basin Street Blues	—

30.7.45   MEZZROW–BECHET SEPTET.

House Party	KJ 143
Perdido Street Stomp	Not issued
Old School, Pt. 1	—
Old School, Pt. 2	—
Blood on the Moon	KJ 143
Levee Blues	KJ 144
Layin' My Rules in Blues	Not issued
Bad Bad Baby Blues	
Saw Mill Man Blues	KJ 144
Minor Swoon	Not issued
The Sheik	—
Boogin' with Big Sid Catlett	—
Baby I'm Cuttin' Out	—

29.8.45   MEZZROW–BECHET QUINTET.

Ole Miss	KJ 142
Bowin' the Blues	KJ 141
Jelly Roll	Not issued
Old School	KJ 141
Gone Away Blues	KJ 140
De Luke Stomp	—
Out of the Gallion	KJ 142

12.10.45   ART HODES HOT FIVE.

Save it Pretty Mama	BN 531
Way Down Yonder in New Orleans	BN 533
Memphis Blues	BN 532
Shine	—
St. James Infirmary	BN 533
Darktown Strutters Ball	BN 531

9.12.45   JOE SULLIVAN QUARTET.

Michigan Square (pseudonym for *Sister Kate*)	Not issued on Disc
Sister Kate	Disc 6003
Panama	Disc 6004
Got It and Gone	Disc 6005
Chicago Blues (pseudonym for *Got It and Gone*)	Not issued on Disc

12.2.46   BECHET–NICHOLAS BLUE FIVE.

Quincey Street Stomp (retitled *Blame It on the Blues*)	BN 517
Old Stack O' Lee Blues	BN 54 (12″)
Bechet's Fantasy	—
Weary Way Blues	BN 517
Weary Way Blues	BN BLP 7008

7.5.46 STELLA BROOKS.

As Long As I Live	Disc 5030
I'm a Little Bit of Leather	Disc 5032
St. Louis Blues	Disc 5031
Jazz Me Blues	—
I'll Never Be the Same	Disc 5032

18.9.46 MEZZROW–BECHET QUINTET.

Breathless Blues	KJ 147
Really the Blues, Pt. 1	KJ 146
Really the Blues, Pt. 2	KJ 146
Evil Gal Blues	KJ 147
Fat Mama Blues	Not issued
You Got to Give It to Me	KJ 148
Hey Daddy Blues	Not issued
Whipping the Wolf Away From My Door	Not issued
You Can't Do That To Me	KJ 148
Groovin' the Minor	—

15.2.47 MEZZROW–BECHET FEETWARMERS.

Royal Garden Blues	WS LP201
Slow Blues	—
Old Fashioned Love	—
Fast Blues	—
Bugle Blues	—

14.7.47 SIDNEY BECHET AND BOB WILBER'S WILD-CATS.

Spreadin' Joy	Co 38320
I Had It but It's All Gone Now	—
Polka Dot Stomp	Co 38319
Kansas City Man Blues	—

23.7.47 SIDNEY BECHET QUARTET.

Buddy Bolden Stomp	Not issued on Co
My Woman's Blues	Not issued
The Song of Songs	—
31.7.47 *My Woman's Blues*	Not issued on Co
The Song of Songs	Not issued on Co
Just One of Those Things	Co 38318
Love for Sale	Co 38321
Laura	Co 38318
Shake 'em Up	Co 38321

18.12.47 MEZZROW–BECHET QUINTET. Chicago

Where Am I?	Not issued
Tommy's Blues	—
Chicago Function, Pt. 1	—
Chicago Function, Pt. 2	—
19.12.47 *I Want Some*	—Chicago
I'm Speakin' My Mind	—
I Ain't Gonna Do It Blues	—
The Blues . . .	—
. . . and Freud	—
Kaiser's Last Break	—

229

20.12.47 *I'm Going Away from Here*   —Chicago
     I Got You Some   —
     I Must Have My Boogie   —
     Funky Butt   —
     Delta Mood   —
     (Untitled Original)   —
     (Untitled Original)   —

Late '47 (No Band Name Printed on Labels)
     Sensation Rag   *V of A DS265*
                 (16")

     Summertime   —
     What Did I Do to Make You So Black and Blue —

RUDI BLESH ALL STAR STOMPERS.
     Sugar   *V of A DS1669*
                 (16")

29.1.49 SIDNEY BECHET'S BLUE NOTE JAZZMEN.
     Tiger Rag   *BN 562*
     Tin Roof Blues   *BN 561*
     Sister Kate   *BN 573*
     Nobody Knows You   *BN 571*
     When the Saints Go Marching In *BN 563*
     I've Found a New Baby   *BN BLP7014*

31.1.49 SIDNEY BECHET AND HIS CIRCLE SEVEN.
     I Got Rhythm   *Cir J1058*
     September Song   *Cir J1057*
     Who   —
     Song of the Medina (retitled *Casbah*) *Cir J1058*

—.2.49 SIDNEY BECHET'S JAZZ LTD. ORCHESTRA.
                   Chicago
     Maryland, My Maryland *JLtd 201*
     Careless Love Blues   —
     Egyptian Fantasy   *JLtd 101*

23.3.49 SIDNEY BECHET'S BLUE NOTE JAZZMEN.
     Basin Street Blues   *BN 561*
     Cake Walking Babies *BN 562*
     Fidgety Feet   *BN 571*
     At the Jazz Band Ball *BN 563*
     Tailgate Ramble   —
     Joshua Fit de Battle ob Jericho —

Early '49 SIDNEY BECHET.   (Probably N.Y. Radio
                 transcription)
     Black and Blue   *Mnre 502*
     September Song   —

14.5.49 SIDNEY BECHET AND PIERRE BRASLAVSKY'S
     ORCHESTRA. (Geneva Concert Recording)
     Sweet Georgia Brown *CSB 4 (12")*
     Summertime   —
     Muskrat Ramble   —
     Tin Roof Blues   —
     High Society   —
     Weary Blues   —

Blues in the Air	—
Ain't Gonna Give Nobody None . . .	—
Southern Sunset	—
Careless Love	*CSB 2 (12")*
Wild Cat Blues	*Not issued*

16.5.49 SIDNEY BECHET AND HIS ORCHESTRA. Paris

Honeysuckle Rose	*BSt 128*
Coquette	*Sw 319*
High Society	*BSt 128*
On the Sunny Side of the Street	*BSt 129*
Sugar	*Sw 314*
I Can't Believe that You're in Love With Me	*BSt 129*
Indiana	*Sw 319*
Festival Blues	*Sw 314*

8.6.49 SIDNEY BECHET WITH BOB WILBER AND HIS JAZZ BAND.

I'm Through, Goodbye	*Cir J1059*
Love Me With a Feeling	*Cir J1060*
Waste No Tears	—
Box Car Shorty (Dixieland Calypso)	*Cir J1061*
The Broken Windmill	—
Without a Home	*Cir J1059*

Late '49 SIDNEY BECHET–CLAUDE LUTER AND HIS ORCHESTRA. Paris

Travellin' Blues	*Vog 5040*
Willie the Weeper	—
Maple Leaf Rag	*Vog 5039*
Panama Rag	—
Apple Blues	*Vog 5168*

14.10.49 SIDNEY BECHET–CLAUDE LUTER ET SON ORCHESTRE. Paris

Ce Mossieu Qui Parlé	*Vog 5013 (12")*
Buddy Bolden Story	—
Bechet Creole Blues	*Vog 5014*
Anita Birthday	—
Les Oignons	*Vog 5015*
Ridin' Easy Blues	—

SIDNEY BECHET.

Blues de Paris	*Vog 5016*

SIDNEY BECHET–CLAUDE LUTER ET SON ORCHESTRE.

Panther Dance	*Vog 5016*

20.10.49 SIDNEY BECHET AND HIS ALL STAR BAND. Paris

Orphan Annie's Blues	*Vog 5017 (12")*
Happy Go Lucky	—

SIDNEY BECHET–KENNY CLARKE.

Klook's Blues (Klook Klux Khan)	*Vog 5018*
*American Rhythm.**	*Vog 5018*

* (This is the same tune as 'Blackstick').

SIDNEY BECHET QUARTET.
Out of Nowhere   *Vog 5019*
Mon Homme (My Man)   —

18.11.49   SIDNEY BECHET WITH HUMPHREY
LYTTELTON AND HIS BAND.   London
Some of These Days   *Mldsc 1103*
Black and Blue   —
Who's Sorry Now   *Mldsc 1104*
Sleepy Town Down South   —
I Told You Once, I Told You Twice   *Mldsc 1105*
Georgia   —

15.11.49   SIDNEY BECHET–CLAUDE LUTER ET SON
ORCHESTRE.   Paris
Temptation Rag   *Vog 5020*
Riverboat Shuffle   —

SIDNEY BECHET–CLAUDE LUTER QUINTET.
Sobbin' and Cryin'   *Vog 5021*

SIDNEY BECHET–CLAUDE LUTER ET SON
ORCHESTRE.
Everybòdy Loves My Baby   *Vog 5021*
Struttin' with Some Barbecue   *Vog 5022*
Sawmill Blues   —

SIDNEY BECHET AND HIS FEETWARMERS.
Wrap Your Troubleş in Dreams   *BSt 152*
It Had to be You   *BSt 140*
Baby Won't You Please Come Home   *BSt 148*
Please Don't Talk About Me   *BSt 140*
Ooh! Boogie   *BSt 142*
After You've Gone   —
I'm Going Away Down Home   *BSt 148*
Margie   *BSt 152*

A Sunday, SIDNEY BECHET–CLAUDE LUTER ET
late '49   ORCHESTRE.   Paris (Concert Recording)
or early '50.
Mon Homme   *Not issued*
Willie the Weeper   —
Ole Miss   *CSB 3 (12″)*
Wild Man Blues   —

19.4.50   SIDNEY BECHET'S BLUE NOTE JAZZMEN.
Copenhagen   *BN 572*
China Boy   *BN 573*
Runnin' Wild   —
Mandy   —
Jelly Roll   —
Shi-me-sha Wabble   *BN 572*

—.4.50   SIDNEY BECHET AND HIS NEW ORLEANS
FEETWARMERS.
Jelly Roll Blues   *Cmd 637*
At a Georgia Camp Meeting   *Cmd 638*
National Emblem March   *Cmd 637*
Hindustan   *Cmd 638*

6.10.50	**SIDNEY BECHET–CLAUDE LUTER ET SON ORCHESTRE.**	Paris
	Ni Queue, Ni Tête	*Vog 5089*
	Moulin à Café	*Vog 5066*
	Maryland	*Vog 5065*
	Careless Love Blues	*Vog 5068*
	Moustache Gauloise	*Vog 5089*
	Francis Blues	*Vog 5064*
	Casey Jones, the Brave Engineer	*Vog 5069*
	Blues in My Heart	*Vog 5069*
9.10.50	*Lastic*	*Vog 5065*
	Madame Bécasine	*Vog 5064*
	Down Home Rag	*Vog 5068*
	Society Blues	*Vog 5067*
	Won't You Please Come Home, Bill Bailey	*Vog 5066*
	Royal Garden Blues	*Vog 5067*
4.5.51	*In the Groove*	*Vog 5093*
	In the Groove	*CSB 2(12″)*
	Promenade aux Champs-Élysées	*Vog 5095*
	Promenade aux Champs-Élysées	*CSB 3(12″)*
	En Attendant le Jour	*Vog 5093*
	En Attendant le Jour	*CSB 3 (12″)*
	Wolverine Blues	*Vog 5095*
	Egyptian Fantasy	*Vog 5091*
	Blues in the Cave	—

8.5.51	**SIDNEY BECHET AND THE ORCHESTRA OF THE DUTCH SWING COLLEGE.**	Hilversum
	Dutch Swing College Blues	*De (Holland) M33199*
	King Porter Stomp	—

7.9.51	**SIDNEY BECHET–CLAUDE LUTER WITH ANDRÉ REWÉLIOTTY ET SON ORCHESTRE.**	Paris
	Kansas City Man Blues	*Vog 5100*
	Together	—
	Apex Blues	*Vog 5101*
	Sleepy Time Gal	—
	Of All the Wrongs You've Done to Me	*Vog 5102*
	My Darling Nellie Gray	—
	Mets Ton Vieux Bonnet Gris	*Vog 5103*
	Sidney's Wedding Day	—

5.11.51	**SIDNEY BECHET AND HIS HOT SIX.**	
	Original Dixieland One-Step	*BN BLP7020*
	Blues My Naughty Sweetie Gives to Me	—
	There'll Be Some Changes Made	—
	That's a Plenty	—
	Ballin' the Jack	—
	Avalon	—

8.1.52	**SIDNEY BECHET ET L'ORCHESTRE CLAUDE LUTER.**	Paris
	Ghost of the Blues	*Vog 5077*
	Strike Up the Band	*Vog 5079*

	Si Tu Vois Ma Mère	*Vog 5076*
	Wabash Blues	*Vog 5079*
	Mouche à Miel (retitled *Pattes de Mouches*)	*Vog 5077*
	Le Marchand de Poissons	*Vog 5076*
	As-Tu le Cafard?	*Vog 5078*
	Dans les Rues d'Antibes	—

21.1.52 SIDNEY BECHET ALL STARS. Paris

That Old Black Magic	*Vog 5118*
Because of You. (Sans Ton Amour)	—
Petite Fleur	*Vog 5119*
I Get a Kick	—
Blues	*Vog 5121*
Girl's Dance	—
(It's No) Sin. (Est-ce un péché?)	*Vog 5122*
You're Lucky to Me	—

31.1.52 SIDNEY BECHET AVEC CLAUDE LUTER ET SON ORCHESTRE. Paris (Concert recordings)

Presentation By Charles Delaunay	*Vog LD060*
Les Oignons	—
St. Louis Blues	—
Muskrat Ramble	—
Frankie and Johnny	—
Maryland	—
Royal Garden Blues	*Vog LD061*
Dans les Rues D'Antibes	—
South	—
Petite Fleur	—
Sweet Georgia Brown	—

12.8.52 Paris (Concert recordings)

Dippermouth Blues	*Vog LD096*
I've Found a New Baby	—
Casey Jones	—
I Got Rhythm (retitled *Pleyel Rhythm*)	—
Society Blues	—
Summertime	*Vog 5131*
Struttin' With Some Barbecue	*Vog 5147*
September Song	*Vog 5131*
High Society	*Vog LD061*
Dans les Rues D'Antibes	*CSB 2 (12")*
Frankie and Johnny	*CSB 3 (12")*
Marchand de Poissons	*Not issued*

7.10.52 SIDNEY BECHET TRIO. Paris

Milenberg Joys	*Vog LD094*
Rockin' Chair	—
Big Butter and Egg Man	—
My Melancholy Baby	—
Limehouse Blues	—
Blue Room	—
Black Bottom	—
I Gotta Right To Sing The Blues	—
Baby's Prayer	*Vog 5156*
Lazy River; Stars Fell On Alabama	—

5.11.52 SIDNEY BECHET–CLAUDE LUTER AND HIS
ORCHESTRE. Paris

Porter Love Song	*Vog LD098*
Embraceable You	—
12th Street Rag	—
Au Claire de la Lune	—
Ol' Man River	—
Showboat Medley	—
You, Rascal You	—
Le Loup, La Biche et Le Chevalier	—

18.5.53 SYMPHONIQUE ORCHESTRE, avec SIDNEY
BECHET, soloiste. Directed by Jacques Bazire.
Paris

La Nuit est une Sorcière—Ballet	*Vog LD190*

28.5.53 SIDNEY BECHET avec ANDRÉ REWÉLIOTTY
ET SON ORCHESTRE. Paris

Pleure Pas Nelly	*Vog 5155*
La Complainte de Infidèles	—
Brave Margot	*Vog 5160*
La Canne—La Fossoyeur	—
Jacqueline (retitled—*Nous Deux*)	*Vog 5162*
Big Chief	*Vog 5163*
Nuages	*Vog 5162*
Elisabeth	*Vog 5163*

25.8.53 THE FABULOUS SIDNEY BECHET.

Rose of the Rio Grande	*BN BLP7026*
All of Me	—
Shine	—
Sweet Georgia Brown	—
Black and Blue	—
Ding Dong Daddy	—

3.10.53 SIDNEY BECHET WITH BOB SCOBEY'S BAND.
Los Angeles (Concert Recording)

Gene Norman introduces Sidney Bechet	*GNP EP1011* (7″)
On the Sunny Side of the Street	—
Muskrat Ramble	—
St. Louis Blues	—
Summertime	—

25.12.53 JAZZ AT STORYVILLE featuring SIDNEY BECHET.
Boston

C Jam Blues	*Story LP 301*
Jazz Me Blues	—
Lady Be Good	—
Crazy Rhythm	—
Indiana	*Story LP 306*
Honeysuckle Rose	—
Bugle Blues—Ole Miss	—

285

On the Sunny Side of the Street	Not issued on Storyville
Basin Street Blues	—

11.8.54 SIDNEY BECHET avec ANDRÉ REWÉLIOTTY ET SON ORCHESTRE. Paris

Le Chant des Canons	Vog 5184
La Complainte de Mackie	—
Some Sweet Day	Vog 5188
When I Grow Too Old to Dream	
When I Grow Too Old to Dream	CSB 3 (12")
Leilie	Vog LD219
Chante, Chante	CSB 3
Temperamental	Vog 5190
Temperamental	CSB 2 (12")
Rose de Picardie	—

—.9.54 SIDNEY BECHET AND HIS VOGUE JAZZMEN. Paris

Crazy Rhythm	Vog M33.331
Lonesome Road	—
Somebody Stole My Gal	—
When You Wore a Tulip	—
When You Wore a Tulip	CSB 2 (12")
Squeeze Me	Vog M 33.331
Chinatown, My Chinatown	—
Chinatown, My Chinatown	CSB 3 (12")

8.12.54 SIDNEY BECHET–CLAUDE LUTER. Paris (Concert recording)

Buddy Bolden Stomp	Vog LDM 30.001
Montmartre Boogie Woogie	—
As-tu le Cafard?	—
Riverboat Shuffle	—
Halle Hallelujah	—
When the Saints Go Marching In	—
Temperamental (Mood)	—
Sobbin' and Cryin'	—
Muskrat Ramble	—
On the Sunny Side of the Street	—
Petite Fleur	CSB 2 (12")
A Moi de Payer	—

8.2.55 SIDNEY BECHET avec ANDRÉ REWÉLIOTTY ET SON ORCHESTRE. Paris

Pourtant	Vog 5193
Un Ange Comme Ca	—
South Rampart Street Parade	Vog 5194
Blues Dans les Blues	—
A Moi de Payer	Vog 5195
Trottoirs de Paris	—

8.8.55 Paris

Basin Street Blues	CSB 2 (12")
Big Chief	—

19.10.55 SIDNEY BECHET avec LES ORCHESTRES DE CLAUDE LUTER et ANDRÉ REWÉLIOTTY.

Paris (Concert Recording)

Old Fashioned Love	*Vog LDM 30.015 (12")*
Charleston	—
Swanee River	—
Southern Sunset	—
Ol' Man River	—
Dans les Rues d'Antibes	—
Panama Rag	—
When the Saints Go Marching In	—
Royal Garden Blues	—
Blues in the Air	*Vog LDM 30.014 (12")*
Wild Man Blues	—
Everybody Loves My Baby	—
Wild Cat Rag	—
I Don't Know Where I'm Going	—
Viper Mad	—
High Society	—
Halle Hallelujah	—
Kansas City Man Blues	—
Les Oignons	—

3.12.55 SIDNEY BECHET avec ANDRÉ REWÉLIOTTY ET SON ORCHESTRE. Paris

Halle Hallelujah	**Vog EPL 7186 (7")*
Les Hommes Sont Genereux	—
L'Enchainée D'Amour	—
Les Blues De Mes Rèves	—
Halle Hallelujah	—
I Had It But It's All Gone Now	—
Blues, I Had It But It's All Gone Now, Halle Hallelujah	—

24.12.55 Paris

Quand Arrive le Samedi Soir	*Vog EPL 7203 (7")*
Dardanella	*Vog EPL 7204 (7")*
Dardanella	*CSB 2 (12")*
Songe d'Automne	*Vog EPL 7204 (7")*

1.2.56 Paris

Bonjour Paris	*Vog EPL 7204 (7")*
El Doudou—Si C'Etait A Refaire	*Vog EPL 7203 (7")*
Laura	—
Laura	*CSB 2 (12")*
Willow Weep for Me	*Vog EPL 7204 (7")*
Stormy Weather	*Vog EPL 7203 (7")*

*(Each side of this disc is a continuous medley performance without separation between tunes.)

16.5.56 SIDNEY BECHET with SAMMY PRICE AND
HIS BLUESICIANS. Paris

St. Louis Blues	Sw LDM 30041 (12")
Tin Roof Blues	—
Darktown Strutters Ball	—
Jazz Me Blues	—
Memphis Blues	—
Dinah	—
Yes! We Have No Bananas	—
Back Home	—

26.6.56 SIDNEY BECHET avec ANDRÉ REWÉLIOTTY
ET SON ORCHESTRE. Paris

Jumpin' Jack	Vog LD 307
Passeport to Paradise	—
Passeport to Paradise	CSB 2 (12")
Coquin de Bonbon	Vog LD 307
Haou Haou Cou Cou	—
Chacun à sa Chance	—
Shake 'em Up	—

29.6.56 Paris

Un Coup de Cafard	Vog LD 307
Le Bidon	Vog 30,066
Le Train de Vieux Noir. (Rock Island Line)	—
Sans Vous Facher, Répondez-moi	Vog LD 307

24.2.57 Paris

Down By The Old Mill Stream	Vog LDM 30.066 (12")
Down By The Old Mill Stream	CSB 3 (12")
14 Juillet	Vog LDM 30.066 (12")
J'ai Deux Amours—Ce N'Est Que Votre Main, Madame	—
J'ai Deux Amours	CSB 3
J'en ai Marre	Vog LDM 30.066 (12")

12.3.57 SIDNEY BECHET–MARTIAL SOLAL. Paris

These Foolish Things	Sw LDM 30.065 (12")
Pennies from Heaven	—
Once In a While	—
I Only Have Eyes for You	—
Exactly Like You	—
Jeepers Creepers	—
The Man I Love	—
I Never Knew	—

23.3.57 SIDNEY BECHET avec ANDRÉ REWÉLIOTTY
ET SON ORCHESTRE. Paris

Au Secours	Vog LDM 30.066 (12")
Premier Bal	—
Premier Bal	CSB 3
La Bagatelle	Vog LDM 30.066 (12")

238

17.6.57 **SIDNEY BECHET–MARTIAL SOLAL.** Paris
- *Embraceable You*   *Sw LDM 30.065 (12")*
- *All The Things You Are* —
- *It Don't Mean a Thing* —
- *All of Me* —
- *Wrap Your Troubles in Dreams* —
- *Rose Room* —

26.6.57 **SIDNEY BECHET** avec **ANDRÉ REWÉLIOTTY ET SON ORCHESTRE.** Paris
- *Amour Perdu*   *Vog LDM 30.066 (12")*
- *Soprano Blues* —
- *Soprano Blues*   *CSB 3 (12)*
- *Écoutez le Trombone*   *Vog LDM 30.066 (12")*
- *Pas d'Blague* —
- *Gypsy Love Song* —

8.7.58 **SIDNEY BECHET** au **FESTIVAL DE JAZZ DE CANNES ET KNOKKE,** 1958.
Knokke (Concert recording)
- *St. Louis Blues*   *Sw LDM 30.094*
- *On the Sunny Side of the Street* —
- *Sister Kate* —
- *I'm Coming Virginia* —

10.7.58   Cannes (Concert recording)
- *Rosetta* —
- *Once in a While* —
- *Sweet Georgia Brown* —

1 or 2.7.58 **BRAVO BECHET–BUCKNER** Paris
- *Weary Blues*   *Sw LDM 30.092 (12")*
- *Ain't Misbehavin'* —
- *Aubergines, Poivrons et Sauce de Tomate* —
- *Sugar* —
- *Bravo* —
- *Who's Sorry Now* —
- *All of Me* —
- *Souvenirs de la Nouvelle Orléans* —
- *I Can't Get Started*   *Sw LDM 30.065 (12")*
- *Blue Festival '58* —

'CONCERT À BRUXELLES'

Early 8.58   Brussels (Concert Recording)
- *Indiana* —
- *Society Blues* —
- *St. Louis Blues* —
- *Swanee River* —
- *In a Sentimental Mood* —
- *All of Me* —
- *When the Saints Go Marching In* —

289

Treat It Gentle

12.12.58	'SIDNEY JOUE NOEL'	Paris
	Silent Night	*Vog EPL 7572* (7")
	Blues du Papa Noel	—
	Spirit Holiday	—
	White Christmas	—
	Les Oignons	*CSB 3 (12")*

Index

242

Other titles of interest